PENGUIN BOOKS

POLES APART

Alison Goldsworthy has been a political adviser and campaigner for more than twenty years. A former Deputy Chair of the Liberal Democrats, she led the team that built the fastest-growing campaigning organisation in the UK. In 2017 she was a Sloan Fellow at Stanford, co-creating its first depolarisation course. A board member of the Joseph Rowntree Reform Trust, Alison has won numerous awards for her work. She has written for the *Telegraph*, *Independent*, *New Statesman*, *The Times* and *Financial Times*.

Laura Osborne is a professional communicator, spokesperson and podcaster, with a background in public affairs and government communications. Currently Corporate Affairs Director at London First, the voice of the city's largest employers, she was previously Communications Director at Which?, the UK's consumer association. Laura has led large teams, working with some of the UK's biggest corporations to apply lessons from communications, consumer insight and behavioural science to making business a force for good.

Alexandra Chesterfield is a behavioural scientist with a master's degree in Cognitive and Decision Science. Forever curious about why we do what we do, she currently works in financial services, leading a team of behavioural scientists to help get better outcomes for employees and customers. For four years, she was an elected Councillor in Guildford for the Conservative Party. She has personally experienced the effects of affective polarisation, both in and out of the workplace.

D0432497

POLES APART

Why People Turn Against
Each Other, and How to Bring
Them Together

Alison Goldsworthy, Laura Osborne
and Alexandra Chesterfield

PENGUIN BOOKS

PENGUIN BOOKS

UK | USA | Canada | Ireland | Australia
India | New Zealand | South Africa

Penguin Books is part of the Penguin Random House group of companies
whose addresses can be found at global.penguinrandomhouse.com

First published by Random House Business in 2021
Published in Penguin Books 2022
001

Typeset in 11.5/16pt Minion by Jouve (UK), Milton Keynes
Printed and bound in Great Britain by Clays Ltd, Elcograf S.p.A.

The authorised representative in the EEA is Penguin Random House Ireland,
Morrison Chambers, 32 Nassau Street, Dublin D02 YH68

A CIP catalogue record for this book is available from the British Library

ISBN: 978–1–847–94297–5

www.greenpenguin.co.uk

For our husbands, Jimmy, Will and Doug.
And our children, Ellie, Anna, Teddy, Evie
and Tomos. We promise, we really are done now.

Contents

PROLOGUE: POLES APART

At a camp in Lebanon in the 1960s, the psychologist Lutfy Diab sought to recreate one of social psychology's seminal studies: the 'Robbers Cave' experiment.[1] Devised back in 1954 by a husband-and-wife team in America, it had been designed to test the extent to which groups would naturally compete for resources when they were scarce but then co-operate when presented with a shared goal. For his version, Diab mimicked the design of the initial study. He brought together a collection of eleven-year-old Muslim and Christian boys and divided them randomly into two groups. Each chose a name: 'The Blue Ghosts' and 'Red Genies'. The plan was to assess first the two groups' tendency to compete, and then their ability to co-operate. In the event, though, the experiment never reached phase two. Diab had to abandon the study when the 'Red Genies' team stole the pen-knife offered as a prize to the more successful group, and threatened a member of 'The Blue Ghosts' with it.

Rather more recently in the United States, three friends were looking for rooms to rent in Pittsburgh, Pennsylvania, a city famous for its steel production, bridges – and universities. Their advertisement on Craigslist gave all the usual details about rent, cleanliness and house rules they desired. It then gave an indication of the sort of flatmates they were hoping to find there. One might have expected a list of desired personal qualities and habits. But apart from a buried reference to cost, the main thrust of the advertisement was as follows: 'We are all open-minded, fun individuals, are open to all religions, genders, sexual orientations and races. No judgement here! However, we hate Trump.' Such a sentiment isn't a one-off. According to a 2019 study among university students in the US, partisan preference is the biggest factor in determining who gets chosen as a room-mate. Students said that they would rather live with someone who was 'not at all clean and tidy' or preferred 'going to bed early' than someone who supported the opposing party.[2]

Both the Lebanese children and the American students demonstrate a fundamental truth: that we form groups and craft shared identities sometimes according to the most trivial, often seemingly irrelevant, criteria. It's a concept that has been widely studied and remarked upon down the ages. One of the earliest enquiries into the phenomenon, by the north-African polymath Ibn Khaldun, even coined a term for it: *asabiyyah*. In his *Muqaddimah* of 1377, in which he sought to 'understand the forces that inform the rise and fall and developments within societies and political structures', Ibn Khaldun identified the way in which views and values spread over time beyond individual tight-knit family groups to incorporate other people. He also identified how, as an 'ingroup' develops, so it comes to create in its collective mind an 'outgroup' of people who are different. Khaldun argued that we seek to both maintain our collective solidarity and fight those we think threaten it.

Rooted in our evolutionary development, the notion of *asabiyyah* survives to this day. As Aimen Dean, who dramatically left al-Qaeda and became an informant for the British intelligence service MI6, told us, 'The word *asabiyyah* [is] the solidarity that one feels with the group that they identify with. But sometimes we use the word *asabiyyah* to mean tribal solidarity, but in a negative way: you're not going to marry my daughter because you are from a different tribe.'[3] Once a group identity is adopted, it changes what we think and do. It also makes it harder to let go of beliefs as they become entwined with who we are.

We can all view ourselves as holding multiple identities that may cross-cut one another: 'mother', 'British', 'nurse', 'progressive/conservative', for example. As these identities become subsumed within labels that carry with them implications about wider attitudes and values – for example, 'gun owner' or 'latte drinker' – they can make us feel either attraction to or repulsion from others. And this attraction or repulsion can be so strong that, in the words of the academics Murat Somer and Jennifer McCoy, it has the effect of creating 'otherwise unrelated divisions, emasculating cross-cutting cleavages, and dividing society and politics into two separate, opposing and unyielding blocks'.[4] Issue-based differences rapidly become differences of social identity. When that happens, people increasingly dislike and distrust those from an opposing side, irrespective of whether they actually disagree on a specific issue. Feelings become more important than facts. Partisan labels come to act as proxies for differences in beliefs, values and behaviour that go far beyond political considerations. This phenomenon is known as affective polarisation, and we'll delve into it throughout the book.

Groupishness can affect people's judgement in unexpected ways. You are more likely to vaccinate your child if the presidential candidate you voted for is elected.[5] If you're a doctor, the course of treatment you recommend for a patient may well be influenced by your own politics and perception of their likely political leanings.[6] If you're a manager, the same consideration will shape your hiring decisions – more so, in some circumstances, than considerations of race.[7] We select those we choose to listen to, from individuals to the media, according to their political viewpoints.[8] We are more likely to find attractive and fall in love with people who support the same political party as us.[9] In the

3

same way, we are less likely to believe a criminal allegation, such as one of sexual assault, if it's brought against someone who belongs to our ingroup.[10] There is no part of our lives, in fact, that goes untouched by the influence of these identity-based partisan labels. So insidious is this that often we're not even aware it's going on.

No one can be blind to the dangers of a perniciously polarised society. The political theorist and scholar of the Holocaust Hannah Arendt rightly said, when considering the impact of totalitarianism, that we have to deal with the problems we face in the present, rather than hark back nostalgically to an earlier time or look forward to a better future. Polarisation, as she so powerfully noted about totalitarianism, is part of the reality in which we live; we ignore its causes and effects at our peril. Polarisation leads to suspicion and distrust. It undermines and gridlocks institutions. As the storming of the Capitol Building in Washington DC on 6 January 2021 demonstrated only too well, partisanship can exacerbate the tendency of those already prone to violence. But violence is far from the only inevitable consequence of polarisation. Where does polarisation leave the intellectual diversity that leads to innovation? Or good governance and decision-making? A society in which trust has broken down can be simultaneously volatile and ineffective. Healthy conflict – where different views can be aired, debated and resolved – is a vital part of how we live, and it occupies a place at the core of a modern democracy, but there are huge risks if partisan conflict becomes all-encompassing, as it eliminates space to engage across the divide.

Humans, like other species, have an innate need to belong to a group. And, as Yale Professor of Psychology John Bargh points out, while the precise form of that group may have changed over time as family and village identities have been overlaid or replaced by others, that doesn't make the groups we belong to any less powerful.[11] Membership confers a feeling of safety and helps us make sense of the world around us. It also brings significant emotional benefits in the forms of pride and self-esteem. It reduces uncertainty. At the same time it fulfils the natural human inclinations to, on the one hand, be superior and win, and, on the other, denigrate and defeat.

While there's nothing new about such tendencies, our propensity to polarise has, thanks to socio-economic circumstances, technological changes and a rising sense of uncertainty, deepened in numerous countries in recent years from the levels seen immediately after the Second World War. Financial shocks have left many people insecure and exacerbated the divides between the haves and have-nots. Access to ever-increasing quantities of information, often of dubious provenance, has left us uncertain and suspicious. Trust in our institutions has plummeted, often enabling populist leaders and governments to step in and fill the void. Our online world, while creating the opportunity for many new networks and connections, has also set up virtual barriers and a distancing that allows us to reject or avoid, rather than engage with the views of those with whom we disagree. To make matters worse, the partisan online world has been monetised, rewarding those who put out emotionally charged content designed to attract attention. The short-term benefits of polarising can offer significant immediate paybacks in money and power, but at what hidden and longer-term social and political costs?

The everyday consequences are there for all to see. In the US, hostility between Democrats and Republicans (as measured on a 'feelings thermometer') has doubled in the last twenty years.[12] Thirty years ago, most Americans said they didn't care whether their child married someone of a different political persuasion to their own.[13] Today, nearly half of Republicans, and about a third of Democrats, say they would be 'displeased' if their child married a member of the opposing party. In the UK, the Brexit issue caused splits across voter groups and often within families (progressive activists are the likeliest to have a politically narrow friendship group).[14] Acrimonious disagreements about the best way to deal with financial deficits have divided citizens in Greece and Portugal. Debates over climate change have split Australians. Hostility to minority groups has driven a wedge between voters in countries from Romania to France. Broad partisan labels that identify 'us' – the ingroup – and 'them' – the 'outgroup' – are bandied about in all sorts of contexts, and not just political. In the process, emotion rather than argument has come to the fore. People will often express more strongly how they *feel* about another group than what they think of the issues that divide them. Indeed, it can be quite possible for them to dislike each other strongly while not disagreeing much on specific issues.[15] Our loyalty to the group poses a huge challenge to society, causing us to interpret the same sets of facts in entirely different ways, and creating entirely different visions of the same realities.

Polarisation distorts our perceptions of the world. Italians believe unemployment rates are more than four times higher than they actually are.[16] British people overestimate the immigrant population of the UK by 54 per cent.[17] People think they hold accurate views, but the odds are that they don't. They believe themselves able to process and evaluate information objectively, but in reality struggle to do so, particularly if an objective assessment would place them out of step with their group. They find it very hard to change their opinions even when they are demonstrated to be wrong or if the situation has changed. These are not failings unique to particular groups. They're common to almost all of us. And they can cause huge damage to us as individuals and to society as a whole.

Are societies destined to pull further apart, or can they find a way to bridge the divide? That is the fundamental question this book seeks to answer. It is also the question that inspired our *Changed My Mind* podcast. We wanted to find out, among other things, whether the tendency to judge others by their assumed partisan identity is spreading to new areas and, if so, how. We wanted to know why strong views on one subject so often shape opinions on seemingly unrelated topics, and why these beliefs are so hard to relinquish. And we wanted to establish whether it is possible for people to change their minds and, if so, what causes them to. This book has its genesis in that podcast and in the enthusiastic response from our many listeners.

Try asking yourself the following questions:

- When was the last time I changed my mind on something substantial?
- When was the last time I challenged myself on why I think what I think?
- When was the last time I spoke to someone who has a different political or world view to mine?
- Does anyone in my circle of friends have a different political or world view to mine?

We expect some of these questions gave you pause for thought. This book explains why, and seeks to offer some answers. In Part One, we go back to first principles, explaining how our beliefs are formed, how those beliefs influence and are influenced by the groups we belong to and form, and why an 'us-and-them' dynamic is so often created. At the same time, we take apart the comforting myth that, both as individuals and as members of a group, we are the enlightened creatures we like to believe, and that those who sit in the opposite camp are ignorant, unquestioning slaves to a false view of the world.

In Part Two, we look at how our polarising tendencies interact with, and are exacerbated by, the world around us. In particular we seek to pinpoint how economic shocks and feelings of uncertainty can cause us to gravitate to extreme positions. We consider the part played by our political systems and our politicians, and the ways in which the institutions designed to protect us can come under threat.

And we explore the ways in which the media and social media trigger more partisan identities and extend conflicts into new areas.

In Part Three, we look at what can be done to tackle pernicious polarisation. How can we reshape our institutions, our groups and, ultimately, ourselves?

It's telling that, historically, much of the most useful research on polarisation has been undertaken by scholars who have witnessed at first hand what its terrible effects can be: Hannah Arendt and the social psychologist Henri Tajfel lived through the era of the Holocaust; the psychologist Muzafer Sherif grew up in a region that experienced the First World War and the Armenian genocide. Today, much valuable work is being done in the US, and is often underpinned by laboratory experiments involving comparatively privileged student volunteers.

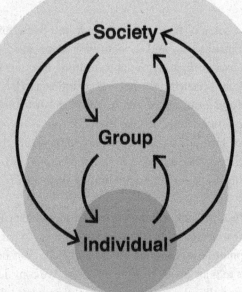

Figure 1: Our interdependent systems

The contrast is noteworthy, and a caveat is therefore required, not least because American students are not necessarily the most diverse group politically, racially or socio-economically. Put bluntly, there is a danger that, amid the research, important voices are going unheard in a country where, for example, some senior figures in social media companies have expressed concern at how political polarisation can dovetail with long-existing prejudices against black Americans. It's an issue that requires further study. It's also an issue that inevitably involves the authors of this book directly: we know we are not immune to our own groupishness and to the illusion of our own objectivity. We have employed many of the techniques described in Part Three in our attempt to present a balanced picture, but we are aware that while we come from different political, professional and socio-economic backgrounds, the narrative and analysis you will read is written by three white British women.

It's easy to take a pessimistic view of our polarised world, particularly in the light of recent events – from the Covid crisis to the American presidential election of 2020 and its aftermath. It's certainly the case that division will never go away completely. We should not expect it to. Nor, actually, should we want it to. A degree of division and disagreement is healthy. It stimulates debate and innovation and challenges groupthink and a desire for the status quo. For some, particularly those structurally excluded from access to the levers of power, adopting a more extreme position is a crucial weapon in what for them is a limited armoury of options to bring about change. But, without a doubt, a high level of polarisation can be destabilising and dangerous. It's this we have to counteract. Arguably, though, since we are all part of the problem, we all have the capacity to be part of the solution.

PART ONE

From Individuals to Groups to Factions

1

WHERE OUR VIEWS
COME FROM

The white nationalist and the social psychologist

Derek Black was brought up in a white, nationalist family in South Florida. His father, Don Black, had moved to the Sunshine State from the Deep South and, when Derek was a young child, had founded the white supremacist website Stormfront. Its bulletin board offered a forum where anti-Semites, neo-Nazis and racists could gather.[1] Derek's godfather, David Duke, was the former grand wizard of the Ku Klux Klan. From an early age, Derek would be taken to conferences where professors and others would propagate myths about the 'scientifically-proven' differences in intelligence between the races. He was regularly exposed to campaigns against entire races or religions that peddled such false beliefs as that Jews control the media and finance.[2] So notorious did his family become that he grew accustomed to the media turning up at their doorstep to get his father's take on a breaking story. Initially, he attended public (state) school. By the time he was ten, though, his parents had decided to home-school him. Assimilating his family's views, he became a public exponent of white nationalism.[3]

Theodore Newcomb[4] was born in Rock Creek, a rural village in Ohio, in the early 1900s. Many of his neigbours were white nationalists. He and his family, however, would have nothing to do with them. Indeed, they were ostracised for standing up to the Ku Klux Klan. Theodore set his heart on following in the footsteps of his father – a Congregational minister – and attended Union Theological Seminary with the intention of becoming a Christian missionary.

Both men subsequently underwent changes of heart and direction. In Newcomb's case, this was partly prompted by a lecturer who argued for the superiority of Christianity over all other religions. Newcomb, of course, came from a deeply Christian family, but he had become interested in anthropology, and the works he was reading on cultural differences and the illusion of ethnocentrism – the notion that one's own particular way of life is natural or correct – clashed with what his lecturer was telling him. He decided to switch to a psychology course, and in 1929 graduated from Columbia University with a PhD in it. Ultimately the man who had once wanted to be a missionary became a major figure in the wholly non-religious field of social psychology.

Derek Black's transformation was even more radical. At college, surrounded by students who fiercely disagreed with him, he initially kept himself to himself, ostracised by his peers. But after accepting an invitation from an Orthodox Jewish student for Shabbat dinner, and striking up friendships over the next two years with others in the student's circle, he slowly began to question his white nationalist beliefs. Ultimately he renounced them altogether. Derek went on to become engaged to one of the friends he had made at the Shabbat dinner and become a vocal campaigner against discrimination.

At one level, such shifts in standpoint on the part of two men from, admittedly, very different backgrounds seem, if not exactly unsurprising, entirely explicable. Humans[5] are supposedly rational[6] creatures who think and act logically. If we come across new views or ideas that challenge our own, we weigh them up objectively. If they seem unpersuasive, we reject them. If they appear convincing, we change our views accordingly. To that extent, Derek Black and Theodore Newcomb's intellectual journeys broadly exemplify the central tenet of rational choice theory – the notion that we are fundamentally motivated to form beliefs that reflect the true state of the world. When new information comes in, we compare it with our prior beliefs, assess its validity on its own terms and then select one of several possible courses of action. We might decide that the information is unimportant or not credible, in which case we will either simply retain our existing view or even, conceivably, feel more assured in it. Alternatively, we might be persuaded by what we've just heard or read, at which point we either become less confident about our current view or reject it altogether.

Rational choice theory provides a framework for understanding and modelling social and economic behaviour. Arguably, it underpins the structure of our entire political system. Rational choice theorists argue that democracy is built on the idea that we are able and willing to examine information and consider choices carefully and even-handedly, weighing up the costs and benefits to ourselves and our families of the programmes offered by different candidates or political parties. It assumes that our support for any given party will be determined by a hard-headed assessment of that party's ability and commitment to represent our interests and world view.

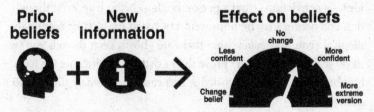

Figure 2: How we think we think

But even if one accepts the basic principles of the theory, it's clear that in practice they operate – at best – in a rather messy way. True, Theodore Newcomb's rejection of the path he had initially set his heart on appears to have been textbook rational choice theory in action: he heard a viewpoint expressed with which he disagreed so fundamentally that he came to re-examine his prior beliefs. But in Derek Black's case one can see that for many years not only were his views shaped by his father and his father's circle, but he also simply lacked access to alternative opinions from people he respected and trusted. Moreover, while it's apparent that his friends at university offered counter-arguments to white nationalism, it was actually their friendship that initially set him on the course that took him away from the views he had held since childhood. In other words, there was more at play here than coldly logical processes. Circumstance and environment on the one hand, and relationships on the other, were also key.

The fact is that, whatever rational choice theory might suggest to the contrary, we are all influenced by a range of factors beyond the rational. Family and peers; the groups we belong to; the cultures of which we are a part – all these shape us. And they shape the beliefs, attitudes and values we draw on when considering and interpreting the facts and arguments we hear every day.

These three connecting forces of beliefs, attitudes and values may sound very similar to each other, but it's important to distinguish between them. And since they are so core to how humans tick, it's perhaps worth teasing them apart a little. Essentially, a *belief* is an idea – a conviction – that a person holds as being true, even though that conviction may be unproven, not based on facts or seemingly illogical (you may *believe* that there are ghosts, even though you've never seen them and can't prove their existence). Beliefs are the basic building block of our knowledge and can be extremely difficult to change.[7]

An *attitude*,[8] by contrast, is an overall evaluation of other people, groups, objects and circumstances. You might *believe*, for example, that a friend is avoiding paying tax, but it's your *attitude* that will determine whether this belief makes you angry or not. Like beliefs, attitudes are vital to us; they offer us shorthand ways of understanding the world. But because they are inherently either positive or negative, they introduce bias into our thinking. And while they can change over time, they can prove remarkably deep-rooted and stubborn.

Values are more abstract than attitudes and beliefs, but they are also more all-embracing. They are the core concepts and ideas that, though they may vary in importance, transcend specific situations to shape our lives.[9] Our view of what is right or wrong, good or bad is shaped by the values we hold. They evoke strongly emotional reponses. If a child is punished for something they haven't done, their sense of fairness is undermined, and they feel despair and anger. Values may not be based on empirical research or rational thinking, but they are central to our self-image. As such they are even more resistant to change than attitudes and beliefs.

How we arrive at our beliefs, attitudes and values is often far from self-evident, both to ourselves and others, but the process starts at an early age.[10] The key role model here, of course, is the family.[11] *The American Voter* (1960) by Angus Campbell, Philip Converse, Warren Miller and Donald Stokes concluded that parents play an active role in teaching their children how to think about the political world, shaping their views of what is acceptable and what isn't, often inadvertently encouraging a psychological, affective attachment to the party they themselves support.[12] What's more, this early shaping of party loyalty tends to be powerful and enduring.[13] Theodore Newcomb and Derek Black both followed in their parents' footsteps until their twenties. Among parents who are also politicians, political dynasties are not uncommon. The Bushes, Gores and Kennedys in the US. The Le Pens in France. The Trudeaus in Canada. The Gandhis in India.

It's not difficult to see why children should behave in this way. In many families they will constantly have the opportunity to overhear what their parents discuss at the dinner table or see how they react to the news, and since children generally have an innate desire to imitate their principal role models they will tend to follow their parents' lead.[14] This is particularly so in families where parents generally agree with one another.[15] Research has shown that, in sending consistent signals to the rest of the family, like-minded adults are particularly prone to raise like-minded children. Roughly three-quarters of children in the US who have parents of the same party will go the same way.[16] Socio-economic status also plays a part here. Access to higher levels of education among those from more affluent backgrounds brings with it greater levels of political interest and knowledge.[17]

Nature and nurture, not nature vs nurture

But it would be incorrect to assume that children are simply blank slates on to which their parents, teachers and others write their beliefs. Genetics plays a hugely significant role too in forming our beliefs and our political make-up.[18, 19] Studies of identical twins (sharing 100 per cent of their genes) and non-identical twins (sharing 50 per cent) brought up apart and together show that political, social and economic attitudes have a strongly genetic component.[20] As our understanding of genetics has deepened so has the robustness of research showing that these components are not just general attitudes or tendencies: views on ideologies and issues as specific as socialism, the death penalty, censorship and divorce[21] have all been shown to have a significant genetic foundation.[22]

This may seem implausible. But it's worth reminding ourselves just how powerful an influence our genes exert on us. Take the story of Jim Springer and Jim Lewis. Identical twins adopted into different families when they were four weeks old, they were not reunited until they were thirty-nine years old, at which point they discovered that, despite their very different upbringings, they were almost unnervingly similar. Both liked the same cars (blue Chevrolets), cigarette and beer brands, shared a passion for the same hobby (woodworking) and had a mutual interest in motor racing. They both stood the same way, held their hands the same way, suffered migraines, had first wives called Linda, second wives called Betty and sons named James. Their test scores on personality measures were almost identical.[23] That they should be so similar in both fundamental and seemingly trivial ways is a striking testament to the power of their genetic make-up. It should come as no surprise, therefore, that mere political tendencies have a genetic component. Theodore Newcomb and Derek Black, or, for that matter, Chelsea Clinton and George W. Bush, acquired world views from their parents and the influence of the wider social environment in which they were raised, but they also inherited their genes.

Recent research[24] has not only confirmed the significant role played by genetics in shaping our belief systems, but also sought to quantify the relative pulls of genetics and social and environmental factors on attitudes to a whole range of different issues.[25] The chart on the next page, which draws on studies conducted across different countries, cultures and time periods, gives an intriguing set of aggregated results.[26]

It's important to appreciate what the chart demonstrates and what it doesn't. It shows that our attitudes to, say, women's rights do have a genetic component, even if social and environmental forces explain more of the differences in views that exist (i.e. the *variance*). It also shows that our genetic make-up explains quite a lot of the differences in views on race and sex, and even more so on authoritarianism and on our overall political leanings. But it would be wrong to conclude from such data that it therefore follows that a specific gene exists for socialism, or conservatism or liberalism or any other political trait. Rather, our genetic make-up, and the complex emotional, biological and psychological structures it creates in our brains,[27] *predisposes* us

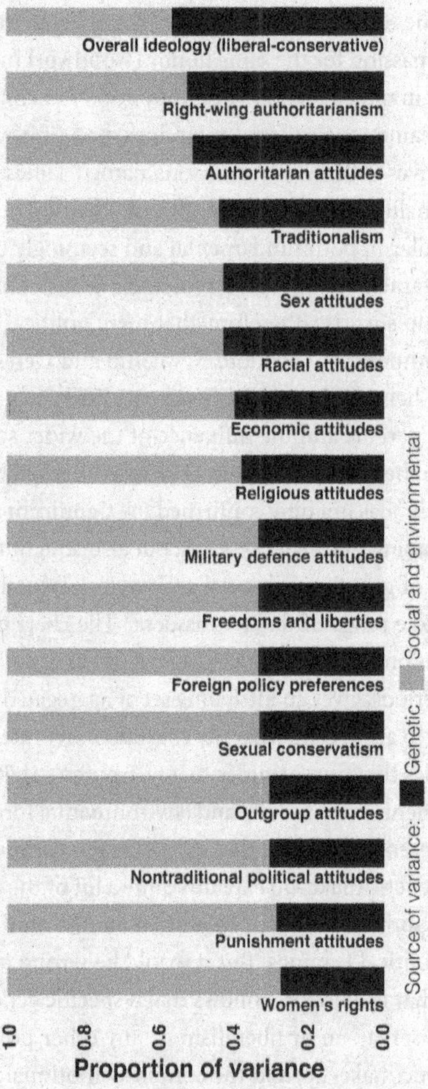

Figure 3: The relative genetic and environmental influences on political attitudes and ideologies[28]

Bars (top to bottom):
- Overall ideology (liberal-conservative)
- Right-wing authoritarianism
- Authoritarian attitudes
- Traditionalism
- Sex attitudes
- Racial attitudes
- Economic attitudes
- Religious attitudes
- Military defence attitudes
- Freedoms and liberties
- Foreign policy preferences
- Sexual conservatism
- Outgroup attitudes
- Nontraditional political attitudes
- Punishment attitudes
- Women's rights

Source of variance: Genetic / Social and environmental

Proportion of variance
0.0 0.2 0.4 0.6 0.8 1.0

to react in particular ways to information, to events, to the people around us. It influences our *sensitivity* to our environment.

The field of epigenetics[29] has proved crucial in helping to explain the processes at work here because it has revealed the role played by 'regulator genes'[30] – that is, genes that switch other genes on or off – in determining how we react to different types of stimulus, whether that stimulus is a sudden awareness of danger or risk, or a reaction to someone who is friendly or unfriendly, or is chemically induced by sugar or alcohol. To borrow an analogy devised by Professor Gary Marcus at New York University, regulator genes are like a computer program that has been coded with a precondition (IF) and an action (THEN).[31] An event takes place – we meet someone new, we hear unexpected news, we are confronted by a problem. Our regulator genes then automatically click in to respond. For example, if we are confronted with a sudden emergency, the amygdala, a primitive part of the lower brain responsible for our fight-or-flight mechanism, will sound an alarm. Adrenaline and stress hormones will then be released, extra blood will be sent to the muscles, breathing will quicken, our blood pressure will skyrocket, glucose will be disgorged by the liver, and non-essential bodily functions will stop. Although these automatic processes generally happen across all humans, the rapidity, strength and sensitivity of the response will vary widely from person to person. Faced with something unexpected, there are those who will experience a panic attack when the system is triggered. Others, though, will display quite muted physiological reactions to even life-threatening events. The rock climber Alex Honnold, who became the first person to achieve a free solo ascent of El Capitan in California's Yosemite National Park in 2017, is an extreme case in point. Even though he climbed the vertical 900-metre granite wall without ropes and could have fallen to his death at any moment, he remained calm throughout. A study of his amygdala showed that, compared to the norm, Honnold's response to threat 'does not show anything'.[32]

21

In other words, as differences in our structural genes explain variations in our physical appearance (such as hair or eye colour), so differences in our regulator genes partly explain differences in our behaviour. It's not a question of nature versus nurture, but of the way nature *interacts* with nurture.[33] Findings in modern behavioural genetics reveal the effect of genes to be interactive rather than directive, let alone determinative.

So why might our genes ultimately map onto the views we hold on things as cerebral as the economy or politics? The answer lies in the fact that at a fundamental level social and political attitudes, to quote Peter Hatemi and Rose McDermott, professors specialising in politics and biochemistry at Penn State and Brown University respectively, 'encompass issues of group living – that is, all those issues surrounding survival, cooperation, and reproduction'.[34] It's certainly the case that the ways in which these issues play out in the twenty-first century are more complicated and nuanced than they were for our prehistoric forebears, but they remain, at their core, the same. Modern economic regulation, welfare programmes and taxation are essentially about how we cooperate and share resources across different groups. Concerns about immigration are about offsetting potential gains and risks posed by outsiders. In the words of Professors Hatemi and McDermott: 'Name a divisive modern political issue and there are numerous evolutionary processes that map to it.'[35] We use the same cognitive and emotional processes in modern politics and society as our ancestors did. Political orientations would not have become part of our genes and core biological processes[36] unless they served to further our survival by helping us to organise our political and social world. The labels used (Republican, Labour, Social Democrat and so on) and the precise details of the issues at stake may vary across different cultures and over time in a way that 'brown eyes' or 'blond hair' don't, but the underlying issues they describe are hard-wired into the human psyche.

And just as humans vary in their physical characteristics, so they do in their political views. As Professors Hatemi and McDermott put it:

> Variation persists precisely because human populations adapt to a wide variety of circumstances, including diverse climates and ecologies, environmental resources and constraints, population pressures, in-group and out-group challenges, and differential threats from predators and pathogens. In order to flourish across the globe, humans depend on biological systems that elicit, and respond to, critical information from the environment at both the individual and population levels. This results in a plethora of discrete attitudes that emerge within a universal structure that not only supports the existence of such values and beliefs regarding one's own personal preferences, but also informs judgments about how others in society should behave toward oneself and others.[37]

In other words, responses and attitudes will always vary, but they are responses and attitudes to a common set of issues and circumstances which often assume a political complexion.[38]

Decades of research into the psychology of authoritarianism, beginning with that undertaken by Else Frenkel-Brunswik and her colleagues in the 1950s, offer a window onto this complex world. Else herself had good reason to be interested in the topic. The middle of three daughters of a prominent Jewish banker, she was born in 1908 in Lemberg,[39] the then capital of Galicia, in the Austro-Hungarian Empire, but, with the rest of her family, had to move to Vienna in 1914 after the outbreak of the First World War to escape the pogroms targeted at Poland's Jewish community. Else thrived in Vienna and in 1930 became one of the few women to earn a psychology doctorate. She then worked at the University of Vienna on psychoanalysis and personality research. But eight years later, she again had to flee anti-Semitism when the Nazis annexed Austria. After marrying a fellow psychologist, Egon Brunswik, the couple emigrated to the US. Because of university rules governing nepotism, she could not receive a tenured position at Berkeley where her husband taught, so instead took up a post as a research associate, seeking to find out what personality traits might make a person more prejudiced, dogmatic and intolerant of others. Along with Theodore W. Adorno, Daniel Levinson and Nevitt Sanford, she then wrote a book that has become a classic: *The Authoritarian Personality.*[40]

Her findings, though challenged and refined since, posit a convincing and fundamental link between an underlying personality type and a particular political outlook. She and her fellow researchers found that most people with an authoritarian personality type are brought up in very strict households where rules are followed to the letter and strict punishment is meted out to rule breakers. They go on to internalise these very strict moral beliefs, feeling insecure if they sense they are not living up to the high standards they set themselves. Ultimately, they come to regard strength and power as admirable qualities, other traits as a sign of weakness, and are prepared to sacrifice a strong sense of self-identity in the interests of maintaining a precarious sense of safety. The world for them becomes a place of opposites and absolutes: good and evil, ingroups and outgroups. Ingroups are strong, powerful and good. Outgroups are weak and bad. There is no room for ambiguity and uncertainty. It's worth noting, incidentally, that later researchers have suggested that there is a hereditary aspect to such a world view.[41]

What's important to note here is that a presdisposition to an authoritarian outlook is not a niche trait. In its resistance to difference, rejection of pluralism and desire for strong order and control, it plays to fundamental human concerns. Karen Stenner, a leading contemporary scholar on authoritarianism, estimates that around one-third of white people in Western liberal democracies have a tendency to prefer 'oneness' (a common authority) and 'sameness' (shared values),[42] pointing out that there is a fundamental division within humanity between those who embrace difference and those who dislike it. Some researchers suggest a link between an authoritarian mindset and a lack of 'openness to experience'[43,44] – identified as one of the 'Big Five' personality dimensions[45] that, along with other factors,[46] reduces the willingness and capacity to tolerate complexity, diversity, and difference.

If an authoritarian outlook can be mapped to aspects of our personality, so can other political and social views. Collectively, the Big Five[47] personality dimensions are thought to encompass and summarise the vast majority of individual personalities:

1) Openness to experience (tendency to be more receptive to new ideas and new experiences and comfortable with the unfamiliar);
2) Conscientiousness (tendency to be responsible, organised, hard-working, goal-directed, and to adhere to norms and rules);
3) Extraversion (characterised by excitability, sociability and emotional expressiveness);
4) Agreeableness (tendency to be more co-operative and caring);
5) Neuroticism (characterised by sadness, moodiness and emotional instability).

A consistent finding among personality researchers is that openness to experience predicts a more liberal ideology, whereas conscientiousness predicts a more conservative ideology.[48] As Professor of Psychology and Politics John Jost and his colleagues explain in their study of conservatism, a psychological need for certainty leads to a preference for the preservation of the status quo, and an equanimity about inequality.

A related approach, albeit narrower in its application than the Big Five personality traits, accounts for differences in our beliefs by drawing on moral philosophy. Professor Jonathan Haidt's is probably the best-known account of moral foundations theory,[49] [50] a theory that helps to explain why moral codes should vary so much across cultures and yet share many similarities and recurrent themes. He draws on a food analogy to explain: 'Cultures vary enormously in their cuisines, which are cultural constructions shaped by historical events, yet the world's many cuisines must ultimately please tongues equipped with just five innate and universal taste receptors.'[51] When it comes to human morality, he argues, there are six different 'intuitions':[52]

1) **Care/harm** (related to our long evolution as mammals with attachment systems and an ability to feel and dislike the pain of others. This intuition underlies the virtues of kindness, gentleness and nurturing);

2) **Fairness/cheating** (related to the evolutionary process of reciprocal altruism, generating ideas concerned with justice, rights and individual autonomy);

3) **Loyalty/betrayal** (related to our long history as tribal creatures able to form shifting coalitions. This intuition underlies the virtues of patriotism and self-sacrifice for the group);

4) **Authority/subversion** (shaped by our long primate history involving hierarchical social interactions. This intuition underlies the virtues of leadership and followership, including deference to legitimate authority and respect for traditions);

5) **Sanctity/degradation** (shaped by the psychology of disgust and contamination. This intuition underlies the religious notion of striving to live in an elevated, less carnal, more noble way);

6) **Liberty/oppression** (related to the hostility and resentment people feel towards those who dominate them and restrict their liberty. This intuition is often in tension with that related to authority. The hatred of bullies and dominators motivates

26

people to come together, in solidarity, to oppose or take down the oppressor).

As with the Big Five personality traits, these 'moral foundations' have political manifestations. Broadly speaking, for example, progressives[53] prioritise avoiding harm and upholding fairness/reciprocity. Conservatives hold these values, too, but also evaluate the world more broadly, placing great emphasis on loyalty, authority and purity. Haidt argues that biology provides us with a 'first draft' of these moral foundations, and that these are then revised during childhood and across cultures. The first draft is not the finished story, of course, but it does influence what comes afterwards. A brother and sister who share similar experiences but possess different dispositional traits will tend to develop different moral and political beliefs and be drawn towards different ideological narratives and groups. While it may not dictate it, our basic biology shapes what we think later on in life.

No explanation of why Derek Black and Theodore Newcomb formed the beliefs they did is complete without focusing on the values we hold. The political science professor Philip Converse once described values as 'a sort of glue to bind together many more specific attitudes and beliefs'.[54] Since they influence what we *believe* we ought to think or do, they may not always hold sway in particular instances, and their relative importance will vary from person to person. But as core, albeit not fixed, predispositions they are very powerful and, like our personality traits and moral reasoning, are shaped and influenced by a blend of our genetic predispositions,[55] our upbringing and our culture. In helping us to navigate our social, economic, and political worlds,[56] they can influence whether we accept or reject particular norms, standards or rules.

According to Shalom Schwartz and his colleagues,[57] it's possible to identify ten basic personal values, across four 'higher-order' dimensions,[58] that are applicable to all cultures:

Number #	Value	Higher-order dimension
1	**Power**: social status and prestige, control or dominance over people and resources	1. Self-enhancement
2	**Achievement**: personal success through demonstrating competence according to social standards	
3	**Hedonism**: pleasure and sensuous gratification for oneself	2. Openness to change
4	**Stimulation**: excitement, novelty, and challenge in life	
5	**Self-direction**: independent thought and action – choosing, creating, exploring	
6	**Universalism**: understanding, appreciation, tolerance, and protection for the welfare of all people and for nature	3. Self-transcendence
7	**Benevolence**: preservation and enhancement of the welfare of people with whom one is in frequent personal contact	
8	**Tradition**: respect, commitment and acceptance of the customs and ideas that traditional culture or religion provide	4. Conservation
9	**Conformity**: restraint of actions, inclinations, and impulses likely to upset or harm others and violate social expectations or norms	
10	**Security**: safety, harmony, and stability of society, of relationships, and of self	

Figure 4: Ten basic personal values

As with the Big Five personality traits and Jonathan Haidt's six moral foundations, these are not uniquely political, but they do map with distinct political attitudes and help to explain differences in broader personal, social and economic attitudes. Bankers and managers, for example, may emphasise power (#1) and achievement (#2); nurses and psychologists may regard universalism (#6) and benevolence (#7)[59] as the key values. In political terms, those who regard power (#1) and security (#10) as priorities will be the ones who also tend to favour nationalist policies.[60] Those[61] who adopt 'Conservation' values (which include #8, #9 and #10) will generally opt for 'militant internationalism' or hawkishness in international relations. The individual value of universalism (#6) best predicts 'co-operative internationalism', in which mutualism and cosmopolitanism are key.

Not only does Schwartz's values table shed light on particular political stances, but it also helps to explain why correlations exist between beliefs on otherwise discrete issues. In purely intellectual terms, there is no reason why, for example, someone who is passionately partisan about global warming should also have a view on, say, gun control. In values terms, though, there is. The Yale law professor Dan Kahan suggests that people develop 'cultural world views' (broadly comparable to Schwartz's higher-order value dimensions) – their vision of a good society – that shape their beliefs about specific policies.[62] Everything from a specific attitude towards social care to an opinion on the UN fits within an invisible grid of 'world views'.

There's an obvious danger of being too reductionist here (some scholars, indeed, question whether one can talk in terms of distinct, separable cultural world views.)[63] And it's definitely not the case that holding to certain values automatically makes one authoritarian or liberal or an anarchist. So much depends on context. Generally speaking, for instance, it's only when people feel they are under threat – particularly when they face what Karen Stenner calls a 'normative threat', or a threat to the perceived integrity of the moral order – that they value openness less and begin to ask for greater force and authoritarian power.[64] A remorselessly authoritarian mind-set is unusual. Nevertheless, the idea that underlying values – granted that individuals will prioritise them differently – can explain how disparate views are fundamentally linked is very useful.

If *what* we think shapes our political selves, there's evidence to suggest that *how* we think has an impact, too. It was Else Frenkel-Brunswik who first suggested that a key hallmark of authoritarianism is deeply rooted mental rigidity or 'cognitive inflexibility'. In her view such a way of thinking makes it difficult for individuals to adapt to new or changing environments. The contemporary Cambridge psychologist Leor Zmigrod similarly argues that there is a link between those who think about things rigidly and single-mindedly and intergroup hostility and extremism. By contrast, cognitive flexibility is linked with tolerance and acceptance of others not like us. As the economist John Maynard Keynes put it, albeit in a different context: 'The difficulty lies, not in the new ideas, but in escaping from the old ones, which ramify, for those brought up as most of us have been, into every corner of our minds.'

Relative mental rigidity or flexibility may sound subjective, and, as Zmigrod[65] explains in her research, in the early days of political psychology they proved difficult to define and measure accurately, particularly when traditional self-report methods were used.[66] However, there are now reliable ways to quantify the extent to which individuals persist with previously established rules, mental heuristics (applied rules of thumb), or behavioural patterns. One such involves getting them to repeat a task over and over again, and then measuring their accuracy rates and reaction times when asked to switch to doing something else. When Zmigrod and her colleagues applied such methods,[67] they found that those assessed as displaying cognitive rigidity also scored highly for nationalism, conservativism and heightened authoritarianism, which in turn predict attitudes to particular contemporary issues like Brexit and immigration.[68] What's particularly interesting here is that the research suggests that, as well as 'hot' emotions, emotionally neutral 'cold' cognitive processing styles may also play a key part in politicised identities.

Rigidity of thought is not the preserve of an individual political group or wing. Indeed, as Zmigrod and her colleagues demonstrated in a study of over 700 US citizens, it's just as observable on the left of the political spectrum as it is on the right.[69] Participants had their mental rigidity measured, and were also invited to indicate their relative feelings of attachment to the Republicans and Democrats by clicking and dragging images of themselves and the two parties closer together or further apart. The results showed a clear correlation between inflexibility of thought and intensity of party allegiance, with participants on both the extreme left and right displaying reduced flexibility in comparison with those whose attachment to either party was weaker. The findings echo other research that shows cognitive inflexibility to be related to nationalism, religiosity,[70] extremist attitudes[71] and general dogmatism.[72]

The perils of seeing the world not as it is, but as we want it to be

If all this suggests that those of us who regard ourselves as moderates have brilliantly flexible minds, that is, sadly, very far from the case. The fact is that most of us find it very hard to change our fundamental views. We think we assess new information objectively, and draw logical conclusions accordingly. Decades of behavioural science research suggest strongly, however, that this is not always – or often – the case. Rather, we typically see, hear and remember a version of the world that fits in with our existing beliefs and world views.

This insight is scarcely new. The Ancient Greek general and historian Thucydides described in his *History of the Peloponnesian War* how 'it is a habit of humanity to entrust to careless hope what they long for, and to use sovereign reason to thrust aside what they do not fancy.' Similarly, the philosopher and statesman Francis Bacon commented in 1620 that 'the human understanding when it has once adopted an opinion ... draws all things else to support and agree with it.' Literature and films abound with plots that turn on incorrect preconceptions. In the popular 2014 Indian movie *PK*, for example, Jaggu, an Indian Hindu woman in love with a Pakistani Muslim, is so convinced that things won't work out that she immediately accepts as genuine a forged letter, supposedly written by her fiancé, calling off the marriage. When it comes to politics, people will take the same evidence to 'prove' contradicting standpoints. When it comes to finding *out* about politics, Republicans watch Fox News while Democrats watch MSNBC. When it comes to science, creationists see fossils as evidence of God, while evolutionary biologists see them as evidence of evolution.

Arguably the first thorough investigation of this phenomenon was 'On the failure to eliminate hypotheses in a conceptual task', a 1960 paper by the cognitive psychologist Peter Wason.[73] He found that when asked to infer a rule governing various triplets of numbers (for example, 2, 4, 6), a proportion of participants (not all) would arrive at a hypothesis and then test only those results that confirmed it, as opposed to instances that would disconfirm it. The philosopher Karl Popper had previously argued that for a theory to be proved scientific it had to be capable of being tested and possibly proved to be false. Wason showed that, however desirable that approach might be, many people operate in an entirely 'unscientific' way.[74] As the Professor of Psychology at Tufts University, Raymond Nickerson, puts it, the 'confirmation bias' Wason identified involves the 'seeking or interpreting of evidence in ways that are partial to existing beliefs, expectations, or a hypothesis in hand'.[75]

Confirmation bias has become something of an umbrella term for the multiple, distinct ways in which our beliefs and/or expectations influence the selection, retention and evaluation of evidence. It has also sometimes been conflated with what is often known as 'motivated reasoning'. In general terms, confirmation bias is an unconscious bias (the 'unwitting selectivity in the acquisition and use of evidence'[76]) and closer to an attentional bias, whereby we pay attention to some things while simultaneously ignoring others. Motivated reasoning, by contrast, implies volition. Or as Gary Marcus, Professor of Psychology at NYU, puts it:

> Our tendency to accept what we wish to believe (what we are motivated to believe) with much less scrutiny than what we don't want to believe is a bias known as 'motivated reasoning', a kind of flip side to confirmation bias. Whereas confirmation bias is an automatic tendency to notice data that fit with our beliefs, motivated reasoning is the complementary tendency to scrutinise ideas more carefully if we don't like them than if we do.[77]

Both serve the same purpose: to frame the world in a readily comprehensible way. A world in which we can feel more certain and less threatened. As the cognitive scientists Mercier and Sperber so accurately put it, we 'are not after the truth, but after arguments supporting our views.'[78]

Motivated reasoning[79] gives us comfort in our convictions and confirmation of what we want to believe to be true. Like confirmation bias, it also removes disconcerting complexity. In what has now become regarded as something of a classic study, the Israeli social psychologist Ziva Kunda[80] demonstrated just how powerful motivated reasoning can be. Volunteers were told they would be playing a history trivia game. They were also told that, to get the hang of it, they would observe someone else (the 'Winner') play the game before they began. Half the group were then told that the Winner would join their team. The other half were told the Winner would join the rival team. In fact, the Winner who demonstrated the game was a stooge, or confederate, set up to play the game perfectly and answer every question correctly. What Kunda found was that attitudes to this seeming paragon of excellence diverged sharply. Those who were told that he would be joining their team in due course praised his 'skills'. Those who thought he would be competing against them were dismissive, tending to attribute his accuracy to luck. Both groups saw exactly the same 'performance', yet came to opposite conclusions.

Kunda's study is not a one-off. Other research has detected motivated reasoning among people of all classes, ages, races, genders and political affiliations, and in all sorts of situations.[81] Take, for example, the study done by Charles Lord, Lee Ross and Mark Lepper at Stanford in 1979.[82] This involved selecting participants known to be either defenders or opponents of the death penalty, and asking them to evaluate two studies (A and B) supposedly designed to test how effective the death penalty was as a deterrent. The literature for study A suggested that the death penalty reduced murder rates in the US states where it was implemented. Study B literature suggested precisely the opposite. Both studies followed almost precisely the same methodology.

Once they had sifted the results, the Stanford researchers found that participants' assessments of the design and conduct of the experiments they were asked to study were consistently skewed by their own beliefs. Those who championed the death penalty prior to the study tended to rate the study that demonstrated its effectiveness highly, and were critical of the one that showed it be counter-productive. Those against the death penalty came to the opposite conclusion. In fact, the opposing viewpoints actually became *more* fixed over the course of the study. As the authors sadly concluded: 'People of opposing views can each find support for those views in the same body of evidence.' It's a phenomenon known as biased assimilation (or biased evaluation[83]), and leads to what is often referred to as 'attitude polarisation',[84] whereby people's response becomes *more* biased in response to a particular body of evidence, rather than less. Quite simply, faced with an argument that runs contrary to our own beliefs and preferences, we will discern so many flaws in it and come up with so many counterarguments that, far from questioning our original standpoint, we end up holding to it more steadfastly. Such mental effort rather puts paid to the cynical notion that people cling to their views because they are too lazy to process new information. In fact, considerable mental effort is required to sift new evidence in order to weed out what we disagree with and bolster our existing views – it would, after all, be much easier simply to accept what we are now being presented with.

Such cognitive asymmetry – where people update their prior beliefs to incorporate new, desirable and confirming information more than new but disconfirming and undesirable information – is extraordinarily powerful. It crops up in every area of our lives. It rears its head, for example, when we're being presented with information about our personality traits,[85] or about our abilities and attractiveness,[86] or about the risks of our experiencing future negative life events.[87] And it persists – however balanced the information we receive might be.[88] Only if the 'new' information is 'desirable', emerging research suggests – in other words is not consistent with our views but still serves our needs – are we more likely to accept it.[89] People will cling on to beliefs even when they have definitively been proved to be ill-founded (a phenomenon known as belief perseverance).[90]

Studies of the brain show how difficult we find it to process and integrate conflicting views we feel strongly about. In one, conducted by a group of researchers at the University of Southern California (USC),[91] a group of people who self-identified as liberals were presented with a mix of political statements they had previously indicated they strongly agreed with ('Welfare and food stamp programs offer necessary help to the poor') and non-political statements that were straightforward facts ('Thomas Edison invented the lightbulb'). Each statement was followed by a counterargument or contradictory evidence. Then the original statement was shown again and the volunteers were asked to report how strongly they now held to it. When pre-scan and post-challenge ratings were compared, it emerged that participants were more prepared to shift their previously held position on non-political statements than they were on political statements.[92]

Scans of the volunteers' brains taken while the study was being conducted suggested the reasons. When volunteers were reading statements that challenged their political beliefs, increased activity was detected in regions of their brains' default mode network, a network linked to self-representation (high-level thinking about who we are, our personal beliefs and values). Those most resistant to changing their minds also showed more activity in the amygdala and the insular cortex – the regions of the brain associated with emotion and decision-making. Their brains, in other words, were struggling to process and integrate opposing views with deeply held beliefs. At the same time the challenge to core beliefs was arousing perceptions of threat, uncertainty and anxiety, much as threats to physical safety might do.

It is not necessarily wrong or irrational to prize new evidence more highly when it is consistent with prior beliefs and less highly when it contradicts them. Indeed in many cases it is 'rational' – or logical – to filter new information in line with what we already know. Professor Tali Sharot at University College London points out that we would, quite understandably, doubt the evidence of our eyes if we saw a flying pig or heard from a friend that they had witnessed one, as such an occurrence would contradict our strongly held prior belief that flying pigs don't exist.[93] The problems creep in when our prior beliefs do not involve real prior knowledge – when they represent something we *want* to be true, even when there's a lack of supporting evidence. Such prior beliefs are not wisdom. They are convictions. As such they are tied up with our group identities, emotions and values rather than our rational intellect.

This perhaps helps to explain why misperceptions – beliefs about policy or politics that are factually incorrect or contrary to the best available evidence – are typically widely held, easily spread and difficult to correct. People do not think they are lacking in knowledge or don't understand – they hold beliefs very strongly. But the very strength of their convictions makes their brains resistant to a change of mind. It's worth noting in this context that those who most vigorously reject the scientific evidence for climate change are also those who believe they are best informed about the subject.[94]

The desire for consistency also plays a vitally important role in explaining why our prior beliefs can be so sticky in the face of new information. Consistency is usually taken to be an important requirement of rationality,[95] possibly the most important. The problem is that the desire to be consistent can be so strong as to make it difficult for us to evaluate new information in an objective way. We also worry about losing face. The very fact that we tend to treat data selectively and partially is testament to the high value we attach to consistency. If consistency between beliefs and new information were of no importance, people would have no reason to guard beliefs against data inconsistent with those beliefs.

Why the aversion to inconsistency? The American psychologist Eliot Aronson argued that the key to understanding whether a particular inconsistency will arouse cognitive dissonance is whether it has implications for our core sense of self – essentially, how we define ourselves.[96] People like to think of themselves as – and be considered – rational, morally upright, worthy individuals. Anything that challenges such assessments is likely to cause dissonance.[97] And that is something we choose to avoid.

Perhaps the most extreme example of an obsession with cognitive consistency is that displayed by the members of the apocalyptic cult described in Leon Festinger's 1956 book *When Prophecy Fails*,[98] co-authored with Henry Riecken and Stanley Schachter. All the cult members were convinced that at midnight on 21 December 1954 aliens would come to take them away in a flying saucer and that before dawn the world would end with a flood, and on the night in question gathered to await the arrival of the aliens. Midnight duly came – and went. And the world carried on. Understandably bewildered, the cult members cast around for reasons why things had not turned out as they should have done. However, the leader of the cult, Marian Keech, was able to reassure most of them. She had received a message, she said, that the God of Earth had decided to spare the planet from destruction on this occasion. As explanations go, this seems transparently weak, if not desperate. But it worked. Far from accusing Marian Keech of clutching at straws, or being downcast or angry, the cult members felt reassured by this confirmation of their beliefs. They stayed together and continued to spread their doomsday ideology to non-believers.

As Festinger said: 'A man with conviction is a hard man to change. Tell him you disagree and he turns away. Show him facts or figures and he questions your sources. Appeal to logic and he fails to see your point.'[99]

FROM INDIVIDUAL BELIEFS
TO GROUP IDENTITIES

The group instinct

> Fish swimming in synchronised unison are called a *school*. A gathering
> of kangeroos is a *mob*. A threesome of crows cawing from their perch
> on a telephone wire is a *murder*. A *gam* is a group of whales. A flock of
> larks in flight is an *exaltation*. But what is a collection of human beings
> called? A *group*.[1]

It's not exactly the most imaginative of terms. But that can't disguise
the fact that the group is key to human existence. Whether it takes
the form of the family, friendship circle, team, tribe or clan, it is central to the ways we organise ourselves and live.[2]

It's also something that we are naturally predisposed to form.
Early humans gathered together to increase their chances of survival.
The group offered them protection from predators, greater chance of
finding and sharing food, access to partners and help with raising
children. Hunting large animals, defending against enemies, and
protecting against external threats would have been impossible

without co-operation, trust, altruism and reciprocity.[3] It's not surprising, therefore, that a sense of which groups we belong to – beyond our family group – begins early. At the age of two, children are capable of understanding which gender group they and others fit into.[4] By the time they're three they are aware of race[5] and tend to be more drawn to friendships with those of the same sex.[6] By the time they're between four and six years old, they will offer predictions on what someone else will be like or what they will do based on that person's gender, race, or ethnicity.[7] Children also use information about who belongs to which groups and the dynamics between those groups to predict whether individuals will harm each other (at around the age of four), help each other (from six years), or be friends with each other (from seven years).[8]

If the group offers physical safety and physical resources, it also fulfils many of our deepest psychological needs.[9] Belonging to a group brings us a powerful and rewarding sense of self-esteem and self-worth.[10] It gives us a sense of social identity, helping us to understand who we are, how to behave and what our relation to those around us is.[11] Who we are is, at least partly, about the groups we belong to. As the psychologists Michael Hogg and Graham Vaughan argue:

> Groups provide us with a consensually recognised and validated definition and evaluation of who we are, how we should behave and how we will be treated by others . . . [Social identity] helps to reduce feelings of uncertainty about who we are, how we should behave and how others will perceive and interact with us.[12]

It is, of course, possible for people to survive on their own, but few choose to do so, and the alternative – isolation – brings with it challenges and drawbacks. During the 2020–1 Covid-19 pandemic, when millions were forced to keep apart from one another and observe social distancing, it was estimated that almost a fifth of the UK population required some measure of mental health support.[13] The prospect of being shut out from a community is hard for most of us to cope with. Indeed it's so hard that the United Nations defines as torture any period of solitary confinement lasting more than 15 days.[14] When researchers at the University of California, Los Angeles, used a functional magnetic resonance imaging scanner to track neural responses to exclusion, they found that people who were left out of a group activity displayed heightened cortical activity in two specific areas of the brain – the dorsal anterior cingulate cortex and the anterior insula – that are associated with the experience of physical pain sensations.[15] It literally hurts not to belong.

And once we form a link with others, we are reluctant to break it. We resist dropping people's names from a mailing list (virtual or physical) because to do so signifies a final dissolution of a social tie. We text friends we no longer see to wish them a happy birthday. We send Christmas cards to people we scarcely remember. Indeed, research has shown that if we receive a Christmas card from a total stranger, we may even reciprocate in order to avoid damaging a relationship that doesn't exist.[16]

What constitutes a group? There's no precise definition on which psychologists, sociologists and anthropologists are agreed, and there is no magic number that determines when a collection of people becomes a group.[17] Clearly, though, for one to exist there needs to be some kind of shared bond. A random collection of people on an aeroplane is, in sociological terms, not a group, since all they have in common is a shared space. Should the plane be hijacked, however, this random collection will now collectively need to decide how to react and interact with one another. They will become more interdependent.[18] In so doing they will become a group, influencing each other's thoughts, values, actions and emotions. Roey Rosenbilth describes such an experience after an attempted hijacking of the plane in which he was travelling from Amsterdam to Detroit. Before the incident, he exchanged 'niceties' with his fellow travellers and then settled down to watch three films. But when one wannabe hijacker started a fire that others managed to extinguish, and all were then detained for five hours, he noted how they became more inter-dependent.[19] Obviously, what draws any particular group together varies widely. In families, kinship is key. In the workplace, shared jobs and tasks lead to group formation and may ultimately inspire friend-ships founded on shared experience.[20]

How much a group, rather than simply being an ad hoc collection of individuals, achieves a sense of mutuality or oneness – what in social science is referred to as *entitativity* – is highly subjective. The so-called Thomas Theorem[21] argues that 'If men define situations as real, they are real in their consequences.'[22] Applied to groups, this suggests that if we perceive a group to be real, it is real in as much as it exists for us, and that if it's real for us our perceptions of its individual members will be modified accordingly.[23] Even so, as the chart opposite shows, it is possible to make some generalisations about different types of group that hold for most humans. Here researchers have recorded the aggre-gated responses of people asked to judge the extent to which particular collections of people can be regarded as groups, on a scale from 1 (not at all a group) to 9 (very much a group). The results are much as one would expect. Not surprisingly, primary groups such as family and close friends receive the highest entitativity ratings, followed by social groups (e.g. work team), then social categories (e.g. women), then col-lectives (e.g. queues). Temporary gatherings such as audiences, crowds or queues are regarded as precisely that: temporary.

Obviously, almost no one defines themselves purely in terms of membership of a single group, and there is a constant interplay between our individual and group (or social) identities. Even within and across those two (individual and group) identities there is con-siderable fluidity, depending on context, with both sometimes at

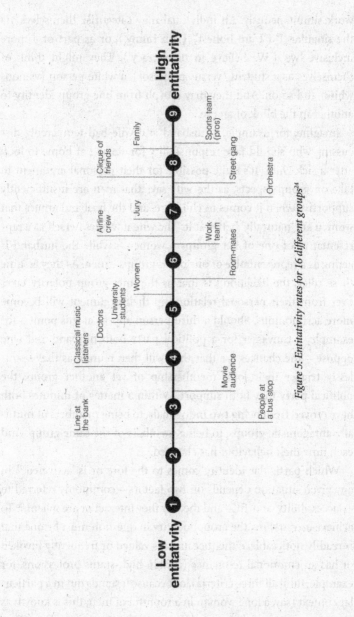

Figure 5: Entitativity rates for 16 different groups[24]

work simultaneously. An individual may categorise themselves via the singular 'I' ('I am honest', 'I am funny'), or as part of a more inclusive 'we' ('We believe in democracy'). They might think of themselves as a student (versus professor), a white person (vs non-white) and so on. And they may morph from one group identity to another in the blink of an eye.

Imagine, for example, a husband and wife bad-temperedly discussing who should take responsibility for staying at home to look after a sick child. It's quite possible for their personal argument to take on group aspects, as the wife says that men are insufficiently supportive when it comes to childcare, and the husband argues that women are 'naturally' better at it. The wife now sees herself as a representative of one of her groups – women – while the husband is acting as a representative of one of his groups – men. As they assume these roles, the likelihood is that as the inter-group polarity takes over from their personal relationship their argument will become more acrimonious. Should a third person appear at this point – for example, a canvasser for a political party both husband and wife oppose – the chances are that they will then reunite as they seamlessly trigger their joint membership of yet another group: the political party they both support. Within a matter of minutes both have moved from being two individuals, to being members of mutually antagonistic groups, to being members of the same group. And each time their behaviour has changed.

Which particular identity comes to the fore or is 'activated'[25] in any given situation depends on two factors – commonly referred to as 'accessibility' and 'fit' – and the way they interact or are salient.[26] To achieve *accessibility*, the group identity in question must be one that is readily noticeable, either because it's valued or frequently invoked or has an emotional resonance (certain high-status professions, for example, fulfil all three criteria), or because it stands out in a particular context (say, a lone woman in a roomful of men; this is known as *situational accessibility*). 'Fit' is all about how much a group or category stands out from other groups or categories on particular attributes (e.g. intellect or creativity or sociability) in a particular situation. The best fit is a group or category which maximises differences *between* groups and similarities *within* groups.

Take, for example, a conference to which designers and accountants – both male and female – have been invited. The likelihood is that, having taken note of the accountants, the designers will identify with the category of 'designer'. However, if an incident takes place that makes the differences between the male and female designers at the party appear more pronounced than those between the designers and the accountants, attendees may then be more likely to categorise themselves as male or female. Acting against type (technically known as *normative fit*) may achieve similar disruption to the initial status quo. If, during a break, the accountants put down their calculators and take to producing ice sculptures, the saliency of the category 'designer' will inevitably be reduced.

But just because the personal or group identity we adopt at any given moment can be fluid, that doesn't make the dynamics and pull of group membership any less powerful. Those looking from the outside at a group – particularly one with high entitativity, such as a family or a sports team[27] – will tend to regard its members more as stereotypes than individuals[28]: uniform and interchangeable.[29] And if they are not well disposed to that group they may automatically assume an individual member to be unfriendly and hostile.[30] Those inside the group are affected by membership, too. They come to identify with the group and its goals, feel an emotional bond with it and value the importance of that bond, particularly if they're not already wholly certain about the correctness of their beliefs. Researchers told women working interdependently on a task that they formed part of a high-unity group. When told that the 'group' failed the women rated themselves more negatively. In a subsequent stage, the same women worked independently on a similar task and showed reduced self-confidence. There was, of course, no group. But the women's view of themselves was nevertheless modified by the assumption.[31] Over time these processes become self-fulfilling prophecies. If we perceive a bunch of individuals to be a group, we are more likely to treat them as such, and they will respond by becoming what we assume them to be.[32] Groupishness[33] fuels groupishness.

Although groups are common to all societies, there is a cultural aspect to them.[34] People in non-Western societies, such as those of India or China, are more likely to think of themselves as group members first and individuals second. Chinese citizens, for example, will typically resist making judgements of an individual unless they know something about the group to which that person belongs. Japanese people similarly tend to start with the group to understand and explain the world around them, hence, arguably, the fourteen different words for 'group' in Japanese.[35] Groups are crucial to the cohesion of Western cultures, too, but people in countries such as the UK and the US tend to perceive the world more through an individualistic lens than a group one, unless that group happens to have achieved particular salience at a given moment.

It's perhaps worth delving a little deeper into the psychological needs that group membership fulfils. Key here is its role in reducing uncertainty.[36] Because we 'belong', we are equipped with a reassuring set of agreed beliefs and values that make navigating an uncertain world that much easier. At the same time, as the basic premise of social identity theory[37] posits, we achieve an enhanced sense of self-worth. Confidence and self-esteem obviously derive to a considerable extent from personal evaluation and achievement ('I'm a doctor', 'I'm clever', 'I have a BMW'). But they derive, too, from the status conferred on us by membership of a particular group. In some instances we may view that status as being so significant for us that we are prepared to signal it visually, as members of political parties frequently do when they don a particular political logo or colour.

The social psychologist Vivian Vignoles and his colleagues suggest that in total there are six forms of motivation that prompt us to seek psychological membership of a group:[38, 39]

1. Self-esteem – the need to maintain and enhance a positive evaluation of the self.
2. Efficacy – the need to maintain or enhance feelings of competence and control.
3. Belonging – the need to maintain or enhance feelings of closeness to, or acceptance by, other people.
4. Distinctiveness – the need to establish and maintain a sense of differentiation from others.
5. Continuity – the need to maintain a sense of consistency across time and situations.
6. Meaning – the need to find significance in and purpose for the self's behaviours and existence.

We will identify with groups that are most able to fulfil these needs. These six factors are not always or even necessarily equally weighted. It's quite possible, for example, for the powerful desire for positive self-esteem to override that of a desire to belong. One of the authors of this book knows from personal experience how her son (then six years old), having loyally adopted his football fan father's team, Everton, out of a sense of wanting to 'belong', was then prepared to risk his displeasure when Everton suffered a losing streak by switching loyalty to the much more successful Manchester United. Whatever paternal pressure may have been brought to bear, associating with Everton was threatening his self-esteem, and he wanted to be associated with winners. Such a desire is extraordinarily powerful. The eminent social psychologist Robert Cialdini and his colleagues found that, even in the pre-social media age, people were prepared to go to great lengths to announce their affiliation with a group when that group was doing well. He showed, for example, that US students wore their college sweatshirts and T-shirts more or less frequently or prominently according to whether their football team had won or lost a game.[40] He also showed that they used the inclusive 'we' significantly more often if the team was successful ('we won') and the third person 'they' more often if the team was unsuccessful ('they lost'). So partisan will people sometimes become that they will react to any criticism of their group as a personal slight.[41]

The effects of winning and losing are biological as well as psychological. Researchers[42] have found that winning or losing a competition has an impact on men's testosterone levels, which rise or remain stable 'to resist a [natural] circadian decline' if they win, and which fall if they lose.[43] That in itself is scarcely surprising. What is remarkable, though, is that this happens even if they are not themselves participating in a game but simply observing their team compete.[44] The same holds true in political elections. One study, conducted during the 2008 US Presidential election, which involved getting 183 participants to provide multiple saliva samples before and after the winner was announced on election night, found that the testosterone levels of male voters who supported the victor, Barack Obama, remained stable, while those of male supporters of the losing rival candidates, John McCain and Robert Barr, fell.[45]

How the group changes us

It may be our individual predispositions[46] that drive us to seek membership of particular groups, but once we are members it is likely we will change. We want to fit in. We want to emphasise our similarity with others. We therefore view ourselves in terms of the defining attributes of the ingroup ('self-stereotyping'), and we adopt that group's prototype, thinking, feeling and behaving as the group typically does.[47] Back in the 1930s, the Turkish-American psychologist Muzafer Sherif[48] famously demonstrated the impact of the group on the individual when he got small groups of volunteers to estimate how much a dot of light on a wall was moving around, after first being tested individually. As it happened, the dot was only appearing to move, owing to an optical illusion called the autokinetic effect. Participants' individual estimates of how far it had shifted varied considerably. But Sherif found that as participants were invited in groups of three to speak their estimates out loud, they rapidly converged on a group average. With some groups the estimate was a high one; with others a low one. In all cases, whatever individuals may have initially estimated, they agreed on a group norm. And that group norm persisted even when participants gave subsequent estimates alone and when new participants gradually replaced the original ones in the group.[49]

This may sound a rather abstract example. The fact is, though, that most of us have undergone much the same experience at school, when we or the people we knew adopted a new persona in their bid to achieve or cement their membership of a particular group. It's one brilliantly and comically captured in the 1995 film *Clueless*. Here 'ugly duckling' Tai is taken up by the 'popular kids' Cher and Dionne, and is immediately given a complete makeover to ensure that she fits in. As the film progresses, we see Tai abandon her beliefs, her interests, the boy she feels closest to, even her individuality, as she strives to fit in with group norms. In technical terms, it's something the British social psychologist John Turner[50] describes as the 'cognitive redefinition of the self'.

As Tai tries to be a group member she also does what people in such situations typically do: she pays most attention to the attitudes and behaviour of the group's most prototypical figure. Cher effectively takes over her life, with Tai slavishly following her rulings and her judgements on everything. Tai comes to demonstrate the basic truth of the argument that, the more strongly someone identifies with a group, the more they change to fit in with the norm.[51] In such circumstances, individual behaviour turns into collective behaviour. An element of depersonalisation creeps in: not to the extent that the individual becomes subsumed within some sort of collective mind, but in a way that involves them expressing their identity in more social, less individualistic ways.

The experience of the fictional Tai at school is mirrored in a fascinating real-life study of student attitudes at Bennington College in the 1930s undertaken by Theodore Newcomb, the American pastor's son who became a psychologist.[52] Bennington at the time was an isolated liberal arts, all-women college in Vermont with about 500 students. It was politically left-leaning and run by charismatic, liberal professors. The students, by contrast, were largely from upper-class, Protestant, staunchly Republican families. What Newcomb discovered was that over time, as the Republican students became ever more steeped in the liberal atmosphere of the college, many underwent a change. First-year students were most likely to prefer the Republican candidate to the Democratic one. By year four of their course, however, they were far more likely to choose the Democratic or radical left-wing candidate.

In his search to explain this Newcomb noted that liberal students tended to garner greater respect from their Bennington peers and to be better integrated into college groups than conservative ones. For their part, conservative students were less likely to be leaders, at least in the eyes of their peers; they felt more alienated at the college, and were likely to spend more time at home. Two follow-up studies of the Bennington women approximately twenty-five and fifty years later found that those who'd graduated as liberals remained liberal. For example, in the 1984 presidential election, 69 per cent of Bennington alumnae expressed a preference for the Democratic candidate Walter Mondale rather than the Republican candidate Ronald Reagan, as compared with the national 35 per cent for women of the same age, race (nearly all were white), and educational achievement.[53] The changes in outlook these women had undergone at college had been permanent.

As to why so many students shifted their political opinions, Newcomb's view was that, unlike those whose political loyalties remained unaltered, they tended to treat the college, faculty and/or fellow students as reference groups whose approval they were anxious to seek and whose approbation gave them a sense of self-worth. 'I think my change of opinions has given me intellectual and social-respect at the same time,' one said. 'As I gradually became more successful in my work and made more friends, I came to feel that it did not matter so much whether I agreed with my parents. It's all part of the feeling that I really belong here.' She added: 'It also meant intellectual identification with the faculty and students that I most wanted to be like.'

Conversely, students who did not go out of their way to seek the approval of the group felt snubbed by it and so didn't change their views. As one put it: 'Probably the feeling that my instructors didn't accept me led me to reject their opinions.' The attitudes of these more conservative students, as with those of their liberal classmates, persisted over the years as they went on to choose new like-minded groups after college – whether friends, husbands or work colleagues. Their stories serve as a reminder of the subtle interplay of genetic disposition, upbringing and life experience in the formation of a group.[54] Bennington, it should be emphasised, changed some students, but it certainly didn't change all. Even so, it offers a case study in the extraordinary power of the group. And the findings of that case study still stand. A more recent study in the US has found that students in their first year of college tend to move towards the predominant political ideology of their randomly assigned room-mates.[55]

Once we're part of a group we don't just take on its views and outlook, we become emotionally tied to it. Members of sports teams will often personally take the blame for a team loss.[56] Members of an unsuccessful research team may stick with it, even if they are offered an opportunity to leave.[57] Activists may elect to jeopardise their own well-being for causes or principles that they are unlikely personally to benefit from (in this context animal rights activists come to mind). In extreme cases, loyalty to the group may even override our natural desire for self-preservation. Sebastian Junger's *War* describes one such instance. 'During World War II', he writes,

> four members of a B-17 bomber crew formed a pact that they would never abandon one another no matter how dire the situation. Not long afterwards, their plane was shelled and went into a terminal dive. The pilot ordered everyone to parachute to safety. As the crewmen donned their parachutes, they discovered that one member of the pact (the ball-turret gunner) was trapped, and there was no time to release him. Realising this, the other three pact members aborted their plans to parachute to safety, remaining on the plane to await their fiery deaths.[58]

Academics[59] describe this phenoneomen – a visceral sense of oneness with a group – as 'identity fusion'.[60] Here, group membership is not a means to an end (for example, increased self esteem) but an end in itself. Violent gangs, terrorist groups or even traders artifically distorting stock prices are all prone to identity fusion.[61]

Group membership can be so powerful that it shapes our perception of facts beyond the group's sphere of activity or expertise. Research[62] by Cass Sunstein and Joe Marks and colleagues at Harvard and University College London found that people given the task of categorising different shapes turned for help to peers with similar political views rather than those who actually knew how to help with the job in hand. The views of participants in a study undertaken by the Yale law and psychology professor Dan Kahan on whether a particular climate scientist was an expert in their field depended on whether they agreed with his overall view. Those who believed that global warming was a real threat accepted his credentials (for example, a degree from Harvard) as evidence of his expertise. Those who didn't dismissed his academic claim to make judgements on the subject. Kahan found a similar pattern among volunteers asked to review experts on gun control and nuclear waste disposal.[63] People never appear to think that their group's position on particular scientific issues is contrary to the consensus view of experts.[64] All are guilty of engaging in biased sampling, counting only scientists who agree with their group's position as experts.

Our partisanship implicitly influences what we think on a range of issues connected to politics,[65] including views on political figures,[66] political facts[67] and support for particular policies. The general tendency to interpret information in line with our prior beliefs, covered in Chapter 1, is likely to be especially pronounced when that belief is connected to group identity.[68] A British Conservative who learns that other party members support a government-funded furlough scheme is likely to regard that programme as conservative by definition, and find values within it that are *consistent* with being a Conservative. For example, they might believe that it 'supports small business' and that 'we must help people to help themselves'. Had the idea come from a rival party, they might have argued that it 'gives money away' or 'squanders government spending'.

It's something that the Stanford[69] University psychologist Geoffrey Cohen[70] observed in his study of attitudes to welfare policies in the US. Participants were first asked which political group they identified with, and then to assess the merit of a welfare policy. Some descriptions of the policy had no information on the 'party line' of that policy; others included the 'party line'. If the description of the welfare policy had no party label, liberals and conservatives alike, he found, would judge the policy purely in terms of their own beliefs. If the welfare policy included the 'party line' on the policy, it was evaluated in purely partisan terms. For example, participants identifying as Democrat in the no-party-line condition viewed a job training programme as helping poor people to 'find employment and support themselves'. In contrast, participants identifying as Democrat in the party-line condition (they were told the Democrats opposed it) called to mind a programme that would 'dump beneficiaries into menial labor'. As Cohen noted, not only were (factual) attitudes towards the policies entirely dependent on the party position on that policy, but different moral interpretations were too. He also found that the effect of the party – the group view – overwhelmed the impact of the policy's objective content and individual's ideological beliefs: levels of knowledge on welfare did not come into play at all.

Were participants aware of the influence their political group identity had on their judgements? No. All were convinced they had made rational assessments based purely on the evidence placed in front of them. They did, however, believe that others, including their allies but especially those of different ideological persuasians, would be swayed in such a way. Geoffrey Cohen's more recent research,[71] with colleagues Stanford professors Lee Ross and Michael Schwalbe, has found further evidence of this 'objectivity illusion', and has convincingly demonstrated that we typically think our own tribe is much more in touch with reality or 'truth' than others. As Cohen, Ross and Schwalbe say,[72]

> when people see their own and their group's beliefs as objective reflections of reality, they tend not only to interpret subsequent information in a biased manner but to use their biased interpretations to reinforce the very belief that gave rise to the bias. As a consequence, moreover, they may come to feel even more confident in their attitudes, and

more convinced in their objectivity, in a potentially repeating recursive cycle.

In other words, they become ever more convinced that their attitudes are the right ones. They also think that such attitudes have been arrived at objectively and in an evidence-based manner.

This worrying tendency to become convinced that the same set of 'facts' prove us to be right and our rivals to be wrong is a major driving force in polarisation. Issues become ideological battlegrounds. As Tali Sharot, Professor of Cognitive Neuroscience at UCL, told us, it follows that if people come to a balanced presentation with opposite prior beliefs, they are likely to polarise. Sharot's research with the author of the bestselling book *Nudge*, Cass Sunstein, and others[73] illustrates this clearly. They presented climate change believers and deniers with information – in line with the widespread scientific consensus – that climate change is a genuine threat to humankind's future. Each group then proceeded to evaluate the information and update their beliefs according to their prior beliefs, leading to what Sharot and his colleagues termed 'asymmetrical updating'. Climate change sceptics changed their beliefs in response to unexpected good news that suggested that average temperature rise is likely to be less than previously thought, but failed to change their beliefs in response to unexpected bad news that suggested that average temperature rise is likely to be greater than previously thought. Those who strongly believed that man-made climate change is occurring responded in the opposite manner.

Group identity vs the real world

As the distinguished social psychology and legal scholars Phoebe Ellsworth and Samuel Gross neatly put it, once an issue represents socially shared values, it constitutes 'a point on which people do not so much form opinions as choose sides'.[74] By this stage specific ideas and policies count for less than partisanship. In political terms, partisanship is one of the strongest predictors of voting behaviour, regardless of more general policy or ideological principles.[75, 76] Over fifty years ago Campbell, Converse, Miller and Stokes noted that specific policies and issues played only a small part in determining which way people would vote, with only 12 per cent of those interviewed having a clear idea of where conservatives and liberals were likely to stand on any given question.[77] When they get to the ballot box, the majority (although by no means all) have made up their minds on which party to vote for.[78]

Our partisan identities influence our reasoning, our perceptions and our memories.[79] Photographs of the large crowd at President Barack Obama's inauguration in 2009 tended to be identified as such by non-aligned voters and supporters of his political ally Hillary Clinton and misidentified as photographs of Donald Trump's less well attended inauguration in 2017 by Trump's supporters.[80] When Steven Frenda[81] and his colleagues asked 5,000 participants to give their memories of past political events (three of which were genuine, two of which were fabricated), they found that conservatives were more likely to falsely remember seeing Barack Obama shake hands with the president of Iran, and liberals more likely to remember George W. Bush vacationing with a baseball celebrity during the Hurricane Katrina disaster. As the researchers explained, events that are congruent with our beliefs promote feelings of recognition and familiarity, which interfere with the source of the memory.

And it's not just our view of the past that is affected in this way. Partisan identities also extend to our view of the future. When Donald Trump was elected President in 2016 Republicans immediately became optimistic about economic growth, Democrats rather less so.[82] The assumption that facts speak for themselves does not always hold true when the group is involved and beliefs challenged. The University of Illinois's Brian Gaines[83] found that during the Iraq War Democrats and Republicans alike took in new information as it became available, but interpreted it very differently. Given the same set of data about American troop casualties, for example, Democrats would interpret them to be more serious, Republicans less serious. New information about the failure to find weapons of mass destruction (WMDs) was interpreted by Democrats as proof that they had never existed, by many Republicans as evidence that Iraq had moved, destroyed or hidden them. In a similar way, in Britain in 2016, a constant stream of new information about the validity or otherwise of the much-vaunted claim that the UK sent £350 million per week to the EU left the majority of Brexit supporters convinced that it did and the majority of Remainers equally convinced that it didn't. The relative percentages – 65 per cent of Leave voters believed the claim; only 26 per cent of Remain voters did – scarcely moved between May 2016 and November 2018.[84] Overall views of Brexit scarcely changed either, as data from as late as December 2020[85] clearly showed.

Our group identity similarly shapes our views when we actually have no strong views. Imagine that a group of people are given balanced information on a wholly unfamiliar issue – say, the risks of a new pandemic – on which they have not previously formed any particular opinion. Given everything we know about group dynamics, we might well assume that they won't carefully formulate a considered response but will react in a more knee-jerk group way. And we would be right.[86] Researchers at Stanford, Harvard and NYU who studied Americans' behavioural and attitudinal response to the Covid-19 pandemic[87] found that it followed strongly partisan lines. Using location data from a large sample of smartphones (and controlling for other factors that might have an impact on social-distancing behaviour, such as local Covid cases and deaths, population density and so on), they showed that areas with proportionally more

Republicans engaged in less social distancing than those with proportionally more Democrats. Survey evidence also showed substantial differences between Republicans and Democrats when it came to beliefs about the severity of Covid-19 and the importance of social distancing. The study did not conclusively pin down the ultimate causes of the divergence in response and attitude between the groups, but it's tempting to posit that part of the reason was that Republicans tended to listen to media outlets that were sceptical about social distancing and the dangers of Covid, and Democrats tended to pay attention to outlets that took the opposite stance.

In short, we distort reality to meet our fundamental human needs – belonging, reducing uncertainty, increasing self-esteem and status within our ingroups – even if the strength of those needs outweighs competing desires to be accurate, and to search for and evaluate information in an even-handed manner.[88] Partisanship causes us to place our group above the need for accuracy and truth, especially if rival partisans appear to be threatening our moral values and access to resources.[89] Or indeed when the saliency of political events, disputes, people or issues is higher.[90]

Back in 1976 Britain enacted the Race Relations Act, which was designed to prevent discrimination against individuals on racial grounds.[91] During the parliamentary debate that preceded the passing of the act in 1975, a Conservative Member of Parliament opposed to the legislation declared that 'there was deep resentment in Britain at the thought of legislation being used to control what were the ordinary dealings of individuals with individuals.'[92] His remark inadvertently sums up the tension at the core of human society. As Henri Tajfel,[93] architect of social identity theory, points out, the MP was right to say that 'individuals' deal with 'individuals'. What he omitted to add was that we often don't treat individuals as individuals. We treat them as members of a group. And in so doing, we bring a freight of preconceptions and prejudices to our judgements.

US AND THEM

The Robbers Cave experiment

Late in the June of 1954, the Turkish-born-turned-American psychologist Muzafer Sherif, his wife Carolyn and their colleagues brought together twenty-two eleven-year-old boys in Robbers Cave State Park, Oklahoma, USA. There were no notable differences between them: they were middle-class, Protestant, shared the same ethnicity and had no history of problems at school. There was therefore no intrinsic difference between the two groups into which they were then randomly divided. Sherif's cover story was that he was running a summer camp. In reality, he had assembled the boys – none of whom had previously met – to test his theory that, when competing for a (limited and desirable) prize, animosity would emerge and the boys would be at each other's throats. In short, in a step on from his earlier work on groups (see p. 49) he wanted to study inter-group conflict.[1]

For stage one of the experiment each group was instructed *separately* to undertake what these days we would describe as 'team-building' activities – for example, cooking and cleaning together, pitching their tents and playing like normal eleven-year-old boys.

Sherif noted that a strong sense of cohesion soon developed. The groups even formed their own clearly defined identities – the Eagles and the Rattlers. They made their own flags and shirts and started to develop their own rituals.

In stage two, the Eagles and the Rattlers were first introduced to each other and then told that the two teams would be competing in a week-long tournament, involving baseball matches, treasure hunts and other tasks. The prize would be a medal and penknife for each member of the winning team. A penknife might not seem desirable to today's tech-obsessed youth, but back in 1954 it was a must-have possession. Members of the losing team would get nothing.

Sherif and his colleagues had designed the tournament to test their theory that, if the two groups were were presented with a scarce and covetable resource (a penknife) and faced with competition from another team, they would become hostile to each other. And the researchers were soon proved right. 'Bums', 'stinkers' and 'cowards': insults flew between the groups with increasing frequency and intensity. There was physical aggression, too. The Eagles burned the Rattlers' flag. In retaliation, the Rattlers raided the Eagles' food. Challenges to fight became common; vandalism broke out; the boys launched attacks on each other's cabins.

Interestingly, as the researchers noted, not only did the language each group used to describe the other become more negative, but the language used to describe co-members became increasingly self-glorifying. Other examples of favouritism towards fellow team members were noted. For example, the two groups were asked to pick up as many beans as they could from a field. Each team's collection of beans was shown via a projector on the wall, and the boys then had to say how many beans each team had collected. As it happened, the number of beans shown on the screen was the same (thirty-five), but because the images appeared quite fleetingly the boys were not able to count them exactly. All they could do was estimate. The numbers they came up with reflected their group bias, each group assuming that it had collected more than the other.

Sherif staged his Robbers Cave experiment in the same year William Golding's dystopian novel *Lord of the Flies* was published. Golding regarded boys as inherently little devils. Sherif didn't hold with this. He believed context is everything. In his view, hostility between groups will certainly develop – even if there is no history of prior tension or clashes, or differences in background or appearance – if they find themselves competing for a goal that only one group can achieve. But even previously hostile groups can be brought together if it is clear that only by co-operating will both benefit. The Robbers Cave experiment was later replicated in the Soviet Union.[2] As we described in the Prologue, it was also attempted in Lebanon. Here, however, it had to be abandoned when intergroup hostility reached dangerously high levels.[3]

It was Gordon Allport, the esteemed Harvard psychologist, who, writing after the Second World War, came up with the maxim that so helpfully sums up what would later become realistic conflict theory: 'Whenever [times] change for the worse . . . in-group boundaries tend to tighten.'[4] Realistic conflict theory holds that when valuable resources are perceived to be abundant, groups will co-operate and exist in harmony; but that when those resources are in short supply and groups become competitive towards one another, prejudice and discrimination will grow. The theory also posits that if the possibility of success for one group is regarded as a failure or loss for another, resentment and discrimination will multiply. At the same time, the members of each group, believing in their inconnected fate, will bond more tightly as they lock down into a winner-takes-all attitude.

For all this to happen, resources don't actually have to be scarce. The mere perception of scarcity is sufficient. If, for example, people in group A believe that members of group B are 'stealing' their jobs, they will feel resentment and hostility even if what they think to be

61

true is not objectively the case. Whatever power they might or might not have to do something about the 'situation', they will develop negative stereotypes about group B and distrust it. Nor do the resources have to be physical in some way, whether they're land, food, water – or jobs. Shortages of a more abstract variety – of prestige, power or social status – can also trigger resentment. Anything that causes people to fear losing what they already have offers the potential for conflict. As Lilliana Mason, Assistant Professor of Government and Politics at the University of Maryland, argues, the threat of loss is 'an essential ingredient' in modern polarisation. At the same time, fear of others gaining what we aspire to but don't have is also an immensely powerful motivating factor.

Real-world examples abound. Brewer and Campbell's study[5] of thirty tribes in East Africa, which showed a link between relative proximity and prejudice, suggests the truth of the fundamental precept of group conflict theory: that tensions arise when people are directly competing for precious resources, such as water. Conflict over control of the verdant and fertile Kashmir Valley, situated between Pakistan and India, has been taking place for centuries, and been exacerbated by the inter-group rivalry of Hindus (who largely support India) and Muslims (who generally support Pakistan). The result has been periods of communal violence and bloodshed. Perception matters, too. In the US the landmark Civil Rights Act of 1964, which prohibited discrimination in several areas, including race, caused many working-class white Americans to fear that black Americans would compete with them for entry-level jobs in companies from which they had once been excluded – and that white Americans would suffer accordingly.[6]

So strong are the pulls of group identity and inter-group rivalry that they can exist even when there is nothing to fight over. In Sherif's Robbers Cave experiment, ingroup solidarity increased and hostility to the 'rival' group became marked the moment each became aware of the existence of the other, and long before they were placed in any kind of competitive environment. Asked about their reaction to and knowledge of another group nearby, both said they wanted to 'challenge them' or 'run them off'.[7]

The social psychologist Henri Tajfel[8] and his colleagues found much the same mindset in the 1970s among schoolboys who weren't even formally part of a group. His experiment was a graduated one. It started off with groups established according to arbitrary and seemingly meaningless criteria ('minimal group paradigm'), and then gradually made them more coherent and logical. To the surprise of the researchers, even members of a group so vaguely defined that it effectively wasn't a group still favoured their 'group' over a rival when placed in a competitive situation.

The Tajfel experiment involved assigning schoolboys to different groups at random for a study supposedly designed to explore visual judgement. After looking at dots on a display screen and being asked to estimate how many there were, each boy was told he was either an over-estimator or an under-estimator. Each was then told that he could allocate points to another boy (who could redeem them for money), who would be identified to him simply as a number and a member of a group – for example, 'number four of the over-estimator group'. What the researchers consistently found was that participants allocated more points to the ingroup than the outgroup. Moreover, as different reward scenarios were enacted, it became apparent that, rather than simply choose options that gave their ingroup the greatest possible absolute number of points, most boys favoured ones that maximised their group's relative advantage over the other.[9] The boys did not know who the ingroup and outgroup members were. They never selected members themselves. And the categories were virtually meaningless. Yet they still wanted their group to win, and they put winning over material rewards. As Tajfel noted: 'It is the winning that seems more important to them.'[10]

This key finding – that ingroup favouritism will emerge even under the most arbitrary (or 'minimal') of conditions – has been widely replicated.[11, 12] If you find yourself put at random in a group of green sock wearers, you will naturally favour other green sock wearers, whether or not you have ever previously expressed a view on socks. In the process, you will come to regard yellow sock wearers less favourably. We may not explicitly discriminate against the yellow sock wearers. But even if we don't, we are effectively putting them at a disadvantage by favouring our group.[13]

Ingroups and outgroups

As was argued in the previous chapter, most humans feel the need to belong to a group and cannot readily survive in isolation. But, as Tajfel and others have shown, membership of a group can rapidly become a partisan act, causing the creation of an outgroup just as it leads to the formation of an ingroup.[14] This much is apparent in Tajfel and Turner's[15] very useful model of what they believe to be the three mental processes involved in dividing the world into ingroups and outgroups and motivating us to favour our ingroups over outgroups. Needless to say, while these processes follow a logical order and series of steps, in reality they occur spontaneously, without much thought on our part.

Figure 6: Our evaluation process

The first step – categorising – is a natural human instinct. We do not just have dogs. We have Labradors, chihuahuas, bulldogs, German shepherds. Experts don't just talk about moss, they distinguish between around 12,000 species, ranging from silky forklet and common haircap to swan's-neck thyme and common tamarisk. We catagorise the books we read, the films we watch and the music we listen to. We categorise within categories: Blue Labour for right-leaning left-wingers in the UK; the Freedom Caucus for Conservative Republicans in the US. We even categorise within a continuum. Our perceptual system, for example, perceives colours as distinct categories even though the eletromagnetic waves that give rise to them occur along a spectrum.

And of course we categorise human groups, through social categorisation[16, 17] – the natural cognitive process by which we place individuals into social groups. We think of someone as being old (as opposed to young), or black (as opposed to another ethnicity). Such thought processes extend beyond 'social structural variables' such as gender, ethnicity, nationality etc., to include many other often more subjective and subtle group memberships,[18] involving partisan loyalties[19] or shared opinions or values[20] where social identity is based on group membership owing to a common cause,[21] rather than organised around a social category. Remainers and Brexiteers. Climate change believers and deniers. Categorisation is so ubiquitous and done so quickly we find it difficult not to think about others in those terms.

There is a story about a man who owned a farm on the Russia–Poland border. So often had the precise location of the border changed – a reflection of the region's complex history – that he wasn't sure which country his farm actually lay in. Was it Russia or Poland? Confused, he paid a surveyor to spend weeks checking measurements and making calculations. Finally, the surveyor came up with an answer. The farm, he ruled, was in Poland. 'Good', said the farmer. 'I don't think I could take those harsh Russian winters.'[22] It's a joke, of course, but it's also a story that nicely illustrates not just the binary categorisations we're all so often guilty of, but the negative and positive associations that go with those categorisations. A farm in Russia is a member of the outgroup where the weather is perceived as worse. The Polish farm is in the ingroup where the weather is perceived as better. The story shows, too, how even geographic categories (in this example, national borders) can have major effects on the human mind, triggering negative evaluations of the outgroup and positive evaluations of the ingroup.

Many of the categories we come up with seem simple ones to us, involving what we perceive to be clear biological, physical or visual differences. But we also categorise when points of difference are more fluid, intangible or complex. Take politics. If I am someone who endorses legal abortion (traditionally a liberal view), but who also believes in small government (a conservative value), what do I categorise as? If I were an entirely rational[23] creature I would match my allegiance to the issue at stake. In fact, I am more likely to simplify things in my mind by making a reductive, *subjective* choice according to where I feel the strongest sense of identification or belonging. Political scientists[24] have repeatedly demonstrated that the vast majority of the public does not think about parties in ideological terms, and that their ties to the political world are instead affective, based on a feeling – a sense of partisan identity – often acquired very early in life. As the political scientists Angus Campbell and colleagues explained back in 1960, identifying with a political group is not only a question of holding a set of beliefs, but also of adopting feelings and values that culminate in a psychological attachment. This helps to explain why political groups may not always cohere in strict ideological terms.[25] One of the authors remembers noticing what a broad church the political party was that she joined, but never being able to articulate why she had joined, other than that she had a strong feeling it was the right thing to do.

Partisan identities in the political sphere can be based on more than party. Significant events can generate affective polarisation, too. Research[26] conducted after the seismic 2016 UK referendum vote to leave the EU by London School of Economics and Oxford University academics, and published in the *British Journal of Political Science*, concluded that Brexit identities 'generate affective polarisation as intense as that of partisanship in terms of stereotyping, prejudice, and various evaluative biases'. In other words, what in some ways started out as an intellectual debate about political sovereignty[27] became one about shared identity that cut across traditional party lines. 'Shared identity' is key here. Merely holding the same opinion as others about specific issues is, in itself, not enough to create such a powerful sense of group. One has to be able to define oneself in much the same way that people of faith can declare, 'I am a Christian' or, 'I am a Muslim' or, 'I am a Hindu'. In other words, articulating one's views in the form of 'I believe that X, Y and Z are the case' suggests far less powerful partisanship than 'I'm a Remainer' or 'I'm a Brexiteer'. Moving from 'I believe that . . .' to 'I am' takes the individual from an assertion about views on an issue to a statement of who they are and who they are not.

It's not difficult to see how the identities people took on during the Brexit debate reflected identities that already existed but were less obviously political. Formed according to age, education and so on, they had been gradually fomented by a leave campaign that was 30 years in the making.[28] What the Brexit debate did was to weaponise them and create salient new identities: 'Leave' and 'Remain'. These labels allowed people to classify themselves as members of a particular opinion-based group that now had an added emotional pull, similar to that identified by Angus Campbell back in the 1960s. The labels also encouraged a sense of differentiation, favouritism towards the in-group, and animosity towards the outgroup. Obviously, in the case of Brexit, this process had a strongly political aspect to it. But it can also occur after a dramatic event, such as a war or a man-made disaster.[29]

It's perhaps not surprising, given the powerful influence of partisanship on all of us, that political scientists are increasingly coming to think of it in its broadest sense as a social category comparable to race, religion or gender.[30] The Harvard lawyer and author Cass Sunstein has even coined the term 'party-ism'[31] to join such other -isms as racism, sexism and classism. The growth of partisanship has another impact, too. Research has revealed that the social categorisation process *distorts* our perceptions, so that we tend both to exaggerate the differences between people from different social groups – 'We're different from them' – and perceive members of groups (and particularly outgroups) as more similar to each other than they actually are.[32] The tendency is particularly strong in the views taken of members of outgroups, resulting in a phenomenon social scientists call outgroup homogeneity:[33] 'Oh, them, they're all the same!'[34] In the UK, for example, Conservatives credit themselves with a diversity that Labour or Liberal Democrat supporters fail to spot. Southerners view themselves as diverse; people in the North regard them as more homogeneous. This overgeneralisation makes it more likely that we will think about and treat all members of an outgroup the same way. It especially applies to groups that are unfamiliar to us (our tribalism is such that we tend not to encounter them) or that seem abstract.[35] In the lead-up to the 2016 Brexit referendum, how many Remainers had Leavers as friends? In Spain, how many supporters of the left-wing Podemos had friends who backed the Conservative People's Party, or vice versa?

It's not hard to see why such centrifugal forces become self-reinforcing. We know members of our ingroup, so we are aware of the many personalities involved. We don't know members of the outgroup, so we form a simplified view of them.[36] We assume that they all possess one particular attribute, or that none do. All Brexiteers must be racists! All Remainers must be members of the privileged elite! Anyone supporting Donald Trump must be stupid! Anyone opposing Trump isn't a patriot! And if we do encounter – and like – any members of the outgroup, we find ways to rationalise our prejudice by treating them as a 'subtype'.[37] During the UK parliamentary expenses scandal of the late-2000s it was common to hear those outside the precincts of Westminster say that MPs were 'all on the take'. It was indeed stated as fact by the family of a newly elected MP to her face as they all sat down for Christmas lunch. When the MP gently pointed out that she was definitely not 'on the take', a sibling looked sideways at her apologetically and muttered, 'Except you – we know you are different.' Her family had created a subtype that allowed them to maintain their overriding belief that politicians were corrupt.

If the *number of interactions* shape perceptions of the outgroup as being all the same, so, too, does the *nature of the interactions*. We tend to interact with another ingroup member as an individual, not simply as a representative of the group. Their likes, dislikes and talents are what are salient to us. We tend to interact with outgroup members in a more superficial way. It's therefore their group membership that remains salient in our minds, and their unique characteristics that recede into the background. We overplay the similarities within the outgroup. By the same token we tend to be unaware of the similarities within our own ingroup.[38]

Once we see members of outgroups as more similar to each other than they actually are, it becomes very easy to fall into the trap of stereotyping (another manifestation of our tendency to categorise everything). Stereotypes are an integral part of our everyday lives, and embedded in our culture, whether on TV, in movies or in social media. They have their place, since they simplify the world around us, so enabling us quickly to evaluate and process information about others. They are part of the bonding fabric of relationships: we share our beliefs in stereotypes with like-minded friends.[39, 40] They can also contain a 'kernel of truth',[41] however exaggerated that might be. Consider the stereotype of the rich US Republican. It is true that Republicans tend to be more affluent than Democrats. To that extent, the stereotype holds good. It's not true, however, as the average American assumes, that 38 per cent of Republicans earn more than $250,000 per year. The real figure is 2 per cent.[42] You might think that these misperceptions are concentrated among people who generally ignore politics. The opposite is true: it's precisely the people who pay attention to political news who tend to labour under the worst misapprehensions. And here lies the problem with the stereotype. It allows us to think efficiently and conserve our mental processes. But it also leads to inaccuracy and bias and, in the process, causes us to depersonalise and dehumanise others before we even know them.

Lord Finkelstein, Conservative peer and Associate Editor of *The Times*, eloquently described this process when he talked about the changes in people's assumptions about him when he switched from being a Social Democrat to being a Conservative.[43]

> People make all sorts of assumptions about your politics and you on the basis that you're a Tory. They really actually do think I do not care if people are poor and I want the N[ational] H[ealth] S[ervice] to collapse ... I remember in some meeting once somebody said to me, in your political life, [is it] more difficult being a Tory or a Jew? Well, I said, funnily enough before 9/11 it probably was being a Tory. Truth is, that it was a sort of a bit of a shock in terms of the way the other people saw me.

Finkelstein's experience is not unusual: when we stereotype, we make all sorts of assumptions and attribute views that the person may not hold at all. We eliminate the room for nuance.

Stereotypes and cognitive monsters

The whole process of stereotyping has been nicely summarised by the social psychologist John Bargh. He refers to stereotypes as 'cognitive monsters', because they are so powerful when activated and because, once activated, they have such insidious influences on social judgement.[44] His view has been summarised as a belief that as traditional groupings like villages and clans 'have broken down, our identities have attached themselves to more ambiguous classifications, such as race and class'. Although we tend to think of members of our own group as individuals, we view people in outgroups as an 'undifferentiated – stereotyped – mass . . . The categories we use have changed, but it seems that stereotyping itself is bred in the bone.'[45]

The type of the wealthy Republican illustrates the way in which stereotypes typically maximise group features that are the most distinctive, and that provide the greatest differentiation between groups (what we earlier referred to as 'distinctness' or entitativity), and that show the extent to which there is similarity within a group and difference between that and other groups. For example, if men assume that women are all alike, they may also think that they all have the same positive and negative characteristics (for example, they are both nurturing and emotional). Women may have similarly simplified beliefs about men (they are both strong and unwilling to commit). The result is that the stereotypes become linked to the group itself in a set of mental representations: they become 'pictures in our heads'.[46] They may be distorted overgeneralisations that exaggerate differences between groups, but they just seem right and natural.[47] So powerful are they that we may feel worlds apart from an outgroup even if our views on specific issues are actually quite similar.

Recent research from Northwestern University[48] demonstrates how insidiously powerful stereotyping others in this simplified, trait-based way can be. The researchers were interested in whether the ways people think about ordinary Democrat and Republican party supporters influence their views of the political parties themselves. What they found was that those who stereotyped others in terms of the groups they belonged to ('liberals', 'conservatives') were less inclined to adopt a polarised stance than those who stereotyped them in terms of their individual characteristics ('ignorant', 'smart' and so on). The stereotypers who fell into this later category displayed 'dramatically higher levels of both affective and ideological polarisation', according to the researchers. Essentially, once we stereotype people according to what we assume people in their group to be 'like', the more likely we are, it seems, to adopt an 'us-and-them' attitude.

And once stereotypes become established they tend, as with many other mental processes, to stick and become self-reinforcing. In other words, we increasingly approach those we stereotype with a mindset that assumes we already know what they will be like. The New York University academics Yaacov Trope and Erik Thompson[49] found that, faced with someone they stereotypically pigeonholed, people were likely to ask him or her fewer questions, and that the questions they did ask were selected and framed in such a way as to confirm their existing views. We assume that a good way to break down barriers is simply to talk to people. Trope and Thompson's findings suggest this may well not be the case. Ironically, those who believe in stereotypes particularly strongly are precisely those highly prejudiced individuals who most need to break from them, and who are most unlikely to do so.[50]

The other problem here is that we tend to remember information that confirms what we already think rather better than facts that might challenge our assumptions.[51] If we believe that bankers are intrinsically selfish and we come across one example of a banker behaving badly, then we tend to remember it. If we believe that bankers are intrinsically selfish and we read a story about one making a large charitable donation, we tend to forget it. As in so many areas of our lives, we perceive stereotypes in ways we can accommodate to our existing beliefs more easily than we modify those stereotypes to fit the reality around us. Ultimately, stereotypes can become self-fulfilling prophecies. We believe in them so strongly that the caricature becomes a reality.[52] If a sufficient number of people believe that men make better leaders than women, they will behave towards men in ways that make it easier for them to lead, and to women in ways that hamper their chances of doing likewise. Men will therefore find it easier to excel in leadership positions, while women will have to work hard to overcome the false beliefs about their lack of leadership abilities.[53] Expectations drive behaviour.

Such assumptions help to explain why female lawyers with masculine names are more likely to become judges,[54] and masculine-looking applicants are more likely to be hired as leaders than feminine-looking applicants.[55] Similar self-fulfilling prophecies can be found elsewhere. It's been shown, for example, that teachers' expectations about their students' academic abilities can influence those students' school performance:[56] the teachers subconsciously behave differently towards those students they have higher expectations for. Other studies[57] have shown how academic performance among black and female students is adversely affected when race or gender is emphasised. When those factors are not stressed, students perform as well as or better than the comparison group.

Most of us assume we don't think in such reductionist ways – and some of us may be right. But research has shown that stereotypical thinking often occurs without our awareness. Not only do we not know that we might be guilty of it, then, but our very lack of self-knowledge makes it difficult for us to correct for it even when we encounter individuals who don't conform to the stereotype lurking in our mind. We may think we are being entirely fair-minded. The chances are that we are not.[58] Such a tendency becomes even more powerful if we are distracted or under time pressure (in other words, when our mental bandwidth is narrower).[59] It's not unreasonable to hypothesise that in our increasingly hyper-connected, always-on world we risk stereotyping even more to help us cope with the world around us.

It's also worth bearing in mind that it takes effort not to react instinctively. We can relax with members of our own group. With members of another group our keenness not to reveal prejudices or assumptions can cause us to experience more negative affect (particularly anxiety).[60] We know what we need to do, but it's hard work and we may well fail.[61]

That said, it would be wrong to assume that our attitudes to outgroups are always the same. Nor is it even the case that the assumptions we make about an outgroup map on to those it makes about us. According to the Princeton psychologist Susan Fiske and colleagues' stereotype content model, when we create stereotypes, we typically do so according to two dimensions – warmth and competence – which in turn drive our emotional response to them.[62] Warmth is essentially tied up with the question, 'What are this group's intentions?' Competence answers the question, 'Is that group able to carry out its intentions?' Warmth is thus linked to friendliness, helpfulness, sincerity and trustworthiness; competence is linked to efficiency, conscientiousness, intelligence and skill. Each, of course, stimulates different responses, and in combination may cause two groups to stereotype each other in an assymetrical way rather than simply as opposites.

Research[63] done in the US (although common stereotypes based on age and socioeconomic status are shared across many countries) shows that middle-class citizens and dominant religions are stereotypically perceived as both high in warmth and competence. By contrast, those who struggle in society – the homeless, refugees, drug addicts and nomads – are stereotyped as low in warmth and competence. These are clearly not comparable stereotypes, and they result in different emotional and behavioural responses. For example, groups perceived as high in warmth and competence will evoke pride and admiration. Those seen low in warmth and competence will trigger disgust and contempt. Sometimes the emotional or behavioural response will be a

	Low Competence (Capability, Assertiveness)	High Competence (Capability, Assertiveness)
High Warmth (Friendliness, Trustworthiness)	**Common:** Elderly, Disabled Children **United States:** Italians, Irish **Emotions Evoked:** Pity, Sympathy	**Common:** Citizens, Middle Class, Defaults **United States:** Americans, Canadians, Christians **Emotions Evoked:** Pride, Admiration
Low Warmth (Friendliness, Trustworthiness)	**Common:** Poor, Homeless, Immigrants **United States:** Latinos, Africans, Muslims **Emotions Evoked:** Disgust, Contempt	**Common:** Rich, Professional, Technical Experts **United States:** Asians, Jews, British, Germans **Emotions Evoked:** Envy, Jealousy

Warmth and competence stereotypes. Common stereotypes, mostly based on socioeconomic status and age, are shared across many countries. Other stereotypes vary by country; persistent stereotypes in the United States appear here (Bergsieker, Leslie, Constantine, & Fiske, 2012, Study 4; Cuddy et al., 2009; Durante et al., 2013, see link to individual countries; Lee & Fiske, 2006)

Figure 7: Warmth and competence stereotypes [64]

mixture of positive and negative. For example, groups or individuals stereotyped as cold but competent, such as rich people or business people, can trigger both envy and admiration.

It doesn't follow that every group that is not your ingroup is automatically an outgroup. There has to be some compelling reason for comparison.[65] The local children's football team do not compare themselves with a UK Premier League side, even though both are playing the same sport. They will, however, compare themselves with the children's football team in the next town. What is being compared is critical, too. Social groups may well consider factors such as earning power. But football teams will focus on relative sporting success. Competition and hostility between groups is therefore not sparked just by competition for resources or status, but by considerations of identity.

Context also matters. We should avoid thinking of certain social identities as inherently attractive or unattractive.[66] Rather, the relative allure of membership of a particular group will vary according to circumstance. A group of psychology students might think they are intellectually superior to a group of fine arts students, or that they are creatively inferior, depending on which yardstick is being applied.[67] If it's in the context of an exhibition they might feel the latter. If it's in the context of a quiz about the human brain they may feel the former, and experience what is technically known as 'positive distinctiveness': a sense of 'We are better than they are . . .' In much the same way, political rivals may be drawn to compare themselves on a scale determined by the coherence of their policies or by the emotions (for example, optimism) those policies inspire. Of course, our natural tendency is to stress whichever comparison scale makes us feel better and maximises the difference between us and the outgroup.[68]

Once an us/them distinction has been made, 'we' will always favour 'us' and, by the same token, disfavour 'them'. It's a fundamental truth. And it's one that has been beautifully illustrated in a psychology study, involving a group of Manchester United fans, undertaken by Professor Mark Levine[69] and colleagues who were then at Lancaster University. First, the fans were invited to complete two questionnaires about the sense of allegiance they felt to their team (for instance, why and for how long they had been supporting them), and their identification with other supporters of their team. Then they were asked to walk to an adjacent building to watch a short film on football. As they did so, they happened to see a jogger slip and fall, grabbing his ankle and shouting out in pain. And this is where, unknown to the fans, the experiment actually started. In some instances, the jogger (who was a plant) wore a Manchester United shirt, and so signalled himself as a member of the Manchester United ingroup. Sometimes he would wear a Liverpool FC shirt, so marking himself as an outgroup member. And sometimes he made his appearance in a plain, unbranded sports shirt. The football fan volunteers were, of course, not only loyal to Manchester United, but had been recently primed to fill in a questionnaire that reinforced their allegiance. Professor Levine and his colleagues were therefore interested to see whether the shirt the injured jogger was wearing would have any impact on the fans' reaction. Would they notice what had happened and offer help or simply walk past?

The results were unequivocal. When the fans thought they were witnessing a fellow fan in need, 92 per cent did something to help him. When it was the Liverpool fan or the jogger in the unbranded shirt in distress, only about 30 per cent stepped in. In psychological terms, perceptions of similarity, feelings of greater closeness and increased feelings of responsibility for the welfare of another member of the ingroup all stimulated the fans to assist, while, simultaneously, that sense of closeness caused the 'cost' of helping to decrease. They were more likely to help someone in a Manchester United shirt because they felt a bond with him. Quite simply, all the necessary factors for intervention were there. It's only fair to note that loyalty to the ingroup was not mirrored by hostility to the outgroup. They didn't administer a sharp kick to the shins of the Liverpool-shirted jogger. They just didn't stop to offer help. The difference in their attitudes to the differently clad joggers was nevertheless stark.

This ingroup/outgroup dynamic influences not only our behaviour but also how we process and evaluate information. The classic study here is one done back in the 1950s, in the wake of a particularly rough football game between teams from two prestigious US universities – Dartmouth and Princeton – in which Princeton's star player suffered a broken nose and had to be taken off. The violence of the match prompted two social psychologists, Albert Hastorf and Hadley Cantril,[70] to try and find out whether Princeton and Dartmouth judged what had happened in the same way. They therefore showed students from the two institutions a film of the game, asked them for their overall impressions, and then specifically whether they felt there to be 'any truth to these charges . . . of dirty play by Dartmouth'.

The answer depended on which school the students attended. More than half of Princeton students said that Dartmouth had played dirty. Only 10 per cent of Dartmouth students were prepared to concede as much. The Princeton students counted an average of 9.8 infractions of the rules. The Dartmouth students spotted only an average of 4.3. Hastorf and Cantril concluded that 'the game' was actually many different games, and that for each onlooker their version of what had happened was just as 'real' as completely different versions were to others. It was as though the students were watching separate matches, in which their side was clearly the hero and the other side the villain.

Why does membership of an ingroup exercise such influence over our minds? The view of most experts is that our group identities act as a kind of heuristic[71, 72] – a rule of thumb or short cut designed to help us process and evaluate information quickly. Simply put, we use the beliefs, policies and values of our ingroups as cues to guide our own. Effectively, we're saying: 'If my group supports this position it must support the core value that I care about.' Such a strategy is one that requires little effort, and so saves precious cognitive resources. It dovetails with a basic precept in social psychology that when people do not have sufficient knowledge or time to evaluate the substance of a message, they typically, but not always, rely on their perception of the status of the person conveying it. Unsurprisingly, political arguments from ingroup sources are generally more persuasive than messages from outgroups.[73] In more technical terms, it's a form of system-one thinking – fast, inuitive, automatic – vs system-two thinking, which is more deliberate, effortful and orderly.[74] This 'heuristic' account suggests people are basically motivated to hold accurate opinions, and that biased views are an unfortunate unintended consequence of people's lack of political interest.

But if we are motivated less by truth and accuracy and more by loyalty to the group, it can actually take more cognitive effort to scrutinise arguments and counterarguments to defend our beliefs[75, 76] – in which case we might expect people with higher reasoning abilities to be more biased. The psychologists Charles Taber and Milton Lodge[77] demonstrated that when it comes to politics, for example, because those with greater levels of political knowledge can come up with a range of counterarguments, they're more likely to stick with a biased evaluation. To that extent, mental or political sophistication, instead of promoting learning, confers the ability to resist unwanted information.

These mental gymnastics can manifest themselves in ways that at first seem surprising. Take maths problems, for example. One would assume that an ability to solve them has nothing to do with loyalty to an ingroup – they're objective maths problems, after all. Yet, as Yale's Dan Kahan has shown,[78] if a maths problem that requires analytical skills has a whiff of politics about it, that will have an impact on people's ability to answer it correctly. What Kahan did for his study was to assess volunteers' natural maths ability, and then ask them to answer questions about crime data for cities that ban handguns, and for those that don't. He found that once that political/ideological dimension was added, mathematical ability ceased to be a reliable guide to the accuracy of participants' answers. Liberals tended to be good at solving the problem when the 'correct answer' proved that gun control reduced crime. Conservatives were better when the answer proved the opposite. In short, people with high numeracy skills were unable to reason analytically when the correct answer collided with their political beliefs. One controversial theory that has been posited is that people who score highly on various indicators of information processing such as political sophistication,[79] science literacy[80] and cognitive reflection[81] are the most likely to express beliefs that align with those of their party. Such individuals, the argument goes, use their advanced reasoning capacities to form and then maintain their identity-affirming beliefs.

Kahan offers another reason why our groupishness motivates us to defend our groups at the expense of the truth. Quite simply most people don't, on an individual basis, have sufficient influence for their opinions to make an impact, so there's no apparent 'cost' attached to what may turn out to be a wrong view. The average citizen, voter or consumer will make no difference to the *incidence* of a particular risk (say, climate change as a result of human CO_2 emissions), nor have power over the *adoption* of any policy to abate that risk (say, introducing a carbon tax). Any 'mistake' he or she makes, therefore, is cost-free. However, there is a cost attached to rejecting the stance that conveys who we are and whose side we are on. It's a social one. And it's huge. Reject the view of the group, and the consequences for our standing with others whose support is vital to our well-being and emotional state can be devastating. Given this, it is perfectly rational to stick to views that express our group identity, whether or not they are factually correct.[82] That doesn't mean that in overall terms there is no cost to a wrong view: for society as a whole it can be disastrous. But groups lack the immediate incentive to arrive at views that will serve the collective good.

From group loyalty to partisanship

Building on neuroeconomic models of decision-making, Jay van Bavel and colleagues[83] offer a more formal way of understanding why people place loyalty to their groups above truth and accuracy. Our brains, they suggest, assign values to the different beliefs we could hold, based on the benefits likely to result from each belief, and we make a decision accordingly. Once a belief has been adopted – and perhaps expressed in public – our brains then measure the outcome and assess its desirability. A good outcome – for example, one that wins approval from others in our group – will shape the formation of future beliefs. A bad outcome will prompt our brain to avoid adopting a similar belief in the future. We learn through experience which beliefs will cost us or benefit us. This influences what we believe and also what we say.

If simply being part of a group prompts us to conform to its views, there is a real risk that as each member of the group reinforces those views they become more extreme. It is something that has been observed in studies across the globe, notably in one in the US conducted by Cass Sunstein, Reid Hastie and David Schkade.[84] The researchers recruited six participants from each of two very different American cities, liberal Boulder and more conservative Colorado Springs. Having checked to ensure that the volunteers had views representative of their community, Sunstein and his colleagues asked each of them to record their views anonymously (and individually) on three topical and controversial issues: climate change, affirmative action (policies positively supporting under-represented/disadvantaged groups), and same-sex civil unions. They then asked the volunteers to discuss their views with others in their group and reach a decision. Finally they asked them to record their opinions individually and anonymously again.

Three findings emerged. First, there was a clear shift in views from those recorded in the initial set of anonymous views to those articulated by the end of each public deliberation. The liberals from Boulder became more liberal; the conservatives from Colorado Springs more conservative. Moreover, when the participants were invited to record their final thoughts anonymously, these did not mirror their initial views, but the more extreme views adopted by the end of the group discussion. As Sunstein, Hastie and Schkade note, there is an important lesson here. Group deliberation not only makes the group more extreme, but has a lasting effect on the individual, to the point where they will state those more extreme views privately and anonymously.

Secondly, group discussion led to greater group consensus. Before people started to deliberate, they privately expressed views that often diverged from those of others in their group. The people were broadly liberal or conservative, but their take on particular issues differed. Discussion, however, brought liberals into line with one another and created close agreement among the conservatives. Brief discussion, in other words, increased group cohesion – and this was expressed in the anonymous post-deliberation expressions of private views.

And thirdly, deliberation significantly increased the differences *between* the views of the largely liberal citizens of Boulder and the largely conservative citizens of Colorado Springs. Before the group discussions, there was considerable overlap on specific issues between the opinions of many individuals in the two cities. Afterwards, there was much less. As a diversity of opinions within each group disappeared, liberals and conservatives became more sharply divided.

In such group discussions, various factors are clearly at play. Our publicly stated views are often a key aspect of how we want to present ourselves, and because we want to be perceived favourably by other group members, we will tend to seek consistency with the overall group position and norms. Those members who are initially only weakly supportive of the dominant view are likely to express unequivocal support for it in a group context, while those who disagree will tend to keep quiet to avoid censure. The political scientist Timur Kuran describes this as 'preference falsification'[85] – a term that usefully captures the way and extent to which the preference we express to others diverges from a view we might hold in private.

We're all guilty of it, even if it's only when, in a desire to be polite, we tell someone who has produced an inedible meal that it is delicious. We also experience a similar phenonemon in the workplace (where it comes under the umbrella of what is termed low 'psychological safety'[86]) if we feel unable to speak up with an idea or admit a mistake. Preference falsification is a form of self-preservation. But because it distorts how the members of a group express their individual preferences and beliefs it can contribute to polarisation. As Kuran explains:

> intolerant communities are never homogeneous. There are shades of opinion. Many members have reservations about specific policies. The differences don't get much notice, however. One reason is that the communities are themselves intolerant toward internal differences. They treat compromise by their members as treasonous. In reaction, community members hide their reservations. They pretend to share their group's values and objectives in total, when in fact they have their differences.[87]

Group polarisation is a numbers game, too. If one idea starts to gain traction, particularly if it comes from a member of the ingroup, it will generate more arguments in its favour and so more adherents.[88] At the same time, the counterargument will be lost in the noise. Without its restraining or challenging presence, the dominant idea will tend to become more absolute. Confidence also plays a part. When people lack confidence, they tend to be tentative and therefore moderate, knowing that their own views may be wrong. But as they gain confidence, uncertainty vanishes and their beliefs may become more extreme. As they win support from others, their confidence grows, and the belief becomes that much more extreme.[89] Ultimately, once affective polarisation has taken root, an echo chamber is formed in which ideas acceptable to the ingroup are repeated again and again, becoming easier to remember and thus reinforced. Simultaneously, 'unacceptable' ideas are withheld and so become increasingly difficult to bring to mind.

Ultimately, the tendency towards extremes in a group, and the polarising effect this has, can mean that 'we' refuse to countenance something that 'they' advocate even if it's actually in our own interest to do so. The Berkeley academics Amy Lerman, Meredith Sadin and Samuel Trachtman[90] tracked this tendency in their research on attitudes to the health reforms (in the form of the Affordable Care Act) that Barack Obama introduced in the US in 2010. Praised by Democrats as a force for good, the act was denounced by Republicans as expensive, unwieldy and, in its championing of government intervention, ideologically wrong. Not surprisingly, therefore, Republican voters proved far less likely to sign up to it than their Democrat neighbours. As the then *Salon* journalist Simon Maloy put it: 'The ideological satisfaction of resisting "big government" outweighed the practical benefit of access to medical care.'[91] This inevitably had serious consequences for individuals' health. One Republican supporter, Luis Lang, for example, whom the Berkeley academics cited in their study, had gone with the party line in not signing up for Obamacare, and jeopardised his health when he was diagnosed with a partially detached retina. His partisan decision literally risked blinding him.

Has the us/them divide got worse? It's difficult to make an unequivocal assertion, as manifestations of 'them' and 'us' change over time and there's no single, consistent way to measure them. That said, there are signs that – in some Western countries, at least – polarisation has intensified.[92] In the US in 1960, according to Gabriel Almond and Sidney Verba, 5 per cent of Republicans and 4 per cent of Democrats said they would be displeased if their son or daughter married someone from the opposite side of the political divide.[93] In the UK at the same time the figures were 12 per cent for Conservatives and 3 per cent for Labour supporters. By 2008 the US percentages had skyrocketed to 27 per cent for Democrats and 20 per cent for Republicans,[94] and while the figure for UK Conservatives had stayed roughly the same at 12 per cent, for Labour it had risen to 19 per cent.[95] Alford et al's conclusion was that in the twenty-first century political identity matters more when it comes to marriage than physical characteristics or such personal qualities as kindness.[96] Indeed, when asked to judge the relative attractiveness of different faces, people tend to rate as more attractive those labelled as sharing their political beliefs[97] (women are especially choosy in this regard). The dating site e-Harmony, in a 2018 survey of its US users, found that 78 per cent of women and 47 per cent of men had started to record their political preference as a dating criterion.

Political preferences also have a bearing on who we choose to share a house or flat with, as the Craigslist example mentioned in the Prologue demonstrates. When Seth, a political activist and academic, advertised a spare room in his two-bedroom flat in north London on Spareroom.co.uk in 2017 he included the caveat 'No Leave voters need apply.' The following day Spareroom intervened to say that the wording contravened their policy of 'positive preferencing', whereby advertisers are free to broadcast their own political views (and say they would like to share with someone similar), but can't say 'no Tories' or 'no Labour supporters'. Seth therefore changed the ad to read, 'Remain voters only, please', and found a new tenant. This is very much of a piece with the 2019 US study mentioned earlier that showed that students felt more strongly about political partisanship than social habits when considering prospective room-mates.[98]

We haven't yet reached the point where we will buy a house or flat only in areas where we can be confident that our neighbours share our mindset – length of commute, local schools and so on are still prime determinants. But there is evidence that there are plenty of exceptions. In India, in cities such as Hyderabad, for example, Muslims tend to seek out other Muslims to live with, Hindus other Hindus. There are good practical reasons for this: if you actively practise a faith, you need to live close to an appropriate place of worship. But as religious and political identities converge in places like Hyderabad, this has meant that in practice Hindus, who disproportionately support Prime Minister Narendra Modi's Bharatiya Janata Party, live together.[99] Affective polarisation may not always influence where we live, but in many places it has political implications for *who* we live with.

The partisan consumer

The us/them divide is also increasingly expressed through what we wear, what we drink and what we buy. In countries with higher average disposable incomes, an element of people's identity is lived through the brand choices they make, in what has been described as the blurring of the so-called 'authentic', non-commercial spheres of life. In other words, people don't just buy goods but forms of self-expression.[100] The wonderfully-titled paper 'Why Do Liberals Drink Lattes?' convincingly argues that the answer is not that there is some taste-driven correlation between coffee preferences and partisanship, but that we may well choose to signal and amplify our membership of a particular group by making a particular lifestyle choice associated with it.[101] Or as Cleopatra Veloutsou and Luiz Moutinho,[102] Professors of Brand Management and Marketing respectively, argued some years back: 'Postmodern consumers use products and brands for their own purposes as well as a medium to help them define themselves and express their identities within society.'

In their 2009 article 'Brand relationships through brand reputation and brand tribalism', the two authors go so far as to talk in terms of tribal loyalties rather than market segments, in their description of people 'who have a link because of a shared passion or emotion [as] not just consumers but also advocates'. What we buy and consume may say more about us than we think. Those two activities are very immediate. The pollster Deborah Mattinson, who in 2018 examined how the political parties were perceived in the UK, found that people had strongly visual and specific images of them: Conservatives dine on quail and pheasant (a longstanding perception); Labour, 'once the party of cloth caps, bingo and pie and a pint, [is] now seen as the party of hippy students whose idea of fun is going on a demo and who drink expensive designer beer and eat quinoa.'[103]

Such characterisations help to explain why people react to brands and advertising campaigns so strongly. It's not a new phenomenon. Gandhi was fully aware of their power when he promoted *swadeshi* (the use of indigenous goods) in his campaign for independence. In Massachusetts during the build-up to the American War of Independence, non-consumption became politicised. Citizens were encouraged to 'save your money, save your country',[104] with ladies encouraged to wear locally grown linen and avoid imported goods such as tea.[105]

As Thomas Roulet demonstrates in *The Power of Being Divisive*,[106] brands and their advertising also play in to the 'us-and-them' aspect of the group dynamic. People want to make their political identities visible, and are willing to pay for products that proclaim partisan membership of one group and so – sometimes explicitly – signal opposition to another. He offers the example of the 'Trump vs Everybody' T-shirts sold by Nine Line Apparel, a company set up by two US veterans which donates a portion of its profits to wounded veterans. 'I think people love the story,' one of the founders said:

> Two soldiers who wanted to start a business and give back to disabled vets in the process. We stand behind our products and we've built a reputation as an organisation that gives back, because we've got a bigger, more important mission than simply meeting our bottom line. That and, you know, people like wearing shirts that talk shit about ISIS.[107]

Selling, in its own words, relentlessly patriotic apparel, the brand uses slogans such as 'Family, faith, friends, flag, firearms: five things you don't mess with', tapping in directly to the partisan dollar.

The fact is that partisanship directly influences what consumers buy, whether they are aware of it or not. As the academics Christopher McConnell, Yotam Margalit, Neil Malhotra and Matthew Levendusky, who have studied the matter closely, summarised in a 2017 article, consumers were 'almost twice as likely to engage in a transaction when their partisanship matched the seller's'. And in their full study they went further: 'These effects of partisanship are at least as large as the effects of religion, another well-known and salient social cleavage.'[108] The authors found that even those 'with only modest ties . . . are willing to forgo economic gains to express their partisan identities.' Another study conducted during Ghana's 2008 elections found that co-partisans were offered lower prices. Kristin Michelitch observed that taxi drivers who consistently offered lower fares to people who shared their ethnic background extended the courtesy to political allies at election time, while forcing supporters of political rivals to pay higher prices.[109]

Such commercial leverage places corporations in a potentially tricky situation. If they're not partisan they may lose out. If they're too partisan – or pick the 'wrong' side of the divide – they may alienate previously loyal consumers. In the highly competitive UK cider market Magners decided to go after the younger, trendier market. Their rivals Strongbow, in response, opted to emphasise their appeal to working-class drinkers. As the *Harvard Business Review* reported: 'The strategy succeeded: Although hipsters began to view Strongbow negatively, its appeal among traditional cider drinkers intensified – and as polarisation increased, so did sales. Strongbow has maintained its leading position in bars and pubs, and in 2009 its sales in the fast-growing off-trade market rose by 23% – beating sales in the overall cider market by 6%.' Another approach, adopted by the baked-goods behemoth Betty Crocker, was to diversify its product range with healthier options while still offering its standard lines, in the hope of creating a 'larger pool of potential buyers' without alienating those who preferred its traditional fare.[110]

For Gary Coombe, the CEO of Gillette, speaking in 2019,

This millennial generation expects brands to play a broader role in society than has ever been true in the past. It was very simple in the old days. Your brand delivered a functional benefit. You created a piece of advertising to demonstrate that on TV and you moved on. You did not really comment on anything else, actively avoiding it in fact. That is simply not the case anymore.[111]

With debates about toxic masculinity and sexual harassment gathering impetus post #MeToo, Gillette made the decision to ditch its 'the best a man can get' slogan in favour of 'The best men can be', launching a TV ad campaign to reposition the brand and call out outdated conceptions of what it is to be a man. Writing about the ad in *Forbes*, Dr Kim Elsesser, a former lecturer on gender at UCLA and author of *Sex and the Office*, argues that the ad first presents men as aggressive before showing their ability to change the narrative for the next generation. She argues that this creates a mixed message: most men are aggressive, it seems to say, but this behaviour is wrong. Male viewers are therefore subconsciously torn between what is presented as the norm (aggression) and what is presented as the correct option (non-aggression).[112] Her point is that if the key purpose of the ad is to change behaviour, the second part alone might have been more effective. However, if the motivation is to signal a clear division, the approach succeeds.

Gary Coombe was evidently overwhelmed by the reaction to the new advertising campaign: 'Within twenty-four hours, I had upwards of 250,000 views [to a LinkedIn post of the video ad] and, in the comments section and in private messages, I had everything ranging from an invitation to speak at the UN to a death threat.' He also saw a spike in people saying that they were likely to purchase a Gillette product, and an increase in consumers who said Gillette shared their values: a significant rise from 42 per cent before to 71 per cent among those who watched the new ad. He noted that 'whilst we reconnected with the millennial generation and did it very quickly, building awareness with positive emotional equity, there were a group of consumers, typically over-50 white men, who simply were offended. But this is one of the realities of brands taking a stand.'

In similar vein Nike made the decision to link its brand with a major social issue – in its case the Black Lives Matter movement – employing to front their campaign the NFL star Colin Kaepernick, who in 2016 sat and then knelt through the US national anthem in protest against systemic, racial oppression.[113] Brandwatch data indicates that there was an immediate boost for the brand:

There were 2.5 million social posts the day of the launch. The brand was on everyone's radar, and not just athletes' and sneaker aficionados'. The campaign paid off in different ways, too. Sure, some conservatives tried to burn their Nikes, but the brand was able to connect to many new and existing customers on a whole new level. Online sales increased by 31 per cent the Labor Day weekend following the ad's release. A few months later, sales were still booming, with a 10 per cent income increase driven by strong revenue. The already prominent brand showed a new, courageous face to the public and, overall, it was a big success.[114]

Some of those boycotting the brand posted about their decision to switch to buying Converse, not realising that Nike owns them too.

Gillette and Nike's success suggests a business case for taking a polarising view on an issue. Take a stand on a major social or moral debate and you will build loyalty with customers who agree with you and so see sales rise. Leaving aside, however, whether or not the brand in question keeps up its immediate advantage or suffers financially from any backlash in the long term (Gillette's immediate gain, for example, was not sustained),[115] the question arises whether in weighing in on a polarising issue, big corporations might not be contributing to the noise rather than effecting a genuine change. The *Atlantic* journalist Helen Lewis argues that corporate interventions can make it *look* as though the issue is being tackled, which raises the risk that people are being divided on issues without there being any clear outcome except the division itself.[116] Arguably, therefore, some corporations may be increasing – albeit unwittingly – the them/us divide.

Such moral and ethical business dilemmas – so uncommon a few decades ago – show the extent to which polarisation has spilled out beyond the political and social areas of our lives. Today, there is a view that CEOs should move beyond business decision-making and take a stance on broader issues. The January 2020 Edelman Trust Barometer,[117] which collates results from surveys of 34,000 respondents in twenty-eight markets, found that 92 per cent of employees say CEOs should speak out on issues of the day, including retraining, automation, the ethical use of technology, income inequality, diversity, climate change and immigration – all keenly fought and divisive areas for debate. Research suggests, though, that this new dimension to business poses a real challenge for CEOs, not just in terms of 'getting it right' but even in deciding whether to engage in the first place.[118] Twenty-two per cent of global millennials have said that they have stopped or reduced their interactions with a business because they disapproved of the stance taken by its CEO. Only 12 per cent have said that agreement with the social or ethical standpoint taken by a CEO has prompted them to support that CEO's business. The potential losses of engagement, in other words, can outweigh the potential gains. And in the US a partisan divide has also emerged over whether CEOs should take an activist role in the first place,[119] with 64 per cent of Democrats thinking they should, compared to 32 per cent of Republicans. In a hyperpolarised world, CEOs now tread a fine line.

PART TWO

The Triggers of Division

THE ECONOMIC FACTOR

Catalysing division

We are starting to see how our beliefs and behaviour are a product of our own wiring and the groups we identify with. But these processes need to be understood in context: polarisation does not happen in a vacuum. Nor is it a constant state: it has ebbed and flowed throughout history. Beyond our inherent personal and social natures, there are other, fluctuating forces at work which at any given time may reduce or intensify our tendency to polarise. Economic and social factors; politics and our political structures; messages delivered through the media and social media platforms – all these interacting elements have a huge impact on our perception of 'us' and 'them'. And they form the focus of the next three chapters.

The destabilising effects of inequality

Throughout history economic hardship, downturns and fear of limited or dwindling resources have, as Sherif's Robbers Cave experiment demonstrated, triggered dissent, protest and conflict. However, it is not just the fear of having less that sparks tension. The worry or suspicion that we are not faring as well as our neighbours can have much the same effect. If we're all poor, we may, to an extent, feel like we are in it together. If, on the other hand, we think we're being left behind and that inequality is widening, we feel aggrieved.

Inequality is an immensely powerful driver of social division. Studies have shown that the growing gap between the richest and poorest in society (technically known as the Gini co-efficient) often accompanies an increase in polarisation and support for major, sometimes even radical, political change. It's something that the academics Noam Gidron, James Adams and Will Horne identified in their analysis of polarisation based on seventy-six election surveys across twenty Western democracies between 1996 and 2015.[1] In particular, they pinpointed rising inequality as a major factor in opening up wider 'us-and-them' divides. It's also a phenomenon that has played out many times since the 2008 financial crash – the worst since the Great Depression of the 1930s – which drew a firm line between the 'haves' and the 'have nots'. In Portugal, for example, unemployment reached nearly 18 per cent.[2] Half a million people took to the streets of Lisbon.[3] In Greece, unemployment sky-rocketed to 27 per cent. Months of social unrest followed and, in Athens, tear gas was deployed by police to control angry crowds.[4] Both countries concurrently experienced significant spikes in polarisation.

Meanwhile, in the US, as the crash started to take hold, 15 per cent of manufacturing jobs disappeared between December 2007 and June 2009.[5] By September 2008 it had become clear that the financial system was on the brink of collapse. The usually unflappable Chair of the Federal Reserve Bank of America, Ben Bernanke, would appear at meetings with his lip literally quivering. President George W. Bush stepped in to oversee the introduction of an emergency multi-trillion-dollar rescue package (the Troubled Assets Relief Program, TARP) to try and ease the pain. Even so, there was a perception (however right or wrong it may have been) that the bail-out helped the elites while it abandoned the manufacturing sector. Accordingly, a 'them-and-us' narrative gained traction. It's scarcely a unique experience for Americans. Back in the 1960s, as the civil rights movement gained momentum, a sense of dispossession among the most economically deprived white groups within the country helped drive support for the nakedly racist policies of the 1968 presidential hopeful George Wallace.[6] Again, relative inequality proved a powerful driver of political discontent.

It's important to note that it's not just a growing gap between rich and poor that powers a sense of inequality. In a world where the richest few per cent have seen their wealth increase substantially over recent decades, the simultaneous stagnation and even relative decline of earnings among those in the middle-income bracket have also fed the forces of polarisation. A 2019[8] report on the then thirty-six countries that made up the Organisation for Economic Co-operation and

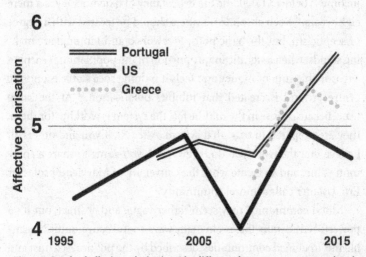

Figure 8: Levels of affective polarisation (the difference between survey respondents' thermometer ratings of their in-party vs the average of out-parties) in America, Portugal and Greece in the aftermath of the 2008 financial crash. Higher values denote higher levels of polarisation.

Development (OECD),[9] ranging from Canada to Korea, has shown that each generation of middle-income people since the baby-boom generation came of age has seen its economic power diminish, and its relative size reduce. Housing has become more expensive as a proportion of earnings. Thanks to the expansion and costs of tertiary education, more young people have entered the jobs market with higher levels of debt. Social mobility has declined. Today, a real sense of dispossession is apparent among many younger adults in Western democracies.

Middle-income earners have traditionally been viewed as the glue that holds society together. They are the people who have a sufficient stake in the status quo to want to preserve it.[10] The political scientists Adam Przeworski and Fernando Limongi have even put a financial figure on that 'stake', suggesting that in those countries where the average income is over $6,000 per annum, democracy can survive 'come hell or high water', but that where the average per capita income is below $1,000, the life expectancy of a democracy is a mere eight years.[11] Such absolute numbers should be treated with a degree of scepticism, but the basic point Przeworski and Limongi are making stands: when a significant proportion of the population is earning a reasonable sum of money and feels it is doing so, a stable economic centre ground is created that inhibits polarisation.[12] At the same time, because those in the middle feel the system is working for them, they are prepared to trust that system. After all, if you and others all believe that the work you do is rewarded, you come to share a common value, and so create what the University of Maryland professor Eric Uslaner calls a 'moral community'.[13]

'Moral community' may seem rather vague and abstract, but it's a powerful entity nonetheless. In many ways, moral communities resemble the 'imagined communities' described by the political scientist and historian Benedict Anderson. Anderson's study of nationalism considered the ways in which, for example, the invention of the printing press and the greater availability of Bibles that followed, simultaneously weakened one community (the Roman Catholic Church, which had previously had a stranglehold on Western Christianity) and created new ones (Lutherans, Calvinists and so on).[14] Those who believe in the American Dream offer a good example of a moral community, in that they are united by a common belief: that anyone, regardless of where they are from and who they are, can succeed through hard work and dedication.[15] That the American Dream has become somewhat tarnished in recent years, as social mobility has declined and inequality grown, helps to explain why the moral community shaped by it has tended to splinter and polarisation has risen.[16] Ironically, as the economist Raj Chetty has shown, these days you are twice as likely to achieve the American Dream if you live in Canada than if you are a US citizen.[17]

And once the core belief of the moral community falters, faith in the institutions which that moral community once supported and which in turn helped to underpin it, can slump. Or, as Jack Citrin and Laura Stoker at the University of California, Berkeley, put it: 'Trust declines when governments and institutions fail to meet expected goals or follow prescribed norms.'[18] In the US, for example, trust in government fell from a high of around 80 per cent in the early 1960s to a historic low of below 20 per cent after Donald Trump's 2016 election.[19] A comparison of data from 1981 to 1990 and 2006 to 2013 revealed precipitous falls in confidence in national legislatures in Australia and the UK (as well as the US), and marked declines in countries such as Finland and Norway. Indeed, an *increase* in confidence in national legislatures was recorded in only five industrial democracies of the nineteen analysed.[20] After the 2008 financial crash, trust in government among the fourteen EU countries that are members of the OECD fell from nearly 50 per cent in 2009 to just under 43 per cent by 2012.[21] In all cases a sense of inequality was shown to be a key driver of disillusionment.

What should be of particular concern to politicians here is that such disillusionment is so marked among younger people. Dr Roberto Foa and fellow academics at Cambridge, for example, who have looked at a huge dataset that recorded the responses of close to five million people in 160 countries between 1973 and 2020, have noted the negative power of 'economic exclusion'[22] and described how, as Millennials and Gen Xers have grown older, they have become steadily less satisfied with democracy.[23] They have also pointed to 'the impact of the eurozone crisis in the periphery and decades of rising wealth inequality [that] have left younger citizens facing growing difficulty in finding secure employment, owning a home, starting a family, or getting ahead in life independent of inherited wealth and privilege'. If today's youth have less reason to believe things will improve for them under the democratic status quo, they have less reason to uphold those institutions.

If disillusionment with political institutions is one consequence of a sense of inequality and dispossession, the other is, of course, political fragmentation and polarisation. The German academics Manuel Funke, Moritz Schularick and Christoph Trebesch, having crunched the numbers from 827 elections across twenty countries over 140 years, have concluded that voter behaviour changes after a systemic financial crisis.[24] Politics becomes more unstable. Government majorities reduce. Populist parties typically see a surge in support. The gridlock that often ensues then slows recovery, leading to a repeating loop of inequality and political division. Other researchers concur, suggesting a close link between rising inequality and support for populist, often extremist, parties.[25] Funke and his colleagues have used historical data to show that the impact on voter behaviour has become more marked with each successive financial crisis since the nineteenth century.[26]

It's certainly the case that the 2008 financial crash was the precursor to a more divided politics in a large number of countries.[27] Many voters across Europe, especially those who bore the brunt of the downturn and subsequent austerity measures, shifted their support to new, reinvigorated or challenger parties, all with a populist bent.[28] In Italy, the nationalist Five Star Movement. In Spain, left-wing Podemos. With each there was a clear 'them-and-us' division. 'They' were the elites who had built and supported the system. 'We' were the citizens the system had let down so badly. Hernan Winkler, a senior economist at the World Bank's Jobs Group, who explored survey data between 2002 and 2014 from twenty-five countries, found that an increase in the Gini coefficient at the local level increased the likelihood of support for a political party 'at the extreme left *or* [our emphasis] right of the ideological distribution'.[29] Dr Foa's team at Cambridge noted that the similarity of left- and right-wing populism, in terms of issues addressed and attitudes adopted, can mean that 'they may be appealing to very similar electoral demographics – including younger voters who are disengaged from mainstream democratic politics'.[30]

Once such divisions get a toehold, a compounding effect tends to set in. Positions become more entrenched; people are less inclined to compromise. To make matters worse, economic factors – which underpinned the initial crisis – come back into play, but in a slightly different form. Business and finance like stability. If that stability seems lacking, they will become cautious and unwilling to invest, so making the economic situation worse. The US academic Marina Azzimonti has charted how polarisation acts as a barrier to investment, creating friction that in turn slows growth and affects household consumption.[31] In a polarised and politically unstable society, she argues, investment falls in the short term, leading to long-term consequences for output and consumption. Tax yields fall as a result, leaving less money for welfare support and even less security for those most affected by the original financial crisis. It can become a self-reinforcing loop.

Azzimonti's general assessment certainly seems to hold for Britain in recent years. While debates still rage as to the ultimate economic impact of the UK's decision to leave the EU, there is no doubt that the instability that came in the wake of the referendum had an effect on investment. Writing before the Covid pandemic, the former joint head of the UK government's economic service Vicky Pryce highlighted the fact that from 2018 to 2019 business investment was down 1.6 per cent and that 'investment intentions in the second quarter, according to the Bank of England, were at their lowest since 2010.'[32] Instability and political polarisation had made investors nervous. Lower investment in turn means less ability for the state to tackle the underlying issues driving discontent.

In the near term humankind is destined for even greater inequality, as the effects of climate change increasingly make themselves felt. Eight hundred million people are already thought to be vulnerable to the ecological consequences of rises in the levels of carbon dioxide in the atmosphere as they battle to adapt to rising sea levels and changing weather patterns.[33] New research from the World Bank estimates that 132 million people will be pushed by climate change into extreme poverty by 2030.[34] Over the next decade or so, as access to essential resources becomes more unequally distributed, the likelihood is that 'us-and-them' divisions will widen on a global scale. At their most severe such divisions could quite conceivably tip over into radicalisation and extremism.[35]

An interesting study of all fifty US states by the Texan academic Alexander Stewart and his colleagues Nolan McCarty and Joanna Bryson in the wake of the 2016 presidential election shows just how psychologically pernicious the societal effects of inequality on polarisation can be. Examining the US presidential cycles between 2008 and 2016[36] they suggest that when the economy was doing well and inequality was accordingly less pronounced, people were more inclined to engage with outgroups (a tendency that, by sparking a more diverse outlook, also led to higher-quality work and an improved bottom line).[37] However, when the economy shrank, people were more likely to take refuge in the safety of their ingroup and far less likely to reach out to others. In short, in uncertain times they craved the certainty of the ingroup, shunned the outgroup and, as they did so, locked themselves into a polarised mindset. This is scarcely surprising. Even a small relative decline in status – whether real (in other words, financial and material) or purely psychological – triggers feelings of resentment and hostility. So when a real economic shock is experienced – say, unemployment – not only is there damage to our self-image or self-perception,[38] but we also experience the corrosive effects of distress, anxiety, depression and helplessness.[39] Seeking support, stability, predictability and affirmation, we turn decisively away from outgroups and find security with our ingroup, helping in the process to reinforce that group's values and prejudices.

Uncertainty

If economic downturns cause instability, they also heighten uncertainty. From an evolutionary point of view, uncertainty is not a universal ill. It motivates us to act and seek information. But we also find it hard to navigate. In the fictional world of Middle Earth, the hobbit Pippin sums up a familiar human emotion when he says, 'I don't want to be in a battle, but waiting on the edge of one is even worse!' In the world of scientific experiments it has been shown that people would rather receive an electric shock for sure than sit in a state of uncertainty wondering whether one might be administered.[40] And in the real world, hearing about a possible change (a restructure at work, say) can be more stressful than knowing for sure it will happen. We crave certainty. As the philosopher John Dewey put it, 'In the absence of actual certainty in the midst of a precarious and hazardous world, men cultivate all sorts of things that would give them the feeling of certainty.'[41]

One of those things is spending more time with people who agree with us, to make us feel more secure about who we are, how we relate to others and our place in society. It's a form of behaviour that has attracted its own theory: 'uncertainty identity theory'. Professor Michael Hogg, who coined it, describes how by identifying with a particular social group we derive a sense of meaning and belonging. Being part of an 'us' validates our world view and sense of self: fellow group members typically agree with our perceptions, beliefs and values and approve of how we behave and what we think; their validation, in turn, helps reduce any sense of uncertainty or social anxiety we may feel. As Professor Hogg puts it:

> Our sense of self is a fundamental organising principle for our own perceptions, feelings, attitudes and actions. Typically, it is anchored in our close inter-personal relationships – our friends, family, partners – and in the variety of social groups and categories that we belong to and identify with – our nationality, religion, ethnicity, profession. It allows us to predict with some confidence how others will view us and treat us.[42]

Professor Hogg's own studies broadly confirm his theory (although, admittedly, more real-world empirical research and refinement on measuring uncertainty is required).[43] His work in Israel is a case in point.[44] Here he was interested to see how uncertainty plays out in a region of the world marked by intercommunal conflict and violence. He therefore set the stage by *priming* people to feel either certain or uncertain (participants were asked to think about things that made them feel certain or uncertain about themselves, their lives, their futures), or *measuring* feelings of certainty/uncertainty directly (via survey questions like 'My beliefs about myself often conflict with one another'; 'My beliefs about myself seem to change very frequently'; 'In general I have a clear sense of who I am and what I am'). He then sought to establish how feeling uncertain or certain would interact with a sense of national identity (Palestinian or Israeli) to produce attitudes that would favour support for extreme actions (for example, suicide bombings) intended to protect and promote that national identity.[45] The results were not unequivocal, but overall suggest that when participants both identified more strongly with their national identity (whether Israeli Jews or Palestinian Muslims) and experienced higher levels of uncertainty, they were more likely to support extreme action.

The workings – and the subtle complexity – of uncertainty can perhaps best be understood through an experiment that the Texas Tech University Professor Zachary Hohman and his colleagues[46] ran in the mid-2000s. Gathering together a room full of volunteers, they first asked them to indicate their political ideology and party affiliation, if any. Next they asked them to read a short speech[47] on the environment by the then president, George W. Bush. After that, participants were randomly put into two groups to prime (that is, activate) either feelings of certainty or uncertainty. One group were asked to focus on aspects of the speech that made them feel *certain*, and write down three phrases from it that most came to mind in this respect. The other group were asked to perform the same task while focusing on aspects of the speech that made them feel *uncertain*. Then, all were asked how strongly they identified as Americans and as members of their chosen political party.

The results were telling. Those participants who classified themselves as strongly Republican or Democrat and who were in the 'uncertain' group, came out with an intensified attachment to their party. Precisely as uncertainty-identity theory predicts, they had elected to counter feelings of uncertainty by identifying more closely with their party. When it came to expressions of national identity, Republicans identified more strongly with nation than Democrats, while Democrats seemed to distance themselves from nation in preference for the party. In other words, Republicans identified strongly with their nation and their party irrespective of their uncertainty, while Democrats who had been primed to feel uncertain identified less strongly with their nation and showed instead a slight preference to identify with their party.

Why the difference? The conclusion the researchers came to was that it was a question of ingroups and outgroups. With a prototypical Republican president in power at the time, the Republican participants felt very much members of the ingroup, and their uncertainty resolved itself in a strong bond with their party and their country. For the outgroup Democrats, however, a sense of shared nationhood was less powerful. They felt that, with a Republican president in place, their own beliefs and values did not fit with the 'nation'. They therefore moved away from that identity, resolving their uncertainty by attaching themselves firmly to party. It's another manifestation of the flexible nature of our identities that was touched on in Chapter 2.

Another study undertaken by Michael Hogg and his colleagues[48] took place against the backdrop of a four-month strike by 70,000 Californian supermarket workers in the winter of 2003/4. Locked out by management in a dispute over pay and conditions, staff camped out in front of stores, while customers who supported them staged a boycott. Meanwhile, management relied on non-union workers to keep the stores running. The academics approached the striking workers on the picket line and asked them to fill in a short survey that measured their feelings of uncertainty (how certain did they feel about their future?), their entitativity (how much of a group did they feel the striking supermarket workers were?), and finally their perceptions of how their own group (the striking workers) and the outgroup (the non-union workers) felt about health care benefits and senior management. What emerged was a close correlation between feelings of uncertainty, perceived entitativity of the ingroup and perceived polarisation between the ingroup and outgroup.

The striking workers, of course, faced real uncertainty. When might they return to work? Would their calls for healthcare and other benefits be recognised by managers? Would they be able to make the following month's rent or put food on the table for their family (one striking shelf stacker said it was like living life 'on a yo-yo string'[49])? At the same time they were acutely aware of the non-union outgroup that had to run the gauntlet of crossing the picket line each day: the outgroup was 'salient'. It was not surprising, therefore, that the strikers who felt relatively uncertain about their future associated very positively with an ingroup, felt a strong sense of belonging, and also perceived their ingroup to hold different views to those of the outgroup on key issues. This was not the case with strikers who felt relatively certain about their future. It was a pattern confirmed by Hogg in a follow-up study focusing – as with his George W. Bush speech experiment – on Democrats and Republicans.[50] Again, among participants feeling uncertain, there was a strong link between the perceived entitativity of the ingroup and seeing Republicans and Democrats as being highly polarised. There was no such link among participants feeling more certain. Taking both studies together, Hogg speculated that when people feel uncertain, they are driven to rely more on their ingroup for indications of how to act and think, and to use the views of the ingroup to make judgements on the outgroup. Uncertainty has a polarising effect.

If Hogg's studies suggest that uncertainty is temporary and linked to specific events, other research seems to show that it can actually root itself in a nation's DNA. Indeed, some argue that one can establish what amounts to an international uncertainty index, whereby it's possible to measure 'uncertainty avoidance'[51] – that is, the extent to which people in different societies are able to cope with uncertainty and ambiguity. In simple terms, countries with higher uncertainty-avoidance scores prefer rules (for example, about food and religion), and have a lower tolerance for unorthodox behaviour and ideas than those with low scores. They also maintain more rigid codes of belief and behaviour. Japan, some Mediterranean cultures (for example, Greek and French), and parts of Latin America (for example, Guatemala) rank among the highest for uncertainty-avoidance, whereas Singapore, Denmark, Great Britain, and the US are among the lowest.[52]

Obviously, any such characterisations run the risk of being not only highly subjective but also reductive. Many would argue that national identity – if it exists – is astonishingly difficult to pin down. Most would agree that for every 'typical' citizen of a particular country there will be an 'untypical' one. Even so, Professor Geert Hofstede, who studied cross-cultural psychology and conducted much of the seminal research in this area, came up with some interesting suggestions as to why particular nations score higher or lower on uncertainty avoidance.[53] He hypothesised, for example, that Japan's higher score had much to do with the country's experience of natural disasters like earthquakes and the consequent desire of its citizens to find and impose order in an uncertain world: 'From cradle to grave', he argued,

> life is highly ritualised and you have a lot of ceremonies. For example, there are opening and closing ceremonies of every school year, which are conducted almost exactly the same way everywhere in Japan. At weddings, funerals and other important social events, what people wear and how people should behave are prescribed in great detail in etiquette books. School teachers and public servants are reluctant to do things without precedence. In corporate Japan, a lot of time and effort is put into feasibility studies, and all the risk factors must be worked out before any project can start. Managers ask for all the detailed facts and figures before taking any decision.

On the flip side, Hofstede explained Singapore's low score in terms of its particularly high Power Distance: 'Singaporeans call their society a "Fine country. You'll get a fine for everything."' And to explain the

UK's low score he argued that the British are happy to 'make it up as they go along', change their plans as new information comes to light, and generally 'muddle through'. Britain's unwritten constitution and development of a case law tradition suggest he had a point. He went on to argue that there are generally not that many rules, though those that exist are adhered to (for example, queuing – which also links to a notion of fair play). And there's an emphasis on the individual, and an accompanying regard for creativity and innovation.

Whether and to what extent any of these characterisations hold water is open to challenge. But there is certainly something to the overarching notion that some societies – for whatever reasons – are more likely to embody uncertainty and the traits that follow from it than others. In particular, as the academics Ronald Fischer and Crysta Derham, who conducted a meta-analysis of uncertainty avoidance,[54] have found, countries that score higher on the uncertainty avoidance index are more likely to favour the ingroup over the outgroup.

Not only have experts categorised and measured uncertainty avoidance, but they have also sought to do the same for global levels of uncertainty from an economic and political perspective. And the current situation is not an encouraging one. According to the International Monetary Fund (IMF) and its impressive sixty-year longitudinal data set, by the start of the 2020s global uncertainty had reached its highest level since the 1960s,[55] having increased significantly since 2012. 'The recent levels of global uncertainty', the authors report,

are also exceptional in a historical context. Looking back at the past sixty years, we see few episodes in which uncertainty has been at levels close to those observed in the past decade. Other notable historical episodes include the assassination of US President John F. Kennedy, the Vietnam War, the gold crisis in the late 1960s and the oil crises in the 1970s.[56]

This doesn't mean, of course, that levels of uncertainty are historically high for *all* countries in the world. But they do largely reflect the increasing role of global factors in driving uncertainty. As one might expect in a more interconnected world, uncertainty spikes are more synchronised in advanced economies than in emerging-market and low-income economies, because these countries tend to move together. Stronger trade and financial links across countries lead to stronger uncertainty synchronisation. At the start of 2020, Kristalina Georgieva, the Managing Director of the IMF, proclaimed: 'If I had to identify a theme at the outset of the new decade it would be increasing uncertainty.'[57] And that was before Covid-19. For humans who are hardwired to find ways to reduce uncertainty,[58] living in a world that is increasingly uncertain is fraught with dangers.

The threat of the outgroup

If uncertainty plays a major role in the ingroup/outgroup dynamic, so does a more general sense of threat. It doesn't have to be the threat of actual physical danger. It could be a particular event or piece of information or attitude that causes concern for the ingroup. And when that happens that ingroup will become even more of an 'us', more of a tribe. Simultaneously, of course, it will become more hostile to the source of the 'threat' – the outgroup.

That in itself should come as no surprise. But what is interesting is how easily threat responses are triggered. A study conducted by Professor Alberto Voci in 2006[59] offers a telling case in point. As an Italian only too aware how culturally split his country is between the relatively wealthy, industrialised north and the poorer, more agricultural south, he decided to see how a group of students, approximately half born and living in northern Italy and half born and living in southern Italy, would react to reading faked perceptions of them by their neighbours at the other end of the country. One half of each group was therefore given information that showed that their neighbours viewed them positively (no threat condition); the other half information that suggested a negative perception (threat condition). The results were unequivocal. When a sense of threat was perceived, those northern and southern Italians who identified strongly as such rated their ingroup more positively. When no such threat was perceived, there was no regional ingroup bias.

The key word here is 'perceived'. It doesn't matter how real the threat actually is. There has only to be the suggestion of one to trigger powerful responses. It's something that New Mexico State University's Walter Stephan and colleagues from Michigan and Stanford[60] explored in their development of what they describe as 'intergroup threat theory (ITT)'. The theory holds that there are two main categories of threat that an outgroup can pose to an ingroup: realistic and symbolic.[61] Realistic threats are the types of threat considered in the last chapter: threats the ingroup perceives the outgroup to pose to their economic and political power, their status and their physical or material well-being. Symbolic threats, by contrast, stem from perceived differences in morals, values, standards, beliefs, world views or attitudes: in other words, all things that involve challenges to the ingroup's culture or way of life. Portuguese people who regarded Turkey's potential entrance to the European Union as a symbolic threat (to their way of life and their culture) were more likely to oppose it.[62] Dutch adolescents who saw Muslims as a symbolic threat were more likely to be prejudiced against them.[63] Perceptions of realistic and symbolic threat tend to be highly correlated[64] and frequently coexist.

There seems little doubt that a mesh of symbolic and realistic threats contributed to the UK's decision to leave the EU in 2016. Immigration affords an example of one of the complex elements involved. Many of those who supported Brexit believed immigrants to the UK, whether from inside or outside the EU,[65] offered both realistic threats (some immigrants, they believed, would be criminals or terrorists; all would compete for jobs) and symbolic threats (immigrants' religion and culture were at odds with those of the UK).[66] Research by the *Economist* revealed that people who lived in regions of the UK where immigration levels had increased by more than 200 per cent between 2000 and 2015 were particularly supportive of Brexit (94 per cent of those constituencies voted in favour).[67] Interestingly, though, those living in areas accustomed to immigration were unfazed by it. The 2018 National Conversation on Immigration run jointly by HOPE Not Hate and British Future noted that Remain support had a strongly urban flavour: 'Cities often have a longer history of immigration,' it concluded, 'so their residents are less likely to be disconcerted by recent immigration from the EU. City residents tend to have more social contact with migrants, a factor that seems to be a key driver of more liberal attitudes.'[68] In a similar vein, the Overseas Development Institute argued that 'overall, attitudes towards immigration generally have an inverse relationship with the number of immigrants. Those countries that host the most immigrants are more positive than those that host fewer.'[69] For those adjusting to an increase in immigration, however, the perceived threat can seem significant.

Intergroup threat theory has been used not only to analyse but also to predict. It was employed, for example, to assess how people in Germany would react to an influx of refugees fleeing a civil war in Syria that had reached heightened levels in 2014–15.[70] The researchers considered the existing proportion of immigrants in each German *Land*, or state, the perception by local residents of immigrants in their state, their perception of the threats posed by immigrants, and an assessment of people's attitudes in general towards immigrants. They found that the actual proportion of immigrants in any given state was not a good indicator of local people's attitudes towards them. Rather, it was the *perceived* proportion of immigrants that counted. Germany ultimately took in one million Syrian refugees. At first, attitudes among native-born Germans stayed pretty static. However, according to researchers, in a 2018–19 survey by the Friedrich-Ebert Stiftung Foundation, '53 per cent of respondents expressed negative opinions about asylum-seekers, higher than the 44 per cent of people who thought this in 2014, prior to the considerable increase in refugee arrivals.'[71] Syrian refugees will actually be net contributors to the German economy in 2021, but of course that doesn't alter the threat many perceive them to pose. ODI researchers have concluded that only greater contact can ultimately change this negative perception.[72]

If a sense of threat can spark reactions based on perception rather than reality, it can also have the effect of prompting people not to act in their own best interests. Like uncertainty it pushes people to crave the status quo – even if the status quo has not served them well. Why do people so often blame victims of injustice rather than the perpetrators? Why do so many poor people oppose the redistribution of wealth? Why are so many people opposed to a rethink of the economy in the wake of worldwide financial crises, meltdowns and bail-outs? According to John Jost, Professor of Psychology and Politics at NYU,[73] a prime motivating factor is threat. People fear that the world they know and understand is being challenged, and this causes them to rush to its defence. The aftermath of 9/11 is a case in point. In the days and weeks after the terrorist attacks on the US, one might have expected to see popular criticism of the US government (however unfair) for failing to prevent them. Instead, the approval ratings of the then president, George W. Bush, shot up 40 per cent and stayed high for almost a year. Gallup polls suggested that Americans' opinions of nearly every authority – the police, the military, Congress – became more favourable. A predisposition to reduce threat drives us to want to keep the world the way it is.

And this predisposition has implications for the leaders we look to. Because we want safety and stability in difficult times, we want leaders who project certainty and confidence. At such moments, the popular management advice to be yourself and admit when you do not know something is actually 'crummy advice', according to the Stanford management professor Jeff Pfeffer. Confidence creates an impression, even if it is wildly inaccurate, of competence. 'When you feel uncertain . . . the people around you on your team need to know you know what you're doing and have confidence.'[74] When people are worried or frightened, the wrong answer is better than no answer. Ignorant confidence is better received than informed uncertainty. Leaders who are trying to do the right thing can fall by the wayside. Leaders who say that they are doing the right thing are popular.

It comes as no surprise, then, that we look to strong leaders in uncertain times. A survey by the Oxford University political scientist Stephen Whitefield of thirteen former communist countries in 2007 found that although most had made the transition to democracies, and although people still remembered days of blacklisting, false imprisonment, torture and execution, the appeal of a strong leader remained.[75] Among Hungarians and Latvians, over 40 per cent agreed with the statement, 'It would be worthwhile to support a leader who could solve the problems facing [their country] today even if he overthrew democracy.' For Bulgaria and Ukraine the figure was over 50 per cent. The Czech Republic and Slovakia scored much lower, but then they had the most experience of genuine democracy. They also had stable economies which, as we've seen, tend to be proof against feelings of uncertainty and threat. A preference for strong leaders, and at its more extreme an abandonment of democracy, is yet another self-reinforcing polarisation loop. Strong leaders, suggests the Oxford historian and political scientist Archie Brown, are the least likely to reach across divides, seek consensus and deliver a transformative, depolarising reset.

THE POLITICAL FACTOR

The political tribe

If uncertainty makes us grip closer to our group identities, this has profound implications for our politics. As we become more tribal, our political allegiances harden. As the ties we establish with our political tribe become stronger, the stage is set for those who can play on our intensified beliefs and values to leverage power and influence. Because the dynamics at work in our brain operate as they do, a polarised landscape to some extent becomes inevitable. It also often draws in those most able to exploit it.

The tribal element in politics has always been apparent. The reforms of Cleisthenes that caused Ancient Athens to be popularly viewed as the birthplace of democracy (despite the fact that women and slaves had no vote) were triggered by division and despotism. The Roman Republic had its rival aristocratic and plebeian elements. As France teetered on the brink of revolution in 1789, representatives of the clergy, nobility and the 'third estate' – the masses – gathered as the political body known as the Estates General and then proceeded to arrange themselves either on the left or the right side of the Royal tennis courts where they met, according to whether they supported the king (in which case they sat on the right), or wanted to see reform (in which case they sat on the left). They thus contributed a left–right metaphor to political vocabulary that has persisted ever since. The Baron de Gauville, who was present at the meeting of the Estates General and was sympathetic to King Louis XVI, recalled trying 'numerous times to sit in different parts of the room' in order to demonstrate that he was 'master of my own opinion'. But he found he was 'condemned to boos from the gallery'.[1]

It's important to bear in mind this innate tribal element – even at times when society as a whole may be relatively united – because one of the great mistakes many political analysts historically made was to assume, as the political scientist Anthony Downs did in his 1957 article 'An Economic Theory of Political Action in a Democracy', that 'the citizens of our model democracy are rational'.[2] Downs advanced the appealing notion that when taking political action citizens are thoughtful, intelligent and enlightened. It's possible to sustain such a view if it really is true that each of us approaches politics as an individual. But since considerable evidence suggests that we view issues and debates through a group lens, it has to be accepted that our decisions in the political arena are prone to be shaped by all the forces that interact with our own psyche to make that group cohere. In short, we don't make single 'smart' decisions.

Politicians who assume that people's political preferences can be swayed by the adoption of particular policies have regularly been disappointed.[3] Tax cuts and giveaways offer a case in point. Announcing a willingness and desire to put money back into voters' pockets works when that happens to chime with their overall set of values. But even such a blatant appeal to self-interest cuts little ice if that view is not part of the group psyche. In 2001, the then UK Conservative Party leader William Hague stood on a popular platform of tax cuts.[4] His party suffered a thumping defeat. In Slovakia in 2012 the right-leaning SDKU-DS[5] advocated populist economic policies, but still lost seats when a secret service wiretap scandal broke. And this was despite the fact that the SDKU-DS had also beaten the drum on restricting immigration – commonly another populist vote winner. In the UK, former Conservative party leader Michael Howard underwent a similar experience when, despite a campaign that placed a populist restriction on immigrants and asylum seekers at its core, he lost the 2005 general election to the incumbent Labour Prime Minister Tony Blair. Blair, who had spent much time pondering the Labour Party's four successive election defeats between 1979 and 1992, rightly concluded that looking at polls on individual policies and assuming that by studying them you had learned something was a 'fallacy' because, as he put it, 'you are separating it from the whole, and in the end it's the whole thing people vote on.'[6]

Voter advice applications painfully expose the gap between rational and voting decision-making. These apps typically guide users through a series of questions about political issues – How do you feel about free trade? How important is tackling climate change to you? Should inheritance taxes rise or fall? – before offering a 'best fit' recommended vote. People have flocked to use them. In Germany, Wahl-O-Mat (vote-o-meter) questionnaires have been completed 85 million times since the app's development in 2002.[7] Over 1.5 million people in the UK looked at Vote Match and Verto during the 2015 General Election. In the run-up to the 2014 European Parliament elections 350,000 French citizens clicked on Vote&Vous.[8] Yet despite such voter engagement, analysis shows that voter advice apps have had no effect on their users' ultimate voting decision.[9] The University of Minnesota's Paul Goren, who has worked on the relative pulls of partisan loyalty and individual issues, expresses the contradiction here very neatly: 'Party identification', he says, 'does not determine value positions, but it appears to shape them'.[10] He doesn't go so far as to say that individual policies have no impact at all. They can and they do. But because the political tribe we identify with exerts such a powerful influence on us, the message sent by a particular policy can be drowned out by wider group perceptions.

And once our group has formed, any issue, from tax cuts to immigration to social welfare to gun control, becomes an opportunity to flourish our group identity and demonstrate which side we've chosen. We're very bad at admitting our partisan limitations when it comes to thinking carefully about and assessing political figures,[11] political facts[12] and support for particular policies. 'Us-and-them' invariably trumps ideas and ideological principles.[13, 14] The sad fact of the matter is that, in politics as in the rest of life, we are not as thoughtful as we like to assume.

That's true for politicians as well as voters. In the US, for example, as issues that caused internal party divides declined (for example, a north–south divide among Democrats on racial issues in the 1960s), so, according to the political scientist Nolan McCarty, the likelihood that politicians would vote with their own party increased.[15] Such political homogenisation suggested to many that it was the elites who were responsible for the polarisation that was taking place. But the evidence points to something rather more complex: a subtle interplay between politicians and voters. A case in point is the study political scientists Douglas Ahler and David Broockman conducted on the voting record of US Congressman Adam Schiff alongside the preferences of his electorate. As Figure 9 shows, although his constituents broadly endorse a progressive agenda across a range of issues, all took a conservative position on one or two acts. Yet Schiff voted with the progressive majority every time. This ultimately leads to Schiff taking an overall more polarised stance than a hypothetical moderate or, critically, those who voted for him.

That doesn't mean that politicians are no more than loyal party sheep. Most political parties – and the voters who support them – are coalitions that have united under a flag of convenience: left- and

Figure 9: The voting record of Adam Schiff and his electorate on a range of issues (P = progressive position, C = conservative position).

| | Survey Response[16] | | | | | Liberal Roll Call Vote | |
	Voter 1	Voter 2	Voter 3	Voter 4	Voter 5	Adam Schiff	Hypothetical Moderate
Act 1 Fair Pay	P	P	C	P	P	P	P
Act 2 Children's Health Insurance	P	P	P	P	C	P	P
Act 3 Economic Stimulus	P	C	P	C	P	P	C
Act 4 Clean Energy	C	P	P	C	P	P	P
Act 5 Affordable Care Act	P	P	P	P	C	P	P
% Progressive votes	80%	80%	80%	60%	60%	100%	80%

centrist Democratic politicians share a party as do the Bernie Sanders supporters and Democrat-supporting Wall Street traders who vote for them; the same holds for Brexiteers and 'one nation' Conservatives. These coalitions contain factions that may regularly fight each other but that will generally unite when faced by a political outgroup – another party. Less common are the individual political mavericks prepared to go their own way and move out of step with party colleagues. John McCain, the Arizona senator who died in 2018, is one example of a politician who broke with the leadership of his party on critical issues such as immigration reform, campaign finance, interrogation methods for suspected terrorists and, towards the end of his life, President Trump's healthcare reform proposals. But he is an exception. Most politicians coalesce around a particular party, especially if there are only a couple or handful of parties to choose from. In a majoritarian system, crossing the floor to join another party is newsworthy precisely because it is so unusual. Starting a new party is even rarer, and the chances that that new party will succeed are vanishingly unlikely. In the UK in 2019, MPs from the Labour Party left to form a new political group. Weeks later they were joined by a number of Conservative colleagues. But within months most of these mavericks had realised that operating outside a party framework rendered their chances of re-election nil. Several then joined the Liberal Democrats. They still went on to lose at the next election. Donald Trump was only too aware of this rule when he decided to stand for president of the US: he knew he had no chance of winning unless he could secure the nomination of one of America's two dominant parties. On the very rare occasions when the existing party mould is broken, the chances are that this is only because of the particular mechanics of the electoral system. So, for example, Emmanuel Macron's presidential electoral success with his newly minted En Marche party was made possible by France's run-off voting system. For the most part, political parties exert reinforcing partisan power over their members.

And loyalty is a two-way street, which offers not just approval and acceptance but possible advancement. The senior political journalist Isabel Hardman, who regularly reviews the scene at Westminster, talks of Government backbenchers who ask UPQs (Utterly Pointless Questions) in the belief that this is the best way to get a promotion.[17] She cites, for example, Conservative MP Alan Mak's question to a Treasury Minister: 'Since 2010 [the year the Conservatives came to power] nearly half a million fewer children and young people are in households where there is worklessness. Will the Chief Secretary confirm that the Government will continue to help households into work and to cut poverty?' The response, unsurprisingly, was yes. Mak obviously viewed this interrogation as successful, as Hardman points out that eight days later he posed a nearly identical question to the Prime Minister. In 2021 Mak was appointed a Government whip, causing journalist Quentin Letts to tweet: 'Years of assiduous loyalty are finally rewarded. A great day for greasers.'

Interest groups and puppet masters

The political landscape is, of course, made up of more than politicians and citizens. There are interest and pressure groups, activists, advisers and donors, some working behind the scenes, others in the full glare of public attention. Some combine multiple roles, varying the exertion of their power as, say, both activists and donors, according to circumstance. Their influence is often hard to measure, and in any case tends to fluctuate. But each group of actors can add force to our natural tendency to polarise.

By their very nature such groups have an agenda to push – whether a new policy they want to see adopted or an overall political world view. Research in the US suggests that while eight per cent of those who regard themselves as politically middle of the road have made a political donation in the last two years, 29 per cent of those who are consistent allies of a political party have done.[18] And such politically active groups have a disproportionate influence, particularly at times of strife. Policymakers are three to four times more likely to make themselves available for a meeting with active political donors than they are for meetings with concerned constituents.[19] In the UK researchers have found that those who have been party donors are disproportionately well represented in the House of Lords.[20] The money trail is especially apparent in the US, where political spending is high and fundraising therefore key (it's estimated that $14 billion was spent on the 2020 presidential campaign).[21] In a country such as the UK, the sums involved are smaller but the influence of some donors is not necessarily any less insidious. The former Conservative minister Guto Bebb has noted that 'the thing about [political] access in Britain, is it is really cheap,'[22] while Peter Geoghegan, the investigative journalist and author of *Democracy for Sale*, told the authors that 'in many regards, I think it makes Britain even more susceptible to money and to donations.'[23]

Even those who individually make quite small contributions collectively pack a potentially distorting punch. According to the US Federal Election Commission, of the $1.3 billion spent for the main candidates during the 2012 Presidential campaign, $621 million was accounted for by individual donations below $200, while those between $200 and $1,000 contributed another $243 million.[24] In the 2016 election, Democratic hopeful Bernie Sanders raised $202 million – 90 per cent of his total budget – from small contributions. In Canada and the UK, small donors represent about a third of the total funds raised for recent campaigns,[25] while in Germany during the 2012 electoral cycle it was round about 53 per cent.[26] These individuals form persuasive networks (peer-to-peer fundraising networks typically raise three times more than ones that are organisationally led).[27] And these networks are most effectively powered by stimulating a strong sense of the group. Shannon Fitzgerald, who led Mayor Pete Buttigieg's digital content efforts for his 2020 presidential bid, has described how his fundraising initiative in part relied on triggering the antipathy of many Democrats in affluent California to what they perceived as a 'coastal elite'. Interestingly, Eric Singler, the nudge expert who worked with Ismaël Emelien to mastermind Macron's presidential campaign in France, has said to us that it focused first on using nudge techniques to find donors, then to recruit party members by creating a sense of belonging.[28]

As it happens, popular membership of political parties has fallen in recent years in many developed countries. In 1960, nearly 15 per cent of the electorate of Europe's democracies were officially affiliated with a political party. By 2000, that had shrunk to 5 per cent.[29] By 2004, New Zealand, along with Brazil, held the dubious distinction of having more former party members alive than current ones.[30] But that doesn't mean that party groupishness has declined. Rather, its nature has shifted. Signing up to and expressing support for a political party these days involves not so much paying a membership due as signalling support by, say, signing a petition to save a local school, signing a birthday card for a candidate,[31] or even via a computer game.[32] At the same time, there has been a rapid expansion in politicised interest groups. Some are more traditional agitators such as Greenpeace;[33] others are more chaotic upstarts like the Tea Party. Such groups do not typically stand for election themselves, and when they do, they are generally unsuccessful.[34] But they can exert immense influence.

Some interest groups can operate perniciously below the radar, using lobbyists and public relations (PR) people to relay their message and relying on these individuals' ready access to politicians and the media to ensure that it is heard. A case in point is the campaign run by the PR company Bell Pottinger[35] on behalf of the Gupta family in South Africa in the mid-2010s. Playing on political fears to pursue business interests, it involved setting up 200 fake Twitter accounts that sent out more than 220,000[36] tweets with hashtags such as #whitemo-nopolycapital and #respectguptas. Websites called WMC [White Monopoly Capital] Leaks and WMC Scams were created. A political group with reported links to the Guptas warned of a coming civil war. The main opposition, the Democratic Alliance, was branded a 'white party' that would be 'cover[ed] up by getting a few black stooges'. Messages were amplified by influencers such as Mzwanele 'Jimmy' Manyi. In a country that had only recently experienced profound racial segregation, the approach was polarising, divisive and incendiary.[37]

It has been shown that politicians are more responsive to the views of fellow partisans and less so to the electorate as a whole.[38] It's worth noting, too, the complementary studies that show that the pressure politicians feel to appeal to as broad a spectrum of voters as possible tends to be experienced most powerfully in a non-polarised environment,[39] and most weakly in a polarised one. In divided times, it makes sense to focus on your own tribe. The polarised environment activates their loyalty and generates solidarity. Political polarisation, in other words, often begets further political polarisation. And as it does so, the loud voices of the partisan drown out those of the moderates,[40] just as, according to Josh Pacewicz at Brown University, politically motivated community leaders in America's Rust Belt swing states are now more to the fore than apolitical ones. Such dynamics suggest an ever-intensifying death spiral. And there are plenty of historical examples of countries that, having started to submit to polarising forces, have been unable to escape them.

But it's also possible to get away from the death spiral, particularly when it's a question of individual polarised groups rather than society as a whole. In such instances, as the political scientist Giovanni Sartori points out, factionalism that could lead to extinction gives way to a reset. Britain's Labour Party, torn apart by internal strife in the 1980s, was able to re-establish itself over time under the leadership of Neil Kinnock, then John Smith, and finally Tony Blair. In the

US, the Republicans under Richard Nixon recalibrated themselves after their election disaster of 1964 under Barry Goldwater.[41] In 2020, the Democrats, pulled in opposite directions by the Hillary Clinton–Bernie Sanders divide, united behind the moderate Joe Biden.

The rules that govern, the people who subvert

When the founding father James Madison made the case for ratifying the US Constitution in *The Federalist Papers* he asserted that 'The reason of man, like man himself, is timid and cautious when left alone, and acquires firmness and confidence in proportion to the number with which it is associated.'[42] Acutely aware of the factional tendency of politics, and a keen scholar of the Roman Republic, which was brought down by factionalism, Madison was determined to create a unifying framework of laws and institutions for America that would both help bring people together and curtail their groupish instincts. Such a framework is often known as the 'rules of the game of a society',[43] and, involving everything from the courts to the judiciary to the military, serves as the foundations on which civic life is built. However, as the late South African political scientist Adrian Leftwich pointed out, it doesn't exist in isolation. There is a constant interplay between the entities and rules that make up the governance of a country and the groups and individuals that operate or seek to operate the levers of power.[44]

A country's constitutional framework can act as a crucial counterweight to that country's tendency to polarise or collapse into authoritarian rule.[45] It's lawyers, not politicians or interest groups, who judge whether an election has been free or fair. It's parliament, not individual political leaders, that has the power to scrutinise new legislation and, if necessary, reject it. It comes as no surprise, therefore, that those with a polarising agenda to push seek not only to capture hearts and minds but also to manipulate laws and institutions to allow them to. If they're able to do that, as the Harvard scholars Steven Levitsky and Daniel Ziblatt argue, it's a short step to sidelining others and tilting the rules of the game, and ultimately locking in their newly built advantage.[46] They may well also seek to manipulate other safeguards against extreme factionalism: the generalised codes of behaviour, such as toleration and forbearance, that are unwritten but shape the way in which society operates and coheres.

Manipulating constitutions and institutions is something we tend to associate with dictators and authoritarian rulers. The Hungarian Prime Minister Viktor Orbán, for instance, introduced a new Fundamental Law, sanctioned by his Fidesz party, that erased all the case law of the powerful, rule-guarding Constitutional Court. He placed political friends and loyalists in key positions: Tünde Handó, the wife of a Fidesz MEP, became head of the powerful National Judicial Office; the Fidesz-backed Péter Polt was appointed chief prosecutor. Potentially embarrassing breaches were swept under the carpet: a 2014 €44 million fraud case involving Orbán's son-in-law went nowhere, despite investigation by the European anti-fraud board OLAF. But such tactics are not the sole preserve of absolutists (those who become absolutists can rise to power, as Orbán did, through democratic means). President Franklin D. Roosevelt (FDR) may regularly end up on the podium in surveys to identify America's best leaders,[47] but he wasn't above trying to expand and stuff the Supreme Court with his apparatchiks when he felt frustrated by that body's rulings against legislation that he was trying to press through.

Given the often noted tendency of political groupings to factionalise, it may come as a surprise to learn that they, too, can be a 'chief practical bulwark'[48] of defence. The fact is, though, that they can prove remarkably effective in keeping authoritarians and extremists – even those with platforms and followings – off the ballot paper. Consider the case of the American car manufacturer Henry Ford, who in 1923 set his eyes on the presidency. When *Collier's*, one of the US's largest magazines, surveyed over 250,000 Americans about their preferred candidate, it found that the incumbent president, Warren Harding, managed to secure just 20 per cent support, while Ford garnered 34 per cent. In another survey, this time of nearly 700,000 readers, conducted by a consortium of local newspapers, Ford picked up 41 per cent of support. But Ford had an ugly side. The *Dearborn Independent*, which he owned, had run a series entitled 'The International Jew: The world's problem'. In 1924, Himmler was to describe Ford as 'one of our most valuable, important and witty fighters'.[49] Such extremism troubled Republican leaders, while Senator James Couzens wondered, 'How can a man over sixty years old who . . . has no training, no experience, aspire to such an office? . . . It is most ridiculous.'[50] Ford may have been a popular choice but, with endorsements withheld and supportive networks closed off, the road ahead for him was blocked, and he faded from political view. Of course, his bid for power came at a time when the Republicans were in the ascendant. In divisive times, grasping for the straw that a polarising figure offers has its appeal.

The transformational leader: myth or reality?

To what extent a leader is able to transform or polarise society, or merely reflects transformation or polarisation that is already there, has been much debated. The traditional view was that there will always be certain powerful, charismatic individuals – whether, in recent times, Hitler, Stalin or Mao Zedong – who are able to wrest a precarious country in a particular direction. Such individuals are generally associated with authoritarian regimes and with aggression. However, a shift away from the status quo is not the sole preserve of dictatorial leaders. On occasion those truly transforming society can give power to those who previously had little. Adolfo Suárez, for example, who became Prime Minister of Spain in 1976, helped engineer a transition from the military rule of General Franco to a pluralist democracy. Once in power, the forty-four-year-old former Franco apparatchik introduced a two-chamber parliament (the Cortes) and universal suffrage – initiatives ratified by a referendum. He then invited the opposition – previously outlawed and persecuted – to the table. In 1977 Spain's Communist Party was legalised. Months later, the first democratic elections were held. Now at the head of a moderate coalition government, Suárez oversaw economic reform, and introduced a new constitution that was duly ratified in a referendum by 87 per cent of the public. Previous political outliers – such as the Communists and the PNV (the Basque nationalist party) – broadly agreed to abide by the new status quo, recognising 'the indissoluble unity of the Spanish nation' and the right to autonomy of the nationalities and regions it composed. Crucially, Suárez also separated the roles of army leader and premier that had helped General Franco achieve totalitarian control. An attempted military coup in 1981 was faced down with the support of the king, thereby securing Spain's hard-won democratic system and Suárez's achievements.

Radical transformation such as occurred under Suárez is rare. It demands an individual prepared to take charge of an existing group but also prepared to give away power should the environment become ripe for change. Since change involves uncertainty and, as discussed in Chapter 4, uncertainty is often a trigger for the certainties of a more authoritarian approach, it's not difficult to see why the Suárezes of this world are rare. Marshal Pétain of France, the defender of Verdun during the First World War, offers a more depressingly common example. During the Second World War he drew on his heroic military legacy to gain support for his Nazi-sanctioned Vichy Republic. Indeed, those who had come within the ambit of his Verdun role proved nearly 7 per cent more likely to collaborate with the Nazis after 1940 than those who hadn't.[51] Those with significant media platforms, such as talk radio hosts,[52] can also tap into the authoritarian leanings of uncertain times.

As Oxford University's Archie Brown puts it in his *The Myth of the Strong Leader*, 'There can be a wide gulf between the image of a strong leader . . . and the more complex reality.' Brown, who identifies Suárez as one of those rare transformational leaders, highlights a tendency to allocate to leaders credit that should, rightly, be spread more widely. Tony Blair, for example, is popularly regarded as synonymous with the political movement 'Blairism' that bears his name. But Blairism required the support and input of others, not least Blair's Chancellor Gordon Brown, who, among other things, made the Bank of England independent and opened the purse strings for significant investments in government welfare programmes. Leaders in democratic countries need supporters and advocates. President Harry Truman was reflecting on this basic truism when he said of his successor, former army general Dwight (Ike) Eisenhower: 'He'll say, do this! Do that! And nothing will happen. Poor Ike – it won't be a bit like the army.'

The political journey of a US president

If there's one political story that demonstrates the dangers of accepting too wholeheartedly either the 'great man' view of history or its opposite – the 'complex influences' view advanced by such thinkers as Herbert Spencer – it's the story of Donald Trump's rise to power. Any close study of America from the late twentieth century onwards can only conclude that the result of the 2016 election was not solely down to either force, but rather to an amalgam of the way individuals interacted with groups and the broader environment. It is worth exploring these in some detail to show the complex, polarising nature of their interactions.

The environmental factor was that outlined in the previous chapter: a sense among many Americans of inequality, uncertainty, declining relative status and, alongside these, a growing dislike of outgroups, all of which had their origins in the economics of the late-twentieth and early-twenty-first centuries. A key moment had come with the signing of the North American Free Trade Agreement (NAFTA) in 1992. Increasing trade liberalisation had set in, which, as subsequent presidential candidate Senator Mitt Romney put it, proved 'good for the nation' but less so for many communities, particularly those involved in industry, who found themselves working for companies that struggled to compete with cheap imports. As Romney went on to explain: 'If you're working in an auto factory in Detroit you're not doing better . . . You had a home, a community. Suddenly the community becomes a ghost town.'[53] Then came the subprime mortgages fiasco and the 2008 financial crash and bail-out. That bail-out had been supported by both Republicans – for whom it went against their small government creed – and the Democrats – who would have to prop up an unpopular outgoing president. The Treasury Secretary, Hank Paulson, recalls theatrically getting down on one knee to beg Nancy Pelosi to support TARP. When she and many of her colleagues did, they saved the economy. Of that bail-out many billions – $182 billion to the insurance giant AIG alone[54] – had gone to bankers. Even though the likes of AIG repaid the government in full (even contributing to a government profit on the deal), there was a sufficient kernel of truth in that narrative to take hold. The rift between the elites or wealthy, and the rest, became a chasm.

Amid this uncertainty and inequality, America's ugly history of racial segregation reared its head again. In 2008, Barack Obama was elected president, the first black man ever to assume that role in the US. Many applauded Obama's assumption of power and his determination to live up to his belief, expressed at the 2004 Democratic Convention, that 'there is not a liberal America and a conservative America; there is the United States of America.'[55] Obama's defeated opponent, John McCain, implicitly acknowledged a social divide in his concession speech, when he talked of the moment as being of 'special significance' for African Americans.[56] George W. Bush, for his part, sensing potential trouble, convened a group of conservative-leaning talk show hosts six days before he left office, to tell them specifically: 'Look, I asked you here for one reason. I want you to go easy on the new guy.'[57] It would have been a naïve person who, given America's troubled history of racial segregation, assumed that all would be happy to see a black man in the White House. It would have been an optimist who assumed that no one would seek to racially leverage Obama's achievement.

From the start, Obama faced a divided country operating in a maelstrom. He had inherited a nation that was economically split, where aspirations to the American Dream felt extinguished for many. A powerful libertarian wing of the Republican Party was so angered by the expansion of government it was willing to fund a backlash against it. And he was a black president in a country that had previously always been run by white men.

So when Obama announced his first major policy initiative, the Affordable Care Act, it should perhaps have come as no surprise that it would become a bitterly fought-over and deeply divisive piece of legislation. That it was based on a policy devised by Mitt Romney, the Republican Governor of Massachussetts, cut no ice with its opponents. It assumed the proportions of a shibboleth, an article of belief that tested whether you were a true conservative. As was pointed out in Chapter 3, so tribal did the issue swiftly become that even those conservative-leaning voters who stood to benefit from it opposed it – yet again demonstrating the way in which a group stance can bulldoze considera-tion of a particular question or issue. Politicians who voiced support found their town hall meetings turning ugly. Former vice-presidential candidate Sarah Palin fuelled the (false) rumour that the act included a provision for setting up 'death panels' that would determine whether individuals were worthy of medical care. Shock jock talkshow hosts like

Laura Ingraham and Rush Limbaugh[58] amplified the story. The wily Mitch McConnell, then Senate Minority Leader, and others sought to use the Affordable Care Act as a political football: 'It set up a referendum in the country,'[59] McConnell argued, suggesting that it could be used to mobilise a debate that would take undecideds off the fence and get them to identify with existing Republican supporters.

Into this frenzied atmosphere stepped a new, well resourced political grouping, the ultra-libertarian Tea Party Patriots (Tea Party). Those resources included at least $200 million from Republican megadonors the Koch brothers, who had been frustrated by the scale and interventionist nature of TARP. But the Tea Party quickly turned their fire on other issues,[60] including the Affordable Care Act. Tea Party activists were urged to 'pack the hall . . . yell out and challenge [the representatives'] statements early . . . stand up and shout and sit right back down.'[61] They proved vocal and successful. When the GOP Representative Joe Wilson shouted 'You lie' as Obama proposed the health care legislation at a joint session of Congress, Wilson's campaign contributions that quarter soared to $2.7 million, 98 per cent from small donors.[62, 63] His Democrat challenger raised about half of that.[64] At the next election Wilson's margin of victory increased – violating the norm of respecting the legitimacy of an opponent had paid off. The Tea Party expanded their sphere of influence. They mobilised in Republican primary elections – for example, helping Marco Rubio wrest control of a US Senate seat from the favourite and established Charlie Crist. Rubio went on to boast that he 'didn't need the [Republican] party' after his victory,[65] signalling a weakening in the ability of long-established parties to act as a bulwark against polarisation. In South Carolina, the six-term congressman Bob Inglis was beaten by a Tea Party candidate whose supporters had chanted 'no bail-outs' outside his office.[66] Senator Lisa Murkowski, whose voting record was among the most moderate of Republicans, was defeated in the Alaskan primary.[67] Seniority was no protection from a toxic political atmosphere in which bipartisanship was viewed as disloyalty. When Eric Cantor, the sitting House majority leader, who had sought to work across the aisle on immigration reform, faced re-election his seat was deluged by Tea Party activists. At one event the conservative talk radio host Laura Ingraham claimed that the Democrats wanted Cantor to win because he was their 'ally' (Cantor had been promoting bi-partisan immigration reform). As a remedy for this perceived disloyalty Ingraham suggested that he should be traded in a prisoner swap with the Taliban.[68] Cantor went from being 34 points up in the campaign to losing out to Tea Party candidate Dave Brat by 11.

As the presidential primary season revved into action for the 2012 election, the move to the right in Republican ranks gathered pace. Nominee hopeful Newt Gingrich played the populist card (by, for example, attacking the mainstream 'liberal' press) and went on to trounce opponents in the South Carolina primary. Alarm bells were ringing, even though in this set of elections moderates prevailed to secure the nomination, Mitt Romney becoming the GOP nominee with Paul Ryan as his deputy. The view of senior Republicans (described in Tim Alberta's *American Carnage*) may have been that Tea Party representatives would 'fall in line. Freshman always fall in line'.[69] But they were beginning to look hopelessly complacent.

Donald Trump had publicly toyed with the idea of running for president for years. His biographer, Gwenda Blair, described it as 'something of a hobby'.[70] To promote his 1987 book *The Art of the Deal* Trump had saved on advertising spend by generating column inches with suggestions of a presidential run. In the following years he donated mainly to Democratic candidates but by 2011 he had switched sides, appearing on stage at the Conservative Political Action Conference. After Obama's victory Trump identified a message that would mobilise a part of the GOP base – that the President had not been born in the US, but Kenya. It was completely untrue, and the subtext of this 'us-and-them' narrative – that it was the first black president whose eligibility was being questioned – was not hard to spot. Trump, though, became the face of the 'birther' movement. After Obama released his birth certificate to refute the claims, Trump tweeted, 'An extremely credible source has called my office and told me that @BarackObama's birth certificate is a fraud.'[71] Each time he issued a comment, he garnered press attention and built his base. The influencer had a platform and a toxic message that polarised and galvanised and, as usual with such messages (see Chapter 3), could not be countered by a statement of the simple truth. Even so, despite this festering malaise, few took Trump's suggestions he would stand for the GOP nomination seriously.

The traditional Republican operators were among the last to recognise the power of the Trump approach. He had no experience of elected office. He displayed little consistency on issues that mattered (Trump had, for example, declared himself both pro-choice and pro-life). There were no top-level political operatives on his team. In any case, there must have been those who, recalling the fate of Henry Ford, reckoned that, when it really came down to it, such a rabble-rouser could not possibly succeed (ignoring the fact that as an outsider Trump, like Ford, did not need to respect the rules of the game). Even when he came second in the Iowa primary in February 2016, few Republican leaders spotted a populist leader on the threshold of power. When RNC Communications Director Sean Spicer had argued vehemently that Trump should be excluded from the primary debates, he was overruled by Chairman Reince Priebus – principally because Priebus feared the consequences of excluding a candidate who had such vociferous Tea Party support. Priebus extracted a loyalty pledge from Trump before agreeing to give him access to the stage. According to *American Carnage*, lawyers later clarified this loyalty pledge was meaningless. Norms are only meaningful when candidates sign up to them, or when failing to do so has consequences.

It's interesting to note here that even those Republicans who had pondered blocking Trump's candidature went on to serve him, as Spicer for a short time became Communications Director, and Priebus Trump's Chief of Staff, before being unceremoniously and humiliatingly sacked (as he descended the steps of Air Force One he joined the presidential motorcade, only to find that his car was pulling out in a different direction). Trump, who had yet to depart the aircraft, was tweeting that Priebus would be replaced, while his Communications Director, Anthony Scaramucci, had described his former colleague as a 'fucking paranoid schizophrenic'.[72] Observers may have wondered if it was the President who enjoyed using his power to make people who had shown him loyalty feel humiliated.

But, as the Republican primaries had raged through 2016, Priebus had lent Trump an air of official legitimacy, putting him on an equal footing with more established players who – partly terrified by the angry online mobs Trump could mobilise – chose to attack each other, not him. As one Republican commentator said, 'No one wanted to bell the cat', as that would involve mutually assured destruction. Instead, Trump watched his seasoned competitors knock each other out, one by one. By July he was claiming the GOP nomination.

Trump had understood how to leverage groupishness for personal gain in an environment ripe for polarisation. He didn't just ignore the rules of the game; he tore them up. His playbook was set. Within weeks Trump was publicly attacking the Muslim parents of a fallen American soldier. Khizr and Ghazala Khan had spoken out against Trump's proposed travel ban on Muslims: 'Go look at the graves of brave patriots who died defending the United States of America . . . You will see all faiths, genders and ethnicities.'[73] Trump responded by denigrating the Khans: 'Mr Khan, who does not know me, viciously attacked me from the stage of the DNC and is now all over TV doing the same – Nice!' There were suggestions that Khan was an extremist. Polarisation had helped win Trump the nomination. It was also to fuel his presidency right to the very end.

THE MESSAGES OF DIVISION

The power of stories

In 1944 Fritz Heider and Marianne Simmel[1] from Smith College, Massachusetts created a short animated cartoon. It featured a series of shapes moving around. Sometimes triangles were inside a box. Sometimes those triangles moved through the box, or bounced off each other. When the film was over Heider and Simmel asked their students to describe what they had just seen. Just one student gave a purely factual account: 'A large solid triangle is shown entering a rectangle. It enters and comes out of this rectangle, and each time the corner and one-half of one of the sides of the rectangle form an opening.' The other students proved rather more imaginative. They invented stories to explain what they had been watching. They even attributed thoughts, feelings and emotions to what were no more than abstract drawn shapes. 'He opens his door,' one said, 'walks out to see our hero and his sweet. But our hero does not like the inter-ruption . . . he attacks triangle-one rather vigorously (maybe the big bully said some bad word).' For this observer a 150-second film had become a narrative with a hero, a villain and a love theme.

The human instinct to create stories is a fundamental one. We tell them to help us make sense of the world. As screenwriting expert Robert McKee puts it, 'Our appetite for story is a reflection of the profound human need to grasp the patterns of living.'[2] Stories can make us feel safe. They allow us to create a shared identity. They sometimes help us to wrap up uncomfortable truths in packages that are readily comprehensible, less incongruent and, accordingly, more consistent and acceptable. Many of the stories we hear from childhood onwards confirm basic human values: fairness, justice, a belief that good will prevail or that hard work and honesty will be rewarded. They help shape us and develop norms from an early stage of life. Research has shown that by nineteen months old, infants expect each person to receive a fair share. At twenty-one months they expect a reward for all who have taken part in completing a task.[3] These expectations are confirmed every day as children find that they receive praise, rewards and even certificates for acts of kindness or good behaviour.

Stories can trigger powerful emotional responses: we may not know the people they feature – and in many stories, of course, they may well be fictional – but we can nevertheless feel a close connection to them and their experiences. The American psychology professor Paul Zak[4] describes how on a long flight, exhausted from back-to-back meetings, he found himself watching *Million Dollar Baby*. The film tells the story of an aspiring boxer (Hilary Swank), written off as being too old to learn. She nonetheless persuades a gruff trainer (Clint Eastwood) to help her and then proceeds – unexpectedly – to win bout after bout. But then the story takes a tragic turn. Swank is illegally sucker-punched by an opponent, hits her head on a stool as she goes down and is left in a paraplegic state. By the end of the film her family have tried to steal her money, and her trainer has agreed to support her in her bid to end her own life. Winner of the Best Picture category at the 2005 Oscars, *Million Dollar Baby* was described by the *Atlantic* as 'shamelessly manipulative and genuinely moving'.[5]

It left Paul Zak in tears. It also left him wondering why, from a neurological point of view, it should have had such a powerful effect.

The answer, he found, lay in the hormone oxytocin. Produced in the hypothalamus, a small section near the base of the brain, oxytocin is an immensely powerful chemical that induces bonding behaviour. It stimulates mothers to bond with their babies. It connects us to one another. And it links us emotionally to stories.

And herein lies one of the great powers and potential dangers of stories. That emotional bonding force they create, in generating a sense of togetherness, can by the same token also generate an outgroup. In his thesis of 'imagined communities' (see Chapter 4), Benedict Anderson described how the rise of the printing press in fifteenth-century Europe led to a growth in the use of the vernacular. This, in turn, he argued, triggered new nationally based emotional connections that ultimately superseded the controlling role that religion, especially Catholicism, had previously played. The stories that printing allowed to be disseminated galvanised the narratives of new 'ingroups' – including Calvinists and Lutherans. Simultaneously, they identified – and demonised – outgroups.

Some stories, of course, explicitly set out to achieve this polarising effect, and do so with devastating force. The German film producer Leni Riefenstahl's *Triumph of the Will*, which follows Hitler over four days of the 1934 Nuremberg Rally, is a case in point. Culminating in a scene where over 150,000 Sturmabteilung (SA) and Schutzstaffel (SS) members stand to attention, the film was intended to signal the rising power of a resurgent Germany, to create a powerful sense of community for those in the ingroup ('All loyal Germans will become National Socialists,' Hitler is heard to say. 'Only the best National Socialists are party comrades!'), and simultaneously, through its appeal to unity and 'purity', to reinforce the notion of an outgroup – an enemy within. What makes its polarising impact particularly powerful is that it's cast in the form of a narrative. As Elmer Davis, the Director of the US

Office of War Information during the Second World War, said, 'The easiest way to inject a propaganda idea into most people's minds is to let it go through the medium of an entertainment picture, when they do not realise they're being propagandised.'[6] The power of a polarised story is something the CIA picked up on with their animated film version of George Orwell's *Animal Farm*. The novel ends with a scene in which the farm animals, looking at their new pig overlords and at the human farmers who had once exploited them, find it 'impossible to say which was which'.[7] The film closes with the farm animals overthrowing the evil pigs: the distinction made here between the 'us' of the farm animals and the 'them' of the (Communist) pigs could not be starker.

Obviously not all stories that adopt a polarising narrative set out to create or exploit division. The good-versus-evil trope, which stretches back to the earliest days of human narratives and fables, and whose tendrils can be detected today in everything from *Star Wars* to *The Lion King*, can often champion the triumph of virtue. But the power of the polarising story to evoke hostility is undeniable. Reactions to the 1915 three-hour epic *The Birth of a Nation* offer a case in point. The film paints a picture of a Civil War America in which black people are brutish, morally degenerate and a very real threat to whites. The racism is brazen. After the film's release riots broke out in several cities. The Ku Klux Klan (presented in the film as a heroic force) experienced a resurgence. The film also sparked the rapid expansion of the National Association for the Advancement of Coloured People (NAACP), who helped lead the protests against its distribution.

Negative political storytelling and campaigning is far from new. When the aristocratic Georgiana Cavendish threw herself into the politics of 1780s Britain, scurrilous cartoons circulated suggesting that she was exchanging sexual favours for votes for her preferred candidate.[8, 9] Lyndon Johnson famously commissioned a TV ad which juxtaposed a small girl counting the petals she is picking from a daisy with a man's voice counting down from ten, to suggest that voting for Johnson's opponent in the 1964 presidential election would lead to nuclear war.[10]

Unlike commercial advertising, which tends to focus on the feel-good boost from wearing or consuming a product, such negative political advertising plays on divisions and fears. And in so doing it can be astonishingly effective. Lyndon Johnson went on to win the 1964 presidential election. In the 1988 Canadian election, fought against the backdrop of the formation of the North American Free Trade Agreement (NAFTA),[11] the Liberal Party created a narrative in which their opponents stood accused of erasing Canadian sovereignty. The Liberals doubled their representation. During the 1992 US presidential race negative advertising was employed by Bill Clinton's supporters. According to Stephen Ansolabehere and Shanto Iyengar it led to an uptick in support for an ultimately victorious Clinton.[12]

For many, Barack Obama's 2008 presidential campaign was characterised by its positivity, notably its focus on the words 'hope' and 'change' that so often appeared on the candidate's posters. But a close study of the Obama camp's TV advertising has revealed that it actually spent more on advertising that promoted a negative message than did those promoting Obama's opponent John McCain via a similarly negative message.[13] Sometimes simply sowing doubt is sufficient. In the 1992 UK General Election – which Labour was expected to win – the Conservatives spread the notion that Labour could not be trusted with the economy.[14] That proved sufficient to persuade some wavering Labour supporters to stay at home. Taking a few points off an opponent through such tactics can be easier than trying to win people over to your side.[15]

More recently, the manipulative impact of story narratives was well illustrated by an ad launched by Volkswagen in 2011 and then later turned against the car manufacturer by Greenpeace. In the original Volkswagen ad a small boy dressed as Darth Vader unsuc-cessfully tries to exert his 'dark powers' on the family dog, various pieces of household equipment and his sandwich. When his father arrives home in a Volkswagen Passat, the boy goes through the same ritual with the car and, unaware that his father has activated them via his key fob, is amazed to see its headlights come on. The soundtrack to the ad is, inevitably, *Star Wars'* 'Imperial Death March'. Shown at that year's Super Bowl, the ad went viral and was branded by *Time* magazine 'the ad that changed Super Bowl commercials forever'.[16]

Volkswagen, however, had run foul of Greenpeace by opposing new European Union carbon emission standards. The environmen-tal group issued a mirror image version of the ad which focused on the good characters in *Star Wars*, with children playing at being Luke Skywalker, Princess Leia, Chewbacca and R2-D2, complete with light-sabers. At the end viewers were invited to 'join the rebellion'. They did so in their millions, and the message was amplified on a cam-paign website that offered 'Jedi training' and invited people to 'ask Yoda to explain the rebellion.' Finding themselves cornered on the Dark Side, Volkswagen announced that it would now work to improve the energy efficiency of its cars. Greenpeace had made clever use of a good-vs-evil narrative. They had also played on another emotion that can be powerfully persuasive: humour. Getting people to laugh with you not only ties the ingroup closer together but also makes it harder for potential members of an outgroup to dislike you. Studies have shown that in situations where laughter is evoked, levels of trust and generosity increase by 30 per cent.[17]

A story can prove notably persuasive when it is accompanied by a suggestion that other people are convinced by it, particularly if those 'other people' are members of one's own group. When, for example, a group who had a broad range of views on abortion were led to believe public opinion was moving in a more pro-choice direction, support for this apparently more popular position grew by 9 per cent, while support for restrictive abortion laws weakened by 12 per cent.[18] Often, too, stories that make people feel initially uncomfortable or even hostile are an essential weapon in the campaigner's armoury, helping ultimately to move the dial on major social issues.[19] But more often – and certainly in a society that is already showing a tendency to splinter – stories tend to be employed merely to confirm existing prejudices and to weaponise them, activating a sense of us/ them, particularly among those who feel their status is declining or fear they are being left behind.

At their most extreme, stories become partisan conspiracy theories that peddle extreme, often bizarre accusations. To outsiders these will seem wholly unsubstantiated and totally preposterous. To true believers, though, because they contain all the elements good stories require, they seem both convincing and compelling. They arouse emotion through their evocation of heroes and villains, good and evil. They offer certainty in an uncertain world, placing random events that might otherwise evoke feelings of fear or powerlessness within a pattern, or pretending that they didn't happen (hence, for example, conspiracy theories about 9/11 or school shootings). And they explain a complex world in simple terms, complete with shadowy organisations that control everything, individuals with unimaginable power, and aliens intervening or taking human form. Ironically, the very fact that evidence for their validity is invariably lacking is a point in their favour. If it's a high-level plot, it follows that those responsible will have covered their tracks. There is an apparent and simple consistency to conspiracy theories that makes them very attractive.

The Pizzagate conspiracy theory in the US demonstrates not just the extreme forms such stories take but their astonishing ability to spread virally. It began with the hacking in 2016 of the personal email account of John Podesta, presidential hopeful Hillary Clinton's campaign manager.[20] As Wikileaks posted the emails online, users of such websites as the anonymous online message board 4Chan[21] started to speculate that what to anyone else appeared entirely innocent messages actually masked horrendous crimes. The word pizza, they argued, was code for child pornography. Pasta meant little boy. Ice cream, male prostitute. All these code words and the crimes they described were, it was argued, connected to a particular pizzeria in Washington, Comet Ping Pong (in 2008 its owner, James Alefantis, had emailed Podesta to ask him to speak at an Obama fundraiser being held there, hence the initial link). 4Chan's users decided Comet's iconic sign included symbols linked to a satanic cult. A photo of an empty walk-in refrigerator was interpreted as evidence of a secret kill room. Lurking in the bowels of Comet's, it was suggested, was a basement where sexual abuse of children regularly occurred.

It was, of course, inevitable that someone in Podesta's role would receive some negative coverage. He supported a candidate who strongly divided opinion. He had led a bitter primary election campaign that had left many of the supporters of the defeated presidential hopeful Bernie Sanders resentful of Hillary Clinton.[22] And he was in a job that regularly involved saying 'no' to people and requests. But nothing can have prepared him for this bizarre conspiracy theory. Needless to say, no element of the story had any truth to it at all. Indeed, there wasn't even a basement at the pizzeria. Yet the rumour spread like wildfire. At one point Comet Ping Pong was fielding over 150 calls a day from conspiracy theorists, many of them death threats. Podesta was harangued at all hours. One conspiracy theorist, Edgar Maddison Welch, who later recounted how 'he had read online that the Comet restaurant was harboring child sex slaves and that he wanted to see for himself if they were there',[23, 24] drove for six hours from his home in North Carolina to 'investigate the case'. Various customers were in the pizzeria as he entered, including children. He was later sentenced to four years in prison for discharging his rifle. It's scarcely surprising that Alefantis should have believed the rumour to have been a 'co-ordinated political attack'.[25]

That some with a clearly political agenda should have helped spread the story is depressing but predictable. Erik Prince, the brother of Trump's Education Secretary (and significant donor) Betsy de Vos, was one such: he 'confirmed' the rumour was true in an interview with Breitbart.[26] Nor is it unexpected that belief in the rumour followed largely partisan lines: 46 per cent of Trump voters thought it to be true, as compared with 17 per cent of Clinton voters.[27] 'The right paid attention to right-wing sites, and the more right-wing they were, the more attention they got,' says the Harvard Law professor Yochai Benkler. More extreme sites would use a (then) 'relatively-credible source' such as Breitbart as a validator, but distort and exaggerate the claims. 'Because they were repeated not only on the very far-fringe sites but also by sites that are at the centre of this cluster, the right-wing disinformation circulated and amplified very quickly.'[28] But the sheer scale of the belief and its persistence does seem extraordinary. Millions of Americans genuinely believed a story that had no evidential basis whatsoever. It took *Rolling Stone* magazine two years (and two teams of researchers) to trace the digital trail.

Why, then, should a story as absurd as Pizzagate prove so 'sticky'? Quite simply, it ticked all the conspiracy theory boxes, and in so doing ticked many of the boxes for a great story. It evoked strong emotion through a narrative of supposedly suffering children. It posited a world clearly divided between good and evil. And in triggering fear in an environment dominated by social and political uncertainty it played on people's natural tendency to pay more attention to negative coverage in the media when faced with news that induces anxiety, whether a terrorist attack, a natural disaster, a financial crash – or an evil conspiracy.[29]

The fear factor is particularly noteworthy here. The University of California Davis Professor Alison Ledgerwood has suggested that negative thoughts are stickier than positive ones, while others have pointed out – not surprisingly, perhaps – that those experiencing stress tend to adopt a negative bias (it's a cornerstone of cognitive psychology).[30] Negativity in its extreme form becomes paranoia, in which state, as Richard Hofstadter observed in his seminal 1964 essay 'The Paranoid Style in American Politics', each person will have a 'special resistance of his own ... to developing such awareness [of how things do not happen], but circumstances often deprive him of exposure to events that might enlighten him – and in any case he resists enlightenment.'[31] In this context it's interesting to note the research from the Massachusetts Institute of Technology that points to fake news being retweeted 70 per cent more frequently than the truth,[32] and to the truth taking nearly six times as long as a falsehood to reach 1,500 people and twenty times as long to be passed on through a chain of ten recipients.[33]

Hofstadter's observation that under certain conditions people will resist enlightenment provides further support for the notion that negative stories in general and conspiracy theories in particular are highly 'sticky' – even when they have been disproved. Take the enduring conviction among Americans that Saddam Hussein was responsible for the attacks of 9/11.[34] No telling evidence for this was ever produced. In fact, as time passed, more and more information came to light that disproved the allegation. Yet as Monica Prasad, Professor of Sociology at Northwestern University, and her colleagues highlighted, 50 per cent of Americans still believed it to be true in 2003. Unconvinced that this was simply due to the fact that the then Bush administration explicitly and implicitly linked Saddam with al-Qaeda (who *were* responsible for 9/11), Prasad and her team dug more deeply. They wanted to establish whether, had the 'information environment' been different – that is, had (Republican) voters been in possession of the facts – they would not have believed that the Iraqi leader was responsible. And what they found was that the provision of correct information would have had next to no impact.

145

For this subset of voters, the fact that the war took place meant they needed a reason for it, and Saddam Hussein – to them – was a good reason. As Prassad and her colleagues put it,

> going to war is a powerful situational heuristic that allows voters to conclude that there is something about their world that justifies going to war . . . They then develop affective [emotional] ties to this conclusion and seek information that confirms it while dismissing information that contradicts it, producing the correlation between information and belief.[35]

This remained the case even when these particular voters were challenged, and even when they were shown a newspaper article in which G. W. Bush himself was quoted as saying there was no link between Saddam and 9/11. Whatever contrary evidence was presented to them, from whatever source, 98 per cent of those interviewed refused to change their minds. Their beliefs, their views and their partisan identity had become inextricably interwoven.

The online factor

Narratives and conspiracy theories that polarise are nothing new. The anti-Semitic blood libel that claims that Jews are guilty of sacrificing Christian children stretches back to medieval times. People have regularly believed that famous figures who died actually survived, whether the Princes in the Tower in the 1480s, President Lincoln's assassin John Wilkes Booth in the 1860s or the Grand Duchess Anastasia Romanov after the Russian Revolution. They have been convinced that events that did take place didn't (the Moon landing) or that events that didn't occur did (aliens built Stonehenge). And they have sworn that famous people weren't all they seemed

(Shakespeare did not write the works of Shakespeare). But if such stories have always existed, it does seem to be the case that in today's more connected world they are much easier to spread frictionlessly and at speed and that, in consequence, they have become more common and more pernicious, their 'stickiness' often acquiring growing force.

In the political sphere, among the earliest countries to appreciate the potential of online negativity were Estonia and Lithuania. Back in 2007 the tech-savvy Estonians had been the first anywhere in the world to adopt online voting.[36] Online campaigning was the natural consequence, and it swiftly acquired a powerfully negative flavour, frequently playing to the anti-Russian feeling prevalent among the country's nearly 1 million voters.[37] Lithuanian campaigners similarly adopted a negative line towards their Russian neighbours. One senior political campaign manager who was active during the 2012 election explained how Facebook had become a vital tool in their propaganda fight: 'Facebook is very important, both for viral campaigning and for negative campaigning which . . . cannot be done in the name of the party.'[38] More recently Viktor Orbán, the Hungarian President desperate to depict himself as a strongman leader, has used Facebook to supercharge a narrative about who is and who is not Hungarian,[39] and to evoke notions of the 'Greater Hungary' that existed until the dismantling of the Austro-Hungarian Empire at the end of the First World War. The Internet, it seems, is an easily harnessed platform from which to promote the certainties and 'them-and-us' divisions of nationalism.

It's worth noting in this context that until 2016 Facebook's line to content creators was that emotional and controversial news stories could expect to receive two to three times as much attention (likes, comments and shares) as more neutral, less emotive ones.[40] Such stories not only stay with us for longer: they also produce a physiological reaction in terms of both arousal/activation and attentiveness.[41] And

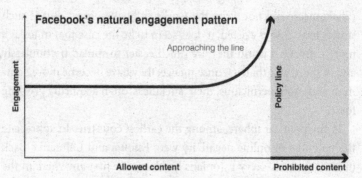

Figure 10: Engagement vs type of content on Facebook

the fact is that the Internet rewards those who spread them, in attention and financial gain. Consequently, as Timur Kuran has said of would-be social media celebrities, for those who seek attention 'the goal is not to go to the middle ground.'[42] The graph above, which draws on Facebook's own research, shows how engagement increases as messages push to the limits, approaching the boundaries of what is deemed acceptable content.[43]

It's not just the ready accessibility the online world affords that makes it so powerful as a campaigning tool, or that it is so cheap to deploy (in the US, for example, where it costs 55 cents[44] to reach people by direct mail, an email can be sent for less than one tenth of a cent).[45] With online reactions virtually instant and easily measurable in addition, messages can be constantly refined to ensure they achieve their maximum engagement. In the 2020 presidential campaign, the Trump campaign tested 5,000 ads a day,[46] using simple A/B tests (in which one approach is tried with one group and a different one with another), to see which were most effective. In the UK 2019 general election the major political parties were testing 3,000 ads a day. Machine learning is now helping to make the process even faster and more effective, and allows it to be scaled to previously unimaginable levels. The environmental group Rainforest Action Network increased the conversion of donors by 866 per cent after it adopted machine learning to hone its approach.[47]

It's therefore no surprise that optimisation techniques, first used on a wide scale politically by Barack Obama's campaign team in 2008, should have become the stock-in-trade of every competent political operative since. In 2008 Obama's team took on a top Google employee, Dan Siroker, to be director of analytics. He proved so successful that he went on to co-found a company, Optimizely, in 2010 to help others do the same thing.[48] In 2012 Obama's digital team used the outcomes of more than 500 A/B tests to optimise the donations process, increasing conversions for the campaign by 49 per cent over twenty months.[49]

Perhaps the most emotive use of the Internet has been by Obama's successor in the White House, Donald Trump. Building on a following of millions built up during his days fronting the television show *The Apprentice*, he employed his chosen weapon, Twitter, to activate his base during the 2016 campaign and throughout his presidency, right up until January 2021, when his account was suspended for contravening Twitter guidelines. Successive tweets by the president sought not only to galvanise supporters but also to attack political rivals, declare policy victories and demonise immigrants, foreign competitors and many others. As Rob Farris and his colleagues reflected, Trump's tweets were then supported and amplified by 'pro-Trump media sources'.[50] The strategy worked. 'Trump's "infamous" tweets were being re-tweeted by a margin of nearly 3–1 over [Hillary] Clinton's tweets', according to Purdue University's Sorin Adam Matei,[51] who also concluded that pro-Trump Facebook activity at times achieved '400 or 500 per cent more interaction'. Some staff at Facebook were so concerned by this turbocharged, often highly questionable use of social media that they left the company to help Trump's political opponents.[52]

Such social media tactics have been widely criticised. The

problem, though, is that online platforms favour them. Negative messaging is perfect clickbait. It grabs attention, retains it and turns it into cash. According to the scholar Rebecca Lewis, 'YouTube monetises influence for everyone, regardless of how harmful their belief systems are. The platform, and its parent company, have allowed racist, misogynist and harassing content to remain online – and in many cases, to generate advertising revenue – as long as it does not explicitly include slurs.'[53] YouTube is, of course, a subsidiary of Google, which controls over 90 per cent of search traffic worldwide. The workings of search engine optimisation (SEO), now a multi-billion-dollar industry in itself, are often opaque. Experts agree that the algorithms employed take account of and prioritise well-known authoritative sources (such as CNN and the BBC). But expert comment still often struggles to achieve cut-through in a medium that so favours the emotional and the manipulative.

Today there is considerable pressure on Internet companies to address online bias, prejudice and false reporting. It's arguable, though, that the very financial basis on which most Internet companies operate makes this almost impossible. For all, attention is everything, because that's what attracts investment and stimulates growth. And since controversial, emotional content is what gets the most attention, that's what serves Internet companies best. Take Twitter, for example. Launched in 2006, with a name defined as 'a short burst of inconsequential information',[54] it went mainstream at the 2007 South by SouthWest conference, an annual gathering of tech entrepreneurs, enthusiasts and the music and film industries.[55] By 2008 27 million tweets were being sent per quarter.[56] Two years later the figure was 65 million tweets per day.[57] Whatever else Twitter was, it certainly wasn't proving inconsequential. By 2010 it had raised $200m as part of a Series F funding round.[58] Three years later, when the company, now with 232 million users, debuted on the New York Stock Exchange, it had achieved a market capitalisation of $31 billion (a 73 per cent rise on its debut).[59] When sums of this order are in play, it is scarcely surprising that decision-making has been primarily geared to what will provide the greatest return on investment. As one insider who has worked for Twitter, Facebook and Google at a senior level told us, 'I don't think it was malicious that they didn't consider the social consequences of their actions; they just didn't think about it and focused on growth.'[60] Twitter clearly recognised the power of narratives and advised clients to leverage it by making their content provocative and passionate. And that is exactly what many did, on Twitter and other platforms, for good – and ill.[61]

The technology of division?

In an era when, according to the UK regulator Ofcom in 2020, 18-24-year-olds spend on average over five hours online each day, many experts have become concerned about the psychological harm that can be done to a life lived too much in a virtual world. [62] *Psychology Today* reported that studies have revealed a link between internet addiction and a reduction in grey matter, adversely affecting the insula – the part of the brain which helps us develop feelings of empathy and compassion. Other studies suggest that excessive screen time can damage our ability to communicate offline. Smartphone addiction is known to correlate with depression.[63] And since depression can feed addiction, it's not hard to see how a vicious circle can be created here.[64]

There is less expert consensus on the extent to which the online world, with its often emotionally manipulative and hostile content and exchanges, exacerbates or merely reflects existing divisions within society. Those who believe the former marshal several arguments in support of their view. They point out, first of all, that it is easier today than it has ever been to share extreme views. It was the Internet, for example, that enabled the far-right anti-Muslim group

Britain First to get a purchase. It has also served the likes of the ultra-nationalist AfD (Alternative for Germany) party well. Experts point out, too, that once such extremist sites exist, they become echo chambers for true believers. A study of Facebook pages revealed AfD supporters, in contrast to those from more orthodox parties, would be far more likely to be exposed to content from sister organisations. In other words, a party whose co-founder, Alexander Gauland, has talked of an 'invasion of foreigners' and described the Nazi era as 'just a speck of bird's muck in more than 1,000 years of successful German history',[65] has members who draw certainly some of their information from sources that are well outside the mainstream.[66]

Strongly partisan groups tend to establish a particular dynamic online. The MIT fellow Kiran Garimella[67] found that their members are more connected to their community than is the case with less partisan groups, are engaged with more by other group members, and receive a higher than average number of retweets and 'favourites'. He also found that those who try to bridge divides by sharing more balanced content paid a price, becoming less central to their network, with the content they provide becoming less appreciated.[68] Group members are, as it were, locked in to their loyalty, and punished if they deviate from the party line. Before even seeing their content, researchers were able to identify partisans with around 80 per cent accuracy *because* of the way their content was liked, shared and favourited.

Exposure to content from the opposite end of the political spectrum doesn't help either. In fact, in can push people to take a more extreme position than the one they originally held. A study conducted in 2018 by a group of academics led by the Duke sociologist Christopher Bail[69] involved paying supporters of the Democratic and Republican parties in the US a small sum each to follow bots that retweeted messages put out by elected officials and opinion leaders with *opposing* political views. Over the course of a month, researchers found that the two groups became, respectively, more liberal and more conservative (the shift was particularly apparent among Republican supporters). What particularly concerned Bail was that as this occurred, moderates on the platform found themselves 40 per cent more likely to be attacked by partisan individuals and that their response was simply to mute themselves. In other words, not only were the poles becoming more clearly demarcated, but the bridges between them were weakening. Simultaneously, a spiral into 'false polarisation' was created whereby people gained distorted views of their opponents because they were hearing only the loudest voices.

Whether or not there's a direct link between extreme opinions expressed online and extreme actions taken in the real world has been much debated. After posts on Facebook were linked to the massacre of Rohingas in Myanmar, the social media company put out a statement saying that they weren't 'doing enough to help prevent our platform from being used to foment division and incite offline violence.'[70] On the other hand, it can be shown that extremists obtain their information from various sources, not just the Internet (Thomas Mair, the neo-Nazi who stabbed the British MP Jo Cox fifteen times and shot her three times, had bought various far-right publications over the years) and, indeed, that the extremist constituency is one whose numbers fluctuate according to events, not just the availability of information.

Eli Pariser[71] and Cass Sunstein[72] popularised the concepts of 'filter bubbles' and 'echo chambers' to describe the power exerted by algorithms in feeds and recommended content. Both argued, forcefully, that by targeting users with material related to what they have already looked at in order to drive advertising revenue, search engines, social media platforms and websites constantly risk both reinforcing particular world views and arguments, and failing to draw users' attention to alternative narratives. So not only are prejudices not challenged but they also receive constant confirmation.

But the 'filter bubble' notion hasn't gone unchallenged, and there are those who think that things are actually rather more complicated than that.[73] When considering groups such as QAnon, it's certainly tempting to assume that their extreme content feeds polarisation. However, it could also be the case that they don't so much draw in new converts as preach to the converted. Or, as Ben Page, chief executive of market research company Ipsos MORI, neatly put it, it wasn't so much a question of being pushed in a particular direction by an algorithm; rather 'maybe the problem was that we didn't have a broad enough group of friends.'[74] In other words, we view content created by 'people like us', and click on the links that will confirm what we already think. Those links may serve to bolster our views. They may possibly make them more extreme. But they don't neccesarily draw in new believers. It's worth bearing in mind that in Christopher Bail's study Democrats became more Democratic and Republicans more Republican. Democrats did not become Republican nor Republicans turn into Democrats.

The picture, then, is a complicated one. It's too simplistic simply to blame social media companies for polarisation, as convenient and tempting as that might be. And it also needs to be borne in mind that while many gather on Twitter or Facebook to talk about, say, sport or TV shows (#gameofthrones, for example),[75] rather fewer use those platforms as sources of information for important political topics. In any case, as pointed out earlier, people do not exist in an online void. They watch the news.[76] They read physical or online newspapers. They talk to friends and family. All information feeds opinion and divides it. Not all information comes from social media. That's not to say, though, that there isn't real cause for concern here. While studies of social media and its relationship with polarisation are still in their infancy, findings so far have been worrying and ominous.

Two other points need to be borne in mind. The first is that the numbers drawn into extremist websites are actually quite low. For all

the hype about QAnon, for example, only a fraction of the US population hold positive views about the movement (2 per cent according to
an NBC News poll).[77] The second point is that while the rise of social
media and the intensification of social and political polarisation in
many countries have coincided over recent years, that doesn't mean
the former has caused the latter. It's certainly true that in the US, for
example, there has been both a rapid expansion in online platforms
and increasing social and political polarisation.[78] But that pattern has
not been matched internationally. A cross-country study of nine
OECD countries by Matthew Gentzkow, Levi Boxell and Jesse Shapiro
confirmed the upward polarising trend in the US and in three other
countries – Canada, New Zealand and Switzerland – over the past
four decades, but showed a declining trend in the remaining five.[79]
And, as Gentzkow et al. have shown, even within the US things are not
as straightforward as they might seem. A study by the same authors
conducted in the aftermath of the 2016 US election revealed that
polarisation had increased most markedly among those people who
were least likely to use the Internet and social media.[80]

That doesn't mean, though, that there's nothing to be concerned
about when it comes to the power of online messages. Until further
research has been conducted, it would be dangerous to dismiss the
views of the likes of Chamath Palihapitiya, who led the team behind
Facebook's explosive growth between 2006 and 2011 and who said
bluntly several years later: 'The short-term, dopamine-driven feedback loops that we have created are destroying how society works. No
civil discourse, no co-operation, misinformation, mistruth.'[81] Nor
would it be right to ignore the suggestion by Sean Parker, Facebook's
founding president, that Facebook (to take just one platform)
'exploit[s] a vulnerability in human psychology'.[82] Social media companies themselves have become sufficiently concerned at the bad
press they have received and the threat of regulation that has come in
its wake to take steps to tackle the issue. Facebook, Twitter and Google

have all hired teams and provided grants to academics to assess whether or not social media in its current form drives polarisation and, if so, to what extent.[83] They have occasionally taken more practical steps, too – from fact-checking (Snapchat), or suspending political advertising (Twitter and finally Facebook), to deleting on a mass scale US accounts that questioned the integrity of the 2020 presidential election. Twitter also introduced a 'moments of reflection' function to encourage people to click through to a link before sharing a post to a story.

There's a further consideration to be taken into account. With the rise of online media there has been an accompanying relative decline in more neutral forms of information gathering and dissemination. Broadcast and print media face considerable competition, both in terms of the proliferation of TV channels that has taken place since the 1980s and the rise of alternative sources of information over the past twenty years or so. In the twelve years leading up to 2020, US newsrooms shed half their employees.[84] In Australia, 3,000 media jobs disappeared in the decade to 2020.[85] Between 2019 and summer 2020 alone, 157 Australian newsrooms closed for good.[86] Equally worrying is that, at a local news level, the void created by the virtual collapse of local newspapers is being filled by partisan outlets. During the 2020 US presidential election, it was discovered that Republican donors were creating local news sites in those regions where local newspapers had shut down, and that they were giving local stories a strongly party political spin.[87]

To make matters worse, those 'traditional' media companies still in existence are all too frequently resorting to playing social media at its own game, focusing on emotionally triggering content to get attention. And they're drawing on the same A/B and machine-learning methods to establish which stories to pitch, how to pitch them and what headlines to employ. They've also learned the social media lesson that negative stories elicit strong emotional responses.

Add that to the left- or right-leaning editorial stance to be found among many traditional media outlets, and the result is the very opposite of impartial. The tech giants are looking to monetise news, too. In 2018, the same year that the News Media Alliance estimated that Google was earning \$4.7 billion[88] from news content, Google announced the launch of the \$300 million Google News Initiative,[89] billed as a way to bring together its initiatives to work *with* the journalism industry, but equivalent to just over 6 per cent of the money it made from it. More channels, more emotionally charged content, fewer qualified staff and the death of local media all play a part in making it easier for partisan actors, domestic or foreign, to influence the information we see and believe.

In a perfect world, firms would gather and sell 'signals' of a true state of the world (in as much as it is possible to arrive at an understanding of that true state). In reality, as the NYU and Stanford economic professors Allcott and Gentzkow have shown,[90] the market for and demand for inaccurate and fake news arises in equilibrium. Inaccurate news is cheaper to provide. Thanks to motivated reasoning (see Chapter 1), consumers like to read content that confirms existing prejudices. There is therefore an incentive for producers of fake news to maximise the short-term profits from attracting clicks and re-shares from consumers, rather than seek a long-term reputation for quality. While some outlets, especially state providers, continue to be tightly regulated in this regard, many are not. It's an unhealthy mix.

And now there's a danger that political parties may want to get in on the act. It's something that has already happened in India, where Prime Minister Narendra Modi has launched an app (now with ratings from over 250,000 users on Apple[91] and in the top 2 per cent of apps worldwide)[92] that promises to offer a 'unique opportunity to receive messages and emails directly from Prime Minister Narendra Modi'. In reality, it acts as a news filter for partisan supporters (typical headline: 'As PM Modi enters 20th year of public life, have a look at his inspiring journey!'), and also makes donation requests ('Support those who put India First. Support BJP through Micro-Donations'). Donald Trump's 'official 2020 app' extended this principle still further, acting as a one-stop shop for Trump's events, and gamifying many features so that users could win points and rewards. Offering social proof to others of one's loyalty to the Trump cause, it also provided an extra dopamine hit. In an era when social media played a crucial role in mobilising demonstrators to storm the Capitol Building in Washington, its full divisive potential still remains to be exploited, just as its effects are still being assessed.

PART THREE

Bringing People Together

RESHAPING INSTITUTIONS

A warning from history

Yugoslavia had been a relative success story. Reformed in the aftermath of the First World War from the former Austro-Hungarian territories of Serbia, Slovenia, Macedonia (now North Macedonia), Montenegro, Kosovo,[1] Bosnia and Herzegovina, and Croatia, it weathered the Second World War and, under the leadership of Marshal Tito, experienced stable and consistent economic growth in the years thereafter. Between 1965 and 1973 its economy grew at 6.1 per cent a year, increasing to 6.4 per cent a year between 1973 and 1980.[2] The Yugoslav government also appeared to unify three otherwise very different cultural groups – the predominantly Catholic Slovenes and Croats, the mostly Eastern Orthodox Serbs, Montenegrins and Macedonians, and the majority Muslim Bosnians and Kosovans. When the country was invaded by the Axis powers in the Second World War, the slogan '*Bratstvo i jedinstvo*' (Brotherhood and unity) took root, evolving into Yugoslavia's guiding inter-ethnic principle. Although intermarriage rates between different ethnic groups stayed fairly static at around 12–13 per cent between 1962 and 1989,[3] the figure was viewed as an indicator that an interconnectedness had developed between different groups.[4] It was certainly higher than rates of intermarriage in America, where the overall inter-ethnic rate in 1994 was just 2.4 per cent, and black – white marriages lower still at just 0.5 per cent.[5]

But after Tito's death in 1980 things spiralled out of control. In April 1987, Slobodan Milošević, a trusted adviser of the then Serbian President Ivan Stambolić, was sent to deal with rising tensions in Kosovo between the minority Serbian nationals and the ruling Albanian Kosovans. When he arrived he proclaimed the party line that 'exclusive nationalism based on national hatreds can never be progressive.' Within four days he had changed his mind. Seeing an opportunity for a power grab, he opted to back the Serbs at a fiery meeting in which false accusations of rape, arson and grave desecration were levelled at the Albanian Kosovans. And he ignored the whispered protestation 'It's all lies' of the Albanian Kosovans' horrified leader, Azem Vllasi, who was sitting next to him. Protestors outside grabbed stones from lorries that had been placed there to provide support 'just in case', and attacked the protective police cordon. As violence and chaos escalated, Milošević left the building to reassure the nationalist protesters that they would not be beaten again.[6]

By 1989, he had displaced Stambolić as president of Serbia. By 1991, Yugoslavia had fractured. In the ethnic conflict that followed, tens of thousands of people perished and millions were displaced. Atrocities and acts of genocide pockmarked Yugoslavia's beautiful hills. It wasn't until 2000 that Milošević finally fell from power. Arrested the following year, he was put on trial at the Hague for war crimes, and died in his cell in 2006.

How did a country that had held together in one form or another for over seventy years polarise and fall apart so quickly? Part of the reason, at least, lies in what was clearly an earlier suppression of true feelings among the population at large – the 'preference falsification' we explored in Chapter 3. In other words, hostility did not come from out of nowhere in the 1980s. Rather, it had always been there, but had previously been concealed because of social pressures not to express it.[7] Under an oppressive regime, masking a private preference or view can be a matter of self-preservation. Even in more liberal societies, there can be a cost in social acceptance to holding views contrary to the norm. The benefit of publicly proclaiming an unfashionable or objectionable view can be close to zero if yours is just one small voice in a chorus of millions of people who appear to think otherwise. In any case, silence and/or conforming to the group norm is easier and less risky.

In Yugoslavia, the 'Brotherhood and unity' rhetoric meant that simmering animosity was repressed, not quelled. Religious and ethnic differences were not aired, even if they were quietly discussed around the dinner table. But once the lid was removed, and the cost of expressing such views fell, the situation rapidly deteriorated, stoked by the actions and words of figures such as President Slobodan Milošević. Once, it had been difficult to express dislike of other ethnic groups. Then it became easy. Then it became difficult not to voice division. The growing violence in turn created 'reputational cascades',[8] whereby people overstated their attachment to a particular identity or set of beliefs to maintain their status within a community whose world view had publicly changed.

A frightening aspect of this was how quickly it all happened. Milošević emerged as a political force in 1987. The descent into civil war began scarcely four years later. The speed of collapse into turmoil has been noted in other major social upheavals and revolutions.[9] As Duke University's political scientist Timur Kuran highlighted in his seminal paper on preference falsification, the French Revolution of 1789, the Russian Revolution of February 1917, and the Iranian Revolution of 1978-79 all escalated very rapidly, as did the Arab Spring in 2011.[10] So unexpectedly quickly did the Iranian Revolution take place, for example, that neither the US's CIA or the Soviet

Union's KGB saw it coming. In September 1977, sixteen months before the end of the monarchy, the CIA concluded that Iran was an island of stability in a sea of turbulence, and that Shah Mohammad Reza Pahlavi was eminently secure. Not even Ayatollah Ruhollah Khomeini, who masterminded the revolution from exile and who would take the metaphorical crown, predicted such a rapid collapse.[11]

Arguably, such processes happen even faster in today's ever-more-connected world. As Timur Kuran, revisiting an old Chinese saying, puts it, 'A single spark can start a prairie fire.' Much attention has been paid, for example, to the way in which social media spread and magnified the messages of opposition that constituted the Arab Spring. There's a danger of overstating the facts here: access to the Internet varied considerably from country to country. Nevertheless it is undoubtedly the case that the ability to rapidly disseminate ideas, news and videos online galvanised people and enabled them to organise swiftly. Academics from the University of Washington note that, in Tunisia's case, 'during the heady days of political change ... Tunisians grew more willing to note publicly that they were tweeting from inside Tunisia,'[12] as the perceived risk of doing so rapidly fell. Alongside social media, increased access to mobile communications, text and email also no doubt played a part in creating the connected-ness that accelerated protest and regime change, though their use and spread is harder to measure.

Given the deep underlying divisions in Yugoslavia, it's a moot point whether anything could have been done to stop the unravelling of the country, once the process was underway. But it is interesting to speculate whether – and to what extent – its institutions could have been future-proofed to help limit or even prevent such a disaster. The country, of course, presented a very particular set of challenges. It was an artificial creation that forced together disparate groups with a long history of conflict. That it lasted as long as it did after the Second World War was largely down to the fact that for nearly thirty years it was dominated by a dictator, Tito, who had the power to paper over the cracks. Arguably, its political system was hopelessly ill-equipped to cope with the complexities of the less authoritarian era that followed Tito's death. If anything, the division of Yugoslavia into Soviet-style republics exacerbated its ultimate fragmentation, since it amplified ethnic and religious divides. Some blame the constitution of 1974 for making matters worse, since it gave greater sovereign rights to the republics (it was also one of the world's longest constitutions). As it was being drawn up, the then professor of the Belgrade Law School Mihailo Đurić argued that although it claimed to be ensuring equality between the republics it was actually creating several conflicting nation states.[13] He was sentenced to nine months in prison for his criticism. Raif Dizdarević, one of the rotating presidents after Tito's death, has similarly reflected that the new constitution focused too heavily on the republics while simultaneously failing to ensure economic reform.[14] The phrase used after Tito's death – 'After Tito, Tito' – shows how little those who came next understood what splintering forces were being unleashed.

The mechanics of political stability

But then it's questionable whether any legislative arrangement – including those to be found in democracies – is foolproof against polarisation. The ideal, of course, is a system that can foster debate, constructively manage difference and effectively scrutinise its leaders', but which structure can guarantee such an outcome in perpetuity is far from clear. On the surface, it might seem, for example, that the most robust political systems involve a plurality of parties, since such a set-up ensures both that many voices are heard and that groups will need to compromise with one another in order to form governments or to get policies through. The evidence, however, doesn't support that simple solution. The adversarial set-up invented and typified by the British House of Commons may seem precisely that (after all, the green front benches where the Government and Opposition face each other are set up to be slightly more than two swords' length apart), but thus far it has proved effective against terminal polarisation. Indeed, those who defend the first-past-the-post (FPTP) electoral system that underpins the British system and has traditionally favoured a two-party set-up, would argue that it ensures precisely the sort of strong government that can operate without the pressures of narrow sectarian interest groups. The question is whether it can continue that tradition in the face of increased polarisation.

Even the oppositional nature of the physical layout of the chamber of the House of Commons is arguably less problematic than it may seem. Both the European Parliament and US Senate, for example, may have opted for more integrated, semi-circular seating, but research has shown that when delegates from opposing groups are seated next to each other, they are actually more likely to vote with their own party.[15] It's also perhaps worth noting that the semi-circular floor of the US Congress witnessed 70 violent incidents between 1830 and 1860 alone, including stabbings, canings and the pulling of pistols.[16] Placing groups in such a setting and in direct contact with each other does not necessarily reduce the tendency to polarise. In fact, it can make things worse.

When it comes to multi-party systems the political science professors Jennifer McCoy and Murat Somer's recent study of eleven countries, from Bangladesh to Hungary to the United States, suggests that while those that have adopted proportional representation (PR) tend to be less polarised than others, this doesn't hold in all cases. Admittedly, it's difficult to make hard and fast rules here because there is no universal system of PR. Some countries have relatively simple PR arrangements. Turkey and Greece, by contrast, have what are known as majoritarian enhancing mechanisms in place, whereby there are high thresholds for winning seats or a bonus allocation of seats to the party with the most support.[17] In other words, small parties are at a disadvantage, large parties at an advantage. But whatever the precise nature of PR in any given country, what emerges clearly from a comparison of the experience of different nations is that PR in itself cannot fully mitigate against or prevent polarisation. Each country's electoral system is intertwined with that country's specific culture and history. There is no one-size-fits-all solution.

The experiences of Belgium and Israel clearly demonstrate that systems that encourage coalitions are not automatically free from polarising tendencies. In 2010, Belgium's PR system delivered an inconclusive election result, which should have triggered the immediate formation of a coalition government. In fact, Flanders supported a Flemish independence movement, while Brussels and Wallonia supported the French Socialist Party, with it taking over a year to break the political logjam.[18] In Israel, where a pure PR system is in place that treats the whole country as a single electoral district, society is divided and unstable coalitions are a constant feature. In theory, that might suggest a political landscape in which horse-trading between different parties leads to governments of national unity. In fact, the opposite can be true, as the largest party looks to more extreme fringe groups to create a workable government. By March 2021 the country had held four elections in two years in an attempt to secure a coalition that could command a governing majority and pass a budget.[19]

That said, certain constitutional fail-safes do seem to help countries resist pernicious polarisation. Notable among these are the ones that directly encourage co-operation and bring dissenting voices together to make progress on something specific. In the UK, select committees tasked with scrutinising particular policy areas tend to be more collegiate than the political parties from which the committee personnel come. They align behind the issues that

167

bring them together, such as reform of personal finance or the future of the justice system, and build stronger bilateral relationships as a result. So strong can that collegiate atmosphere be, it can even cause MPs normally loyal to their party to take a contrary stance. In the early 2010s party whips who had traditionally controlled membership of select committees (by steering votes towards a particular nominated candidate) started to take more of a back seat, leaving choice of committee chairs to the party's MPs. Gradually government-supported candidates began losing out to respected elder statesmen and women who commanded the respect of their peers. It was a development that received national attention when the preferred government candidate for chair of the influential Intelligence and Security Committee, Chris Grayling, lost out to a Conservative colleague of two decades' standing, Julian Lewis MP, who teamed up with the Opposition to secure victory.[20] Lewis paid the price in that he then lost the party whip – a warning to others of what might happen to them if they ever chose to follow in his footsteps.

That doesn't mean that all scrutiny committees are less partisan than the political parties from which its members come. Senate and congressional committees in the US, for example, tend to divide along party lines, complete with constant political point-scoring. That the chair of such committees tends to go to the most senior member of the majority party may have something to do with this. But in other countries these systems have proved effective in fostering constructive debate and building consensus. In New Zealand, scrutiny committees have a public consultation mechanism. In Australia, the Covid-19 committee, chaired by the Opposition, received '463 written submissions, held 35 virtual public hearings, and handled hundreds of questions . . . [it] has already influenced the shape of key legislation . . . and played a central role in the public debate on the efficacy of key government responses to the pandemic.'[21] When there is a bipartisan approach baked into the scrutiny committees' structure, they act as an important check and balance on partisan power and polarisation.

Parliamentary committees are not, of course, the only place where trusted senior figures can join forces to create an agenda that transcends party or partisan divides. The Elders – a group founded by Nelson Mandela and populated by global ex-presidents, former UN secretary-generals, and other world leaders – was set up in 2007 and holds at its core a message of co-operation and conflict resolution. It promises to use its convening power to bring groups together and secure change. It is one of a number of international groups that seeks to call out isolationist and nationalist responses to global challenges.[22] In his book *The Ex-Men*, Giles Edwards talks about the role of the Elders in putting overlooked issues on the international agenda, such as child marriage, and driving them rapidly up the global priority list.[23] As well as using their power to raise the profile of a problem, they also use it to look at issues from another perspective. For example, a group of former Latin American presidents, led by the former Brazilian president Fernando Henrique Cardoso (described as a 'boat-righting, rather than a boat-rocking, kind of guy'),[24] worked effectively together to create a new strategy in the region's war on drugs. Their report, published in 2009, concluded it was time for a new paradigm: 'Treating drug users as a matter of public health; reducing drug consumption through information, education and prevention; and focusing repression on organised crime.' It was an explosive notion at that time, but it helped shift the debate away from an assumption that criminalising drug users was the only possible policy, and start a new conversation about what might actually work.[25] Outside the immediacy of the election cycle, these former leaders can take a stance that might have been too politically costly for them previously; by building consensus and working together across the political spectrum, they are listened to by those who might not respond to them individually. The danger of overestimating the importance of leaders has already been pointed out, but there are clearly times when their status and networks can make a difference – as they have, for example, in Northern Ireland.

A different approach to consensus building occurs in the Netherlands, where a tradition known as the polder model has grown up (the word is derived from the Dutch term for the reclamation from the sea of low-lying land), and been supported by the country's institutions and regulations.[26] The tradition was revived during the economic crisis of the early 1980s to bring together core groups (unions, business leaders, politicians) to bridge divides, build co-operation and forge policy. The recovery plan of the 1980s was possible because the unions agreed to lower wage demands, business leaders capped executive pay and, in addition to committing to maintaining the social safety net, the government introduced tough austerity measures. Recovery was fast, despite the challenging economic conditions (which, as Chapter 4 showed, so easily triggers polarisation). Fast-forward almost forty years, and the Netherlands had the lowest polarisation scores in Gidron's twenty-country comparison. That doesn't mean, of course, that the country has never experienced extreme political forces and polarisation. It has suffered division in the past and again more recently, for example, after the assassination of Pim Fortuyn, the leader of the right-wing populist LPF party, in 2002. Fortuyn had, according to the Dutch and German academics Jasper Muis and Ruud Koopmans, 'succeeded in attracting by far the most media attention of all politicians, and out of the blue the LPF won 17 per cent of the votes'[27] following his assassination a week before polling day. Several Dutch parties went on to adopt variants of his overtly anti-immigrant policies. Even so, widespread polarisation did not take hold and the situation calmed. The Dutch practice of going round the room to ensure that all are heard before a consensus view is reached meant that anti-immigrant voices were heard but did not dominate and that while immigration policy evolved it did not become extreme. The country's strong co-operative tradition held.

Arguably, though, the most successful mechanisms for resisting political polarisation are, paradoxically, the ones that actually include by design a degree of tension or conflict. As the Yugoslavian example shows, when states fall apart, they can do so at speed. Polarisation becomes hard to contain. No system has been designed that can successfully hold it back every time. But those that embody a degree of friction – that slow processes down that might otherwise run out of control, that build in scrutiny, or that seek to enforce previous norms – can prove valuable safeguards. It seems to be the case, for example, that those national governments that have bicameral parliaments, in which one chamber (sometimes referred to as a 'veto player') scrutinises the activities of the other (the Senate and Congress in the US; the House of Lords and the House of Commons in the UK; the Bundesrat and Nationalrat in Austria), can offer a necessary degree of 'drag' that can mitigate against polarisation rapidly taking hold within the system. Given that only a few countries have swapped from having two chambers to just one (and those that have, like Denmark and New Zealand, are small countries that score low for polarisation), empirical proof is hard to come by. But there are certainly case histories that provide food for thought. It's arguable, for example, that the single parliamentary chamber set-up in Hungary meant limited scrutiny, a lack of 'veto players' and access to a supermajority, for the populist leader Viktor Orbán. He was therefore free to impose his own vision of a future Hungary relatively easily. Similar scenarios, with one party winning a supermajority in a unicameral system, have also played out in Turkey and Bangladesh, enabling subsequent unobstructed reform of the constitution.[28]

The other key countervailing force is the judiciary. In their best-selling book *How Democracies Die*, Steven Levitsky and Daniel Ziblatt convincingly lay out the ways in which strong, independent judicial systems can be effective bulwarks against destructive or polarising forces. They allow judges to be the final arbiters on the conduct of elections. Were they legal and fair? They scrutinise legislation. Are the policies the government is seeking to introduce actually legal? They reduce abuse of power and process. Is a particular business or sector seeking to establish too great an influence in political circles? Are contracts being fairly awarded?[29] Conversely, as the University of California's Professor of Law and Political Science Richard Hasen[30] has pointed out, once judiciaries lose their independence and no longer hold governments to account, more extreme stances are not only taken but also prevail. As Levitsky and Ziblatt highlight, once that starts to happen, and authoritarian leaders increasingly appoint their own partisans to oversee legal processes, a point of no return can rapidly be reached. Significantly, one of the first things that the Hungarian premier Orbán did as he sought to reshape his country was to capture the judicial appointments process. Significantly, too, it was ultimately the US judiciary that ruled on the legality of the 2020 presidential election and determined that the result called by all major media outlets on 7 November should stand.[31]

The record of other countervailing forces has tended to be patchier. Regulators, for example, who 'police' various sectors of the economy and civil activity, have a mixed record when it comes to resisting political pressure. Regulatory bodies can be 'affiliated' to a government department and may be required to take some form of political steer, so the degree of independence – politically and financially – varies. There have been many instances when a regulator has been forced to give in to political forces. In the UK in 2015 for example, the then head of the Financial Conduct Authority, Martin Wheatley, was pressured to resign by Chancellor George Osborne after he levied record-breaking fines against banks for breaking the rules. Then-Treasury select committee member John Mann MP, who went on to become chair, called this out as playing politics, 'wrong' and 'undermining the independence of the regulator'.[32] In Hungary, Viktor Orbán has been overt in ensuring that people he approves of are appointed to regulatory bodies. The British record might be better, but it doesn't pay to take regulatory independence for granted. Even when a non-partisan regulator is appointed, challenges remain. Because it can take them time to get a grip on their brief and so fully understand the pressures and trends in play and thus the reforms required, they can prove disappointingly ineffectual at holding those they regulate to account. Many organisations that come within a regulatory remit – particularly those in fast-moving sectors such as social media – have become wiser to this and, as Chapter 6 explained, have now started to take proactive steps to get ahead of increased regulation.

The power of diversity

This need for some sort of 'grit in the oyster' is apparent in all organisations, not simply political, legal or regulatory ones. Because our ingroup tendencies are so strong, we tend to surround ourselves with those who are similar to us and agree with us, and by the same token push away countervailing views and perspectives. Although we reap immediate benefits (including a heightened sense of self-esteem), we fail to appreciate that not only is the ingroup/outgroup dynamic unhealthy for the ongoing robustness of our societal systems, but it is also counterproductive. The fact is that better decisions get made when a range of different perspectives are heard. More mistakes are avoided. New furrows are ploughed.

Evidence from the business sector demonstrates this powerfully. It's certainly true that clarity of vision can be critical in driving business success – as the Nike founder Phil Knight writes in *Shoe Dog*, the power of 'belief is irresistible'.[33] But research has repeatedly shown that alternative viewpoints, ideas, and challenges to the status quo – in other words, the creation of more diverse teams – can boost problem-solving, reduce errors and increase innovation.[34] In 2013, the Australian airline Qantas posted a record loss running into the billions. In 2017, it delivered a record profit. Speaking to a meeting of Deloitte partners later that year, the Qantas CEO Alan Joyce laid this success at the door of diversity, telling those in the room, 'We have a very diverse environment and a very inclusive culture . . . [which] got us through the tough times . . . diversity generated better strategy, better risk management, better debates, [and] better outcomes.'[35] Apple sings a similar tune, arguing that new ideas come from diverse ways of seeing things. We explored some of the reasons for this in Chapter 3. As the Columbia Business School professor Katherine Phillips says, 'When disagreement comes from a socially different person, we are prompted to work harder. Diversity jolts us into cognitive action in ways that homogeneity simply does not.'[36] Boston Consulting Group has tested the benefits, finding that companies with greater diversity in their workforce achieved a 19 per cent innovation-related advantage – that is, they achieved a larger proportion of revenue from innovative products and services (those brought to market in the last three years) than companies with below-average diversity. Different perspectives enhance the likelihood of spotting new market opportunities and currently unmet needs, with a direct impact on the bottom line.[37]

Maggie Neale, Professor Emerita of Management at Stanford, points out the vital importance of what might be termed constructive conflict within an organisation if it is to be truly innovative and creative.[38] Where the space to debate and innovate does not exist, stagnation is a very real risk. Internal groupishness can also lead to internal rivalry, as other teams within the organisation become a focus for competition. Ingroup/outgroup demonisation is all too often the consequence.[39] The culture can be so powerful that those who disagree find themselves less heard or unable to speak freely.

This isn't just true within teams whose specific goal is to come up with new ideas and concepts. There is a growing body of research that suggests partisan diversity at board level can be more product-ive, too. Kwang Lee, Jongsub Lee and Nandu Nagarajan, who studied 2,695 corporates between 1996 and 2009, concluded that alignment in political orientation between the CEO and the independent direc-tors led to 'lower firm valuations, lower operating profitability, and increased internal agency conflicts such as a reduced likelihood of dismissing poorly-performing CEOs, a lower CEO pay–performance sensitivity, and a greater likelihood of accounting fraud'.[40] This was particularly so, they found, among smaller boards where the interaction between the CEO and independent directors was more frequent. It would seem to confirm the truth of the general observa-tion that has been made about like-minded groups: that the psychological cost of disagreement within the team is significant enough to stifle honest debate.

Partisan prejudice can also lead to questionable investment deci-sions. Investors assume that their thinking is entirely rational and based on key economic and financial indicators, but they are as prone to biased thinking as anyone else. Alok Kumar, finance professor at Miami University, and his colleagues have shown that 'investors become more optimistic and perceive the markets to be less risky and more undervalued when their own party is in power.'[41] Bankers overseeing syndicated loans are no different.[42] Even though their spe-cialism demands that they assess risk objectively, US bankers have been shown to change the cost of credit according to whether or not the person they support for the US presidency is elected. According to a study of nearly 3,000[43] syndicated loan transactions in the US, 'misaligned' bankers (that is, ones who did not vote for the winning candidate)[44] charge up to 7 per cent more to lend money than aligned bankers (after the 2016 US election that figure rose to 13 per cent). The researchers conjectured misaligned bankers have different beliefs about the economy and borrowers' credit quality, and are more pes-simistic about future conditions than aligned bankers. It could be proposed that the banker who charges more is acting logically because he or she believes the winning candidate to be bad for the economy. However, the research shows that they are heavily influenced by personal feelings of political optimism or pessimism; indeed, the effect is stronger when partisan disagreement about the state of the economy is heightened. Interestingly, 'non-aligned' bankers in the study performed no better than their 'aligned' colleagues even though they charged higher interest rates. In other studies it has been demonstrated that fund managers are more likely to invest in firms led by co-partisans,[45] regardless of the objective merits of the decisions they are making.

Mission-led start-ups are renowned for their single-mindedness and tendency to reflect the values of the financial elites who invest in them. While on one level this is to be expected, it does raise questions about the impact on polarisation of organisations moulded in the image of one particular group's outlook and beliefs. In such set-ups, the risk is that not only is there a very strong sense of 'us', but also a corresponding 'them' who would never be employed. This has its own implications for cognitive diversity, creativity and innovation.

This insight is borne out by a 2015 experiment designed by the husband-and-wife team Thomas and Karen Gift. The Gifts sent out 1,200 CVs, some indicating support for the Republican Party, some showing support for the Democrats, to employers in areas of the United States known to be either strongly Republican or staunchly Democrat. What they found was that the chances of being called for an interview depended, in part, on political affiliation. The candidate who, for example, stated that they had worked for Barack Obama was less likely to get a call if they applied to a firm in a Republican area.[46]

In recent times, organisational diversity has tended to focus on the crucial issues of race and gender. But there's a case to be made for ensuring a plurality of political views too, not least as, at a fundamental level, these encompass how we share resources across different groups (see Chapter 1). Salesforce CEO Marc Benioff, a Democrat who supported Hillary Clinton's run for the White House, argues that having the former Republican Secretary of State Colin Powell as a mentor and ultimately on the Salesforce board has been hugely beneficial (not that Powell's views as a soft Republican are necessarily that far from Benioff's own).[47] Certainly, the converse – political groupthink – can make companies less alive to the communities they seek to reach and less responsive to changes in society.

Harnessing difference – enabling debate and division that boosts rather than undermines innovation, creativity and productivity – is critical, but so too is emphasising what holds us together. It was this approach that helped frame the reforms of Cleisthenes in Ancient Athens. The city state had been riven by division and famine, but Cleisthenes was able to achieve a degree of cohesion by bringing together groups of free men from the coast, mountains and cities into new units where they could form collective identities to contribute to the larger whole. Cleisthenes may not have had access to the randomised controlled trials of modern-day testing, but his insight still holds: finding areas of common ground in one part of life makes it easier to reach resolution in another. In Cleisthenes' case, the reforms he enacted lasted relatively untouched for hundreds of years.

Contemporary research indicates that group stereotyping and prejudice are more likely when our social identities are uppermost, and that they inevitably reduce when we downplay differences between us. For example, if children from different class, race or gender groups are asked to work co-operatively on a task, their focus will shift from what differentiates them to the goal all are striving for.[48] For Jonathan Haidt, this insight is key. His view is that while increased diversity brings great benefits, it has tended to be handled in a way that reduces, rather than creates, greater trust, because the focus has been on what makes people different, rather than what they have in common.[49] To that extent, he argues, it is better to focus less on what separates people and more on superordinate goals – those shared aspirations that bring us together, rather than apart; goals that supersede an individual group and can only be achieved by working together.

In his work with Karen Stenner,[50] Haidt has taken his view one step further. Stenner and Haidt argue that we should design the world according to how we are, not how we want to be, and that we can do this by building rituals, institutions and processes that focus on what we have in common. This in turn involves understanding some people's need for oneness and sameness; for identity, cohesion and belonging; for pride and honour; and for institutions and leaders they can respect. Clearly, this is not intended to be a get-out-of-jail-free card for people who do not want to see greater diversity in the workplace, in public life or in the media. But it is a reminder that if we do not acknowledge those responses to threat that we explored earlier, we risk resistance and backlash. Haidt is not alone in seeking a way forward here. Many of the twentieth century's heavyweights in liberal political thought have struggled with the problem. How, given potentially irreconcilable differences, can we make peaceful political decisions? The conclusion of the American political philosopher John Rawls was that we need clearly defined ways to debate with one another, while protecting our political institutions, if we are each to remain free. We must find a way to disagree that does not ultimately undermine us all.

RESHAPING GROUPS

The challenges of intergroup contact

In 2015 Jordan Blashek, a former marine and staunch Republican, and Chris Haugh, a former speechwriter in Obama's White House and Blashek's political polar opposite, struck up a friendship that led to a series of road trips across the USA. It wasn't always easy. 'There's something about politics that has its way of creating divides among even people who shared these deep bonds of friendship or family,' Blashek recalls.

> Chris and I found ourselves stumbling into that over and over again. And I remember one fight in particular around undocumented immigration. We were driving through the middle of nowhere in Nevada and somehow stumbled into this conversation about the President's rhetoric and the issue of the border wall and undocumented immigration that just spiralled out of control. And we started levelling these very intense accusations at one another. And it led to this question in both our minds of 'Why are we doing this? Why would I engage with this person?'

Chris and Jordan remained friends, but similar disagreements sparked by their different world views peppered their journeys together and often became intensely personal. Abraham Lincoln is supposed to have said, 'I don't like that man. I must get to know him better.' Chris and Jordan's experience suggests that this alone isn't enough. If friends can polarise so easily over their different world views, what chance is there of ever reconciling antagonistic groups, or at least of making them less hostile to one another?

It's something that the American psychologist Gordon Allport famously explored in his landmark book *The Nature of Prejudice* (1954). In his exposition of what he labelled the intergroup contact hypothesis, he argued that the mere act of physically bringing people together can help promote tolerance and acceptance. He had observed this phenomenon among refugees during the Second World War. And he hypothesised that it might work even in a post-war America riven by racial tensions and enforced segregation. He noted, in support of his idea, that earlier studies had suggested that housing and workplace desegregation[1] reduced prejudice towards black people. To achieve this, various conditions needed to be met. There needed to be equal status (those involved should not be in a hierarchical relationship). There needed to be an uncompetitive environment in which people were invited to work together. There should be a common, desired goal requiring members to work together. And there should be support on offer from social and institutional authorities (so, for example, no official laws enforcing segregation). Some subsequent studies exploring contact theory have suggested that this framework is too elaborate, and that not all these conditions are essential. Basic contact, some argue, is sufficient and is a clearly demonstrated method for reducing hostility between ingroups and outgroups.[2]

There is some evidence to support this optimistic view. A study[3] from 2016, involving ten-minute conversations with voters in southern Florida,[4] found that carefully scripted discussions, known as 'deep-canvassing', led by both transgender and non-transgender canvassers, reduced prejudice against transgender people and increased support for transgender rights, even when the study participants were shown political attack ads. What's more, the effects of these discussions were still apparent three months later. In the course of the discussions an approach known as analogic perspective-taking was employed: voters were asked to recall a time when they themselves had been judged negatively, so prompting them to try to understand how it felt for a transgender person to be viewed in a hostile way. Interestingly, transgender and non-transgender canvassers were equally successful in reducing prejudice (one of contact hypothesis's predictions is that contact with stigmatised groups will be more effective than conversations with their champions). Whether or not it was the analogic perspective-taking that moved the dial cannot be proved absolutely. A second study that focused on abortion did not yield the same results, though the study's authors thought that this might have been because the canvassers in the first study were more skilled at getting respondents to share the perspective of a transgender person than those who canvassed on abortion.[5]

A not dissimilar approach was developed by Dr Elliot Aronson, head of the social psychology department at the University of Texas, in the 1970s. A former student of his had become an assistant superintendent for schools in Austin, and had immediately come face to face with the education crisis that followed desegregation. Riots had broken out among black, Hispanic and white pupils. The student asked Dr Aronson for his help.[6]

The answer that Aronson, in collaboration with his graduate students, came up with was to establish a new teaching method in Austin schools – one that focused on getting children to learn from each other, so that their peers' successes became integrated with their own. Each task they undertook was interdependent (hence the moniker 'jigsaw method' used to describe this approach), and assessments were based on the performance of groups as a whole. For example, if students were studying the Second World War, one group might look at Hitler's rise to power, another the wartime Eastern Front, a third the war in the Pacific, before sharing their knowledge with each other.[7] The idea was to reduce individual competitiveness and emphasise the effectiveness of co-operative behaviour.[8] At first, the children resisted this innovation. Eventually they embraced it. Aronson's view was that such an upfront method of teaching, which grasped the central problem of tension between groups, encouraged listening, engagement and empathy. A subsequent study in two schools in Australia designed to test Aronson's theory found his approach reduced racial prejudice, as well as improved inter-personal relationships and academic performance among the students.[9]

If this suggests that all that is required to move the dial is interaction between hostile groups, the reality is, sadly, not that simple. First, as the south Florida case studies show, these are tricky conversations that require skill and adroitness. What may work in one arena may not be easily replicable in another. Secondly, many of the studies carried out in this field (the majority, in fact) have been conducted essentially in lab conditions: they don't necessarily reflect what might or will happen in the real world because they can't replicate its many complexities. Thirdly, and most crucially, there is evidence to suggest that increased exposure to another group can, in some instances, actually lead to greater, not less, hostility.

The findings of a couple of studies conducted by the Princeton social psychology professor Elizabeth Levy Paluck offer worrying evidence of this.[10] The first, conducted in Rwanda[11] in 2004–5, just a decade after the horrific genocide that took place there, exposed one group to a reconciliation-themed radio soap opera, and the control group to a soap opera about health. Paluck found that those who listened to the reconciliation-themed soap were willing to examine their perceptions of the themes it explored (for example, on inter-marriage, open dissent, trust, empathy, co-operation and the healing of trauma) but did not change their personal beliefs about them.

A second study in the eastern Democratic Republic of Congo (DRC), which has suffered multiple conflicts, took things a step further, in that participants not only listened to a soap opera that focused on community cohesion but then also heard a follow-up talk show discussion of the themes raised. In order to be able to make calibrated comparisons, Paluck used six non-overlapping broadcast regions spread across the north and south provinces of eastern DRC, pairing those that were most similar to one another in terms of urban and rural mix, road accessibility and historical and current levels of violence. She then randomly chose one broadcast region in each pair to air the soap opera on its own, and the other to feature both the soap opera and the fifteen-minute talk show that followed. When she went back a year later to test attitudes among a random sample of 842 people exposed to one or other of the broadcast packages, she found that those who had heard both the soap opera and the talk show were actually *more* likely to say they would not want members of the group they disliked to join their community (49 per cent talk show and 37 per cent baseline listeners). Respondents were also *more* likely to claim that peace would not come to DRC if the people they regarded as an outgroup continued to live there (71 per cent talk show compared to 62 per cent baseline).[12] In addition, Paluck found that the talk show audience might have been more likely to discuss the issues raised with others, but that those discussions were also more likely to be contentious.

Even in those countries and instances where rival factions have been brought together, success has been qualified. A study in post-conflict Iraq by the political scientist Salma Mousa,[13] for example, showed that when both Christian and Muslim footballers were brought together in a single team, interfaith relations among them improved. But even when they'd been training and playing for months, they were unlikely to mix socially or attend events that had a mixture of Christians and Muslims in attendance. Intergroup hostility on the pitch certainly declined. Off the pitch the results were, at best, patchy. The experience of the classical pianist and conductor Daniel Barenboim with his West-Eastern Divan Orchestra has been not dissimilar. Those Israeli and Palestinian musicians who have performed with the orchestra have reflected on the life-changing impact of viewing others as musicians first, not members of rival communities. One reflected that 'the orchestra is a human laboratory that can express to the whole world how to cope with the other.'[14] But the orchestra's inspiring example has had a limited wider impact. As Barenboim himself said, 'People have often described it as an orchestra for peace, which of course it cannot be.'[15] In a twentieth-anniversary interview with the German press agency he reflected that 'Today we cannot play in most Arab countries or in Israel . . .'[16]

Some are more optimistic about this 'shared activity' approach to reducing intergroup tensions. Promising research suggests that by immersing people in stories through live theatre, empathy can be created and attitudes changed.[17] It's also been suggested that community enterprises such as local newspapers and pubs can create venues for shared stories that can help prevent polarisation.[18] For her part, Sarah Corbett, a lifelong campaigner for social justice who in 2009 founded the Craftivist Collective, argues that 'gentle craftivism can help create a safe space for deeper engagement with social change: to reflect on the causes and complexities, what we can do to be part of the solution not the problem and help us channel our anger, sadness or despair into strategic, kind and effective activism.'[19] Her approach involves using the slow nature of craft to encourage reflection, to bring people together to create something and so to reduce tension and confrontation; and she has now shared her technique with 12,000 people worldwide via talks, events, and workshops. Her commitment and achievements are impressive, but even so, it does generally seem to be the case that contact-based approaches can only have a limited effect when it comes to reducing polarisation, not least because the people who become involved are not drawn from society as a whole but from those who chose to 'opt in'.

It's interesting in this context to consider the mixed fortunes of what is known as deliberative democracy, whereby representative groups (typically comprising twelve to twenty-four people) are brought together to discuss a complex social issue. Participants are given time and information to encourage them to generate *explanations* – rather than justifications based on values, hearsay, or feelings – for their positions. The approach has certainly been shown to have a similar benefit to contact theory in that, by bringing people together in the context of a shared goal (in this case resolving an issue), it can lessen hostility. But its record is patchier when it comes to the group practically resolving the issue at hand.

Deliberative democracy is designed to create a different space for debate and to bring the decisions we face in society closer to the voting public. It removes both the over-simplification of policy information that people usually receive (for example, from the media) and some of the biases of presentation and processing of that information (for example, via social media or a particular spokesperson). The challenge, though, is how to move from well-meaning discussion, which may indeed lead to consensus or at least a lessening of tension, to genuine change on a major, divisive issue.

Quintin Oliver, a conflict resolution specialist and the man behind the successful referendum for a 'Yes' vote on the Good Friday Agreement in Northern Ireland, told us that for deliberative democracy to work, three essential ingredients first have to be in place: a purpose; a promise; and a deadline. All three were reflected in the deliberative assembly that considered the legalisation of same-sex marriage in the Republic of Ireland, and the subsequent vote. The assembly, which comprised sixty-six citizens broadly representative of the public, thirty-three political representatives and an independent chair,[20] had a clear purpose: to consider arguments and evidence to make recommendations. It secured a promise: for the government to hold a referendum on the issue. And it gained a deadline: the vote in 2015. Had any of those elements been lacking, it could have been largely ineffectual. Without a clearly defined purpose it might have disintegrated into fruitless polarised debate and the deliberately soft-toned Yes campaign might have been very different in nature. Without securing a promise to take the issues to a public vote, any recommendations it made could have been accused of being unrepresentative of the population. It's worth noting that Ireland's record with citizen assemblies has been mixed. Two had a concrete outcome. A further seven, however, led nowhere, though their adherents might claim that they helped lessen tensions nonetheless.

The deliberative process put in place by (the then) Omagh District Council in Northern Ireland on the future of local schools in January 2007 exhibits both the positives and the negatives of such endeavours. In August 1998 an IRA splinter group, the Real IRA (which opposed the peace process), had detonated a bomb in Omagh that killed twenty-nine people and injured another 220. The exercise in 2007, the first deliberative polling done in such a divided community, was designed to change Catholics' and Protestants' perceptions of one another and to create an Omagh less divided along sectarian lines. At the outset, most of those surveyed appeared to hold reasonably positive views of the others. At the midpoint of the process, the team running it started to fear that the responses it was reviewing suggested that beneath this ran a veiled hostility. At the end it did seem that the polls were more positive than they had been at the beginning.[21] However, whether or not greater goodwill was established, it had little if no practical effect beyond the increased positive feelings between those involved. Schools remained segregated along religious lines, as did leisure facilities. Any changes in perception or increases in goodwill were, by the limited nature of the process, insufficient to outweigh the lack of a concrete mechanism for change.

Deliberative processes also tend to come unstuck if they run up against partisanship in the political assemblies that ultimately make the decisions. Part of the reason why the same-sex referendum vote in Ireland took place and was successful was because there were already overwhelming majorities for marriage equality before the referendum campaign started.[22] It also helped that it was tied to a concrete process of updating the Irish constitution. By contrast, Dr Lucy Parry's work on deliberative democracy and foxhunting in the UK shows that the political divide on the issue was too strong for a deliberative process to make headway. She argues that

a more deliberative approach may help animal advocates to be taken more seriously and have their voices heard by those in power. However, any debate that divides along party lines will struggle to forge a constructive deliberative path in Parliament. So divisive is the outcome of this issue that any new process introduced will be vulnerable to attack from both pro- and anti-hunting advocates.[23]

Emphasising similarity

But if the road to mutual group understanding is riddled with potholes, there is one general approach that seems to work in many different contexts: emphasising similarity. It's something *Die Zeit* experienced when it set up its 'Germany talks' project with its online readers in 2017.[24] It posed the question: Would people of different political persuasions like to be linked up with one another to have facilitated discussions? The answer was yes, with 1,200 meeting for face-to-face discussions. The result was enduring bonds, reflective discussion and no reported 'incidents'. The project grew into 'Europe Talks', expanding to over 16,000 people. On the surface, this would appear to show that reasonable people who disagree with one another can be brought together. In fact, of course, all these people already had something in common: they were readers of *Die Zeit* or one of its partner outlets, and again they actively chose to be involved.

The power of emphasising similarity was also experienced in 2016 by Canon Linda Taylor, then serving at an Episcopal church in Saratoga, California. The Sunday after a mass shooting in Orlando the church's prayers called for an 'end to gun violence'. Many in her congregation were unhappy, arguing politics has no place in church. Several weeks before, Canon Taylor had learned about Living Room Conversations, an organisation that facilitates discussion between people with different viewpoints. A key aspect of their work is to provide a framework for sharing experiences rather than opinions on an issue, thereby helping to identify common ground in spite of disagreement. When participants in Saratoga tried this approach, they found it valuable in understanding each other's positions – including on the role of politics in church. Canon Taylor has gone on to introduce the conversations in other churches when invited to do so, and the broader Living Room Conversations model has grown across the US.[25]

All this is reminiscent of the final stage of the Robbers Cave experiment described in Chapter 3. Having placed two groups of boys in situations where they rapidly became hostile to one another, Muzafer Sherif and his colleagues wanted to see whether there were ways in which the conflict between the Eagles and the Rattlers could be reduced. The first attempt involved bringing the two groups together in neutral settings and with no competitive activity. It was unsuccessful. The Eagles and the Rattlers remained as hostile to each other as before. Then, the psychologists tried something different. They cut off the water supply. As Gina Perry explains in her book on Sherif,[26] to reinstate it, the boys would have to find the water tank and work together to shift the rocks the researchers had placed over the valve.

> Slowly, with the sun beating down and their water canteens emptying,
> the boundaries between the groups began to blur ... [first the boys]

took turns lifting and carrying the rocks away. But, realising there was a better and faster way of getting the job done, they soon formed a chain, passing the rocks down the line and working as a single team.[27]

With a relevant and tangible 'superordinate' goal in play, the animosity previously expressed by the two groups quickly began to dissipate.[28] The insults dwindled. Aggression vanished. Cross-group friendships began to form. Pursuing a common goal highlighted what the boys had in common and averted focus from what was different.

If an appeal to a shared value or goal can create common ground, so can an appeal to a shared identity. The former US president Jimmy Carter has said that he feels the breakthrough moment in his attempt to broker peace between the Prime Minister of Israel, Menachem Begin, and Anwar Sadat, the President of Egypt, came when he activated his shared identity (and responsibility) as a grandparent with Begin.[29] Negotiations between Israel and Egypt had proved fraught in the aftermath of the 1967 Six Day War and the 1973 Yom Kippur War. At the US presidential retreat at Camp David in 1978 things seemed hardly more promising. Then Carter gave Begin a set of photographs of the two men with Sadat, each addressed to each of Begin's grandchildren. 'I handed it to him,' Carter later recalled,

And he started to talk to me about the breakdown of the negotiations and he looked down and saw that I had written all of his grandchildren's names on the individual pictures and signed them, and he started telling me about his favourite grandchild and the characteristics of different ones. And he and I had quite an emotional discussion about the benefits to my two grandchildren and to his if we could reach peace. And I think it broke the tension that existed there, that could have been an obstacle to any sort of resolution at that time.

It activated for both the motivation needed to find compromise: rather than 'winning' or 'being right', it tapped into the need to think about the longer term and to be pragmatic, to approach the negotiations from their shared perspective as grandparents. In 1978, Begin and Sadat were jointly awarded the Nobel Peace Prize. Three years later Sadat was assassinated by a terrorist group opposed to his rapprochement with Israel.[30]

The evidence of the Israel–Egypt summit may seem anecdotal. However, there is empirical evidence to back up the basic principle behind it. In Chapter 3 we described Professor Mark Levine's football experiment,[31] which showed that Manchester United supporters were more likely to help a passing jogger who had tripped and fallen if he, too, appeared to support the same team. In a second study, Manchester United fans were asked to talk not about their team but about what they liked about being a football supporter. When the fans primed in this way were then confronted by the fallen jogger, the help they offered was determined not by whether the jogger was a Manchester United supporter but by whether he was a football fan. In psychological terms, those conducting the experiment had activated a superordinate category membership. When *Manchester United supporter* was uppermost, that was who was helped. When *football fan* was most important, participants in the study were as likely to help a victim in a Liverpool shirt as they were one in a Manchester United shirt. Previous intergroup rivalries – you are Liverpool, I am Manchester United – become submerged within a more inclusive or common categorisation: football fans. Group identities, it would seem once again, are not as immovably fixed as we might think.

The University of Pennsylvania political science professor Matthew Levendusky[32] conducted a similar, though more politically directed experiment in the US. He wanted to see whether priming national identity ('Americans'), rather than partisan identity ('Republican' or 'Democrat'), would serve to bring fellow countrymen together. Levendusky's basic prediction was straightforward: priming American national identity will reduce affective polarisation. But he also predicted that people who have 'aligned' identities – that is, people whose general ideological outlook matches their partisan orientation – and those who have particularly strong partisan identities will be more resistant to this type of priming.

At the start of the study, people had to state which party they most identified with. One group was then asked to read an article about the strengths of America and Americans and write a paragraph about what made them proud to be American. The other group – the control group – was asked to read a brief apolitical news story and write a short paragraph about an apolitical topic. After that, members of both groups were given a whole range of questions. One involved rating the Democratic and Republican parties on a 100-point 'feeling thermometer', with zero the 'coolest' measure and 100 the 'warmest', most positive ranking. Another sought to establish a trait scale (how well a series of traits described the opposing party). Another consisted of getting participants to list their likes and dislikes of the opposing party.

Overall, the results showed that those who were primed to focus on their shared American identity were more positive about those who supported a rival party by about five degrees on Levendusky's feeling thermometer. In the control condition, people who strongly identified with a particular political party were about nine degrees cooler towards the outgroup than those whose loyalty was weak or lukewarm. In other words, priming halved the gap between rival partisans, regardless of race, gender or intensity of pre-existing political views. Cleverly, Levendusky added an additional element to the study through his employment of a real-world scenario to mimic the experimental stimulus: the annual Fourth of July holiday. His prediction was that, thanks to all the national symbols and celebrations that accompany the holiday, people interviewed on or close to that day would have the most positive impression of rival political parties and their leaders. This turned out to be the case, as did his prediction that those interviewed further away from 4 July would score lower on the feeling thermometer. We do not know how long such effects last – we should expect them only to be temporary and know that they are eliminated in the peak part of campaign cycles. But they do suggest that dislike can be softened by activating attachment to a broader community.

During their road trips together, Jordan Blashek and Chris Haugh found that a good way to reduce tension was to 'strip away the labels'. 'We learned to identify each other not as Democrats or Republicans with beliefs motivated by partisan ideology, but instead as the deeper identities that we both carried that matter to us,' said Jordan.

> So, for me, it was as a Marine, and I wanted Chris to understand my perspective ... And similarly, I learned to see Chris as a journalist and someone who grew up in [liberal, progressive hotbed] Berkeley and ... around activists his whole life. And it gave me a much deeper appreciation for why he approached issues the way he did. We were able to have much better conversations and we think everyone can do that.

What Chris and Jordan learned informally is known in psychological circles as self-affirmation: a way of focusing on boosting our perception of ourselves via an alternative identity or attribute that helps to offset the prevailing group label. Self-affirmation, academics have found, increases openness to new information from 'them' and makes each group less defensive of its position. Lab studies[33] have shown that when people are asked to reflect on their own positive attributes – for example, by writing them down – they react more open-mindedly to information that goes against their partisan identity.

Identifying with a group in the first place is (partly) down to the desire to maintain self-esteem and positive self-image. We like to think of ourselves as upstanding and moral so that we can feel good about ourselves. Favouring our ingroup and disparaging the outgroup is an easy way to achieve that goal; being open to the other side both minimises that all-important perceived difference from the outgroup and threatens our standing with our ingroup. Who wants to risk not appearing to be loyal? However, if we first think about our own positive attributes (attributes not connected with our group), the boost we receive in self-esteem neutralises the negativity we would usually experience from a dalliance with 'them'. Self-affirmation, it seems, gives people the inner security they need to accept new ideas that they would otherwise reject, and to abandon old ideas to which they would otherwise cling. By meeting the need to feel good, affirmation opens the door for other motives like accuracy and objectivity to prevail.[34]

Messengers and messages

If one way to reduce inter-group hostility is to emphasise what groups have in common rather than what separates them, another way is to introduce high-profile, high-status individuals who have the power to get across a particular belief or idea. During the Second World War, Carl Hovland and his colleagues at Yale, who were closely involved in US war propaganda, discovered that when it comes to making an impact it's as much (if not more) a matter of who delivers the message as what that message actually is. They talked, for example, of attractive communicators and credible communicators and the power they wield. Post-war psychologists[35] have confirmed their findings, and have shown that since most of us do not typically have detailed evidence and arguments for why we believe what we believe politically, we tend to rely on easier and more visible signals transmitted by messengers we recognise, like and trust. In their book *Messengers*, Joe Marks and Steve Martin pulled together decades of scientific analysis of what makes an effective messenger to develop a framework with eight characteristics: four 'hard' messenger effects (socio-economic position, competence, dominance and attractiveness), and four 'soft' messenger effects (warmth, vulnerability, trustworthiness and charisma). As Joe Marks puts it: 'We have on the one hand hard messengers, who derive influence from having superior status. And on the other hand, we have soft messengers, who people feel connected to in some way. A superior messenger would be high on all of the traits we found.' Such messengers, of course, have the power to do considerable harm. But they also possess the power to deflect groups from extreme stances.

This was all put to the test in 2015, when a researcher sought to establish whether 'elite influencers' could help amplify the message that inter-communal hatred would not be tolerated.[36] To do so, they created Twitter bots to respond to white males who were using racial slurs. These bots had a cartoon black or white avatar, and their relative status was signalled by the number of Twitter followers they were supposed to have (the more Twitter followers, the higher the status). If someone with a history of using offensive words online directed the N-word towards another user, they would receive a bot tweet that read, 'Hey, man, just remember that there are real people who are hurt when you harass them with that kind of language.' Overall, such interactions led to a reduction in the use of the N-word on Twitter over the following weeks. However, the effectiveness of individual bots was very much down to their colour and perceived status. If a racist was confronted by a white bot with numerous followers, he would tend to rein in his activities more than if the bot had fewer followers. If the bot in question was a black male with few followers, it would be largely unsuccessful.

Another study[37] explored the same phenomenon, this time in the real world in the educational sphere. By encouraging a small set of students in twenty-eight public middle schools in New Jersey to take a public stance against typical forms of conflict at their school, overall levels of conflict – measured subjectively by student-reported norms and administratively by school-reported disciplinary events – reduced by about 30 per cent. The improvement was even larger in schools in which the small group contained many 'social referent students' – that is, students with high status among their peers. To put this into perspective, by leveraging the outsized influence a few students have over social norms and behaviour, the intervention reduced the total number of disciplinary events from 2,695 to 2,012 across the 11,938 students in participating schools.

If the identity of the messenger is crucial, so too can be the way in which a message is framed. If you're in a supermarket and see a pack of mince on the shelf that is labelled '95 per cent fat-free', you are more likely to buy it than one that is labelled 'Contains 5 per cent fat'. Studies have shown that people are more likely to buy a burger described as 75 per cent lean than one described as 25 per cent fat,[38] and have more positive attitudes towards medical procedures when average survival rates are given rather than average mortality rates.[39] It therefore makes sense that messages framed in a way that appeals to 'us' are likely to be more effective. Across three studies,[40] academics from Columbia University showed that the way in which environmental levies and carbon reduction were framed had a direct impact on their acceptability to different groups. Democrats were not concerned whether a 'carbon fee' was described as a tax or an offset. Republicans and independents, on the other hand, reacted more favourably when the word 'tax' was absent, preferring 'offset'. Although these weren't real-world studies, the effects were pronounced.

In Chapter 3 we discussed the case of Luis Lang, a life-long Republican who was an outspoken critic of the Affordable Care Act (known as the ACA, and by its partisan-loaded label Obamacare), and so never bought health insurance. But was he an isolated case, and what was it about the message he so disliked? Three academics from the University of California, Berkeley, Amy Lerman, Meredith Sadin and Samuel Trachtman,[41] set to work to find out the extent to which partisan identity had an impact on the uptake of Obamacare and whether reframing it might lead to its wider adoption. That there was a strongly partisan aspect to it immediately became apparent. Looking at self-reported survey data, they found there was a significant gap between the uptake rates among Republicans as compared with Democrats. They also found that Republicans, who have a long tradition of being more wary of state involvement in healthcare, were significantly less likely to enrol for health insurance through government exchanges. However, when the researchers altered the overall framing of Obamacare by couching it in terms of enrolment in a health insurance website, rather than a government website, they found that Republicans were – by 20 percentage points – more likely to enrol. Polarisation was having a huge impact on uptake.

Opinions have always shifted over time and, as they start doing so (as one generation replaces another), even those holding older, more 'traditional' views may well adapt them to fit in with new norms. However, there's no doubt that such processes can be facilitated by the way in which new norms are expressed. If people are told that their views are outdated, they may double down. Messages that seek to include rather than reprimand them will be more effective. Psychology PhD student at Stanford Gregg Sparkman, who specialises in how to get people to behave in more eco-friendly ways, argues that telling people to eat less meat can be counter-productive. It implies that they are doing something wrong, which challenges their positive sense of self, which in turn makes it more likely they will react negatively. However, if the message is presented in a non-confrontational way, as a dynamic norm (for example, 'Meat consumption in the US has gone down by about 12 per cent since 2008'), it implies that more people 'like you' are starting to cut back on how much meat they are eating, and so removes the uncomfortable sense that you might be in conflict with your group. Studies have found that when 'people learned about the trends over time, they were much more likely to reduce their meat consumption and express greater interest in curbing how much meat they ate'.[42] Sparkman goes on to argue that 'when we see other people change, it can convey to us a lot of really important information. It can help facilitate personal change.'

It is difficult to reshape groups in such a way as to reduce polarisation. But that doesn't mean that it is impossible.

RESHAPING OURSELVES

The challenges of changing your mind

Humans are individuals before they are part of a group. But who each of us becomes is, at least partly, about the groups we belong to. We each feel that our beliefs are entirely our own, chosen at will, consciously considered. We don't see, or don't acknowledge, that they are formed from a mix of innate predispositions (our biology) and the unwritten rules and norms we learn from our social world: the groups we identify with, be they family, friends, peers, gender, race, sexuality, religion, or nation. You may assume that the acquisition of new information will lead you to update or change your views, but often it doesn't. Changing your mind, more often than not, requires you to grapple with your own identity. Admitting that you were wrong feels personal, requiring you to trade off your yearning for accuracy and truth against the unwillingness to lose face or the respect of the people who matter to you: your ingroups. Asking you to change your mind can be like asking you to change your tribe.

The difficulties involved help to explain why most of the people we interviewed for this book and our podcast series found it hard to recall a time when they had ever changed their mind to a significant

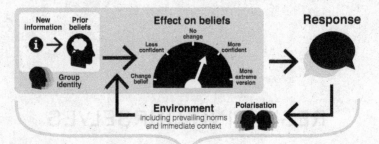

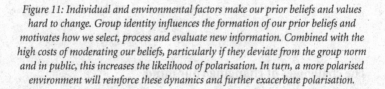

Figure 11: Individual and environmental factors make our prior beliefs and values hard to change. Group identity influences the formation of our prior beliefs and motivates how we select, process and evaluate new information. Combined with the high costs of moderating our beliefs, particularly if they deviate from the group norm and in public, this increases the likelihood of polarisation. In turn, a more polarised environment will reinforce these dynamics and further exacerbate polarisation.

extent. Most reckoned they never had. Some thought they might have done, but couldn't remember why and when. As the former leader of the Liberal Democrats in the UK, Jo Swinson, acknowledged: 'The cost of changing your mind is actually quite high. I think that's one of the difficulties.'[1] All the more so if the stance you have now come to doubt was taken publicly. Research has found that the public at large are singularly unimpressed when leaders change their minds on moral issues, even if they happen to support the newly adopted position.[2] Who wants to be called a flip-flopper, or have 'U-turn' screamed at them? It makes leaders look indecisive and disloyal to their group. One of the reasons why Senator John Kerry's 2004 US presidential bid floundered was that his opponent, George W. Bush, harped on about Kerry's changes of position on the economy, on terrorism and on the war with Iraq, to sow seeds of concern about a lack of credibility.[3] And when we acknowledge that we may have got something wrong, we are often punished for it. Research has found that apologies from public figures who have expressed controversial views are either met with indifference or criticism.[4]

As to why we seem conditioned to forget that our current views may be different from the ones we held before, one likely explanation is our desire to avoid the high mental and emotional cost of being inconsistent. Our brains sense dissonance, and in response record discomfort. Not remembering is both more efficient and more comfortable. It's a mental process similar to that which women go through after childbirth. Studies show that some mothers come to remember labour as having been less painful than they originally described it (although the pain is never forgotten entirely!). From an evolutionary perspective, the memory of pain serves an important purpose – it's a red flag to remind us of a threat to our safety. But it would not make sense for women to be able to recall entirely the pain of childbirth given the existential threat to the future of the human race that would pose.[5] Fewer studies have been carried out on the mental processes involved in belief change, but two pieces of research undertaken by Michael Wolfe, Professor of Psychology at American University Grand Valley State, do at least seem to show how poor our awareness of changing our minds is after the event.[6]

It's interesting to note at the same time, though, how quickly people accept change once it's actually occurred. It's something that Kristin Laurin, Associate Professor of Psychology[7] at the University of British Columbia, noticed with consumers in San Francisco after a ban on plastic water bottles was introduced. Using Facebook ads to recruit participants, she found that those who completed a survey on the Tuesday immediately following the ban (and before people had time to adapt their behaviour) reported more positive attitudes towards the policy than participants completing the survey before the ban came in. She observed much the same pattern of behaviour in Ontario when a smoking ban was introduced in parks and on restaurant patios. Those who, having completed an initial survey about their smoking habits, completed a follow-up one *after* the new law came into force reported that they had spent less of their time smoking in what were now banned areas (parks and restaurant patios) than they had in the first survey. By contrast, the reports of those who completed a follow-up survey *before* the law came into force were far more consistent. It was almost as though smokers were adjusting their memories after the new law came in to minimise the extent to which it affected them.

A third study Laurin and her colleagues carried out before and after Donald Trump's inauguration as US president provided further confirmation of this feat of mental gymnastics that we all seem so prepared to perform. People who had previously disapproved of Donald Trump now became more positive – not converts, certainly, but far less negative. As Laurin explains:

> It's hard to understand why seeing someone give what you judge to be a disappointing performance would make you more confident in their abilities to lead the country. It's not rational – it's rationalisation: when something becomes a part of the present reality, even when it's something you don't like, you find ways of tricking yourself into thinking it's not quite so bad.[8]

Jo Swinson offers a British example of this tendency. 'I fought against the Conservatives for five years to bring in gender pay gap reporting,' she says. 'But then they sort of pretended that it was their idea, and now have been saying, we have done this, it's great.'[9]

Laurin likens this phenomenon to a 'psychological immune system': an unconscious mechanism whereby brain space is freed up for the everyday challenges of living by removing the dissonance that would otherwise be felt. For his part, Thomas Gilovich, a psychology professor at Cornell, calls this process 'sweet lemons rationalisation'.[10] Because we can't change reality when things we dislike or that cause us harm come to pass, we instead change our minds about them, persuading ourselves that they're not really that bad. At one level it's a useful coping tool, allowing us to move on when confronted with things outside our control. At another level, it can be dangerous, inviting us to comply with things that may actually be bad for us or that go against our better judgment. Dissonance theory describes this as induced (or forced) compliance. It's a phenomenon that helps to explain why people are so often complicit in regimes that are inconsistent with their personal beliefs, attitudes or values.

That doesn't mean, of course, that we never change our minds, or that we are never aware we are doing so. In some areas of our lives we change our minds all the time.[11] What to have for lunch. What clothes we choose to buy. What job we want to do next. Maybe even what partner we choose to spend our lives with. Some of these decisions are scarcely trivial ones. And sometimes, over time, our deeper values and norms change too: our attitudes to smoking, say, or to working mothers, or to gay marriage or to transgender rights. Part of this is reflective of effective campaigning, but it is also driven by new generations entering the picture, each influenced by unique historical moments and wider socio-economic trends. Research published in the *Economist*[12] shows that 'support for gay marriage has risen by some 30 percentage points within each generation since 2004, from 20 per cent to 49 per cent among those born in 1928–45 and from 45 per cent to 78 per cent among those born after 1980.' The eminent political scientist John Zaller went so far in his 1992 book *The Nature and Origins of Mass Opinion*[13] as to argue that public opinion is actually extremely unstable on matters large and small, and that even the simple act of ordering or reframing questions in a survey will lead to wildly different answers.[14] This may be because many people do not have strong views to start with, or the views are not connected to a group identity. More broadly, it does seem to be the case that we will abandon a position if the evidence against is overwhelming (though how overwhelming is unclear) and if we haven't already taken a decisive position on it.[15]

201

The unpersuasiveness of facts

What, then, *does* change our minds? Not, as a general rule, facts. Although new facts may alter aspects of our perception of a particular notion or event,[16] they are a weak tool when it comes to changing our minds.[17] The behavioural scientist Steve Martin puts it like this:

> We over rely on information. We think that the best way to influence, [to] change people's minds, is to inform them into change. I have this point of view; I have all this logic that sits behind me. And so therefore, if I simply tell everyone else about it, they'll see the light, the results will change as well. What's interesting and slightly disconcerting is the fact that there's very little evidence [that] supports the idea that information is a good lever of effective influence.[18]

It's something that became all too apparent in the UK during the 2016 Brexit debate. The former Prime Minister Gordon Brown's pollster and founder of BritainThinks, Deborah Mattinson, has described how campaigners on both sides initially assumed that rational, fact-based arguments would be the ones that would work. Hence the view of some Remainers that the visit of President Obama to the UK and his speech in London on the economic dangers of Brexit would be a game-changer. But Dominic Cummings, the campaign director of Vote Leave, had the key insight that it was emotional connection, not fact-based arguments, that would win out: 'perhaps [he] understood this all the way through,' Deborah suggests, 'which is very smart and quite dangerous'. Deborah and her team followed the arguments and counterarguments via diaries kept by 100 people in ten locations. These, she argued, showed that those on the Leave side 'talk[ed] all the time about kind of emotional things, like taking back control'. On the Remain side, however, voters were 'plagued by rational economic arguments'.[19]

Time and time again, facts have proved poor persuaders. In seven separate national survey experiments conducted over eleven years in the US, Daniel Hopkins and colleagues from the Universities of Pennsylvania, George Washington and California, Berkeley[20] investigated whether correcting Americans' misperceptions on immigrants would change attitudes. Americans are (like the citizens of many countries) prone to exaggerate the size of the foreign-born population and the size of many minority groups; such misperceptions are linked to unfavourable views of immigration. It therefore seems logical to assume that if those who are hostile to immigrants are given correct information about how many there actually are, they will modify their views accordingly. However, that is not what Hopkins and his team found. Having randomly assigned accurate and inaccurate information about immigration policy and levels of immigration to participants in their study, they found that the provision of accurate facts and figures did have an impact on people's *knowledge*. But that new knowledge had no knock-on effect on *attitudes*, even among those who discovered that their previous assumptions were wildly out of kilter with reality. What this suggests is that, in this case, at least, facts don't form opinions, as we'd like to believe. Rather opinions come first, and facts are interpreted to support them. This points to a wider truth touched on in Chapter 1, that many of our attitudes are rooted in predispositions established early in life and reinforced by the groups we interact with, and that, consequently, mere information is often insufficient to shift the dial.

Fresh facts can actually make misperceptions worse. The US and UK academics Brendan Nyhan and Jason Reifler[21] have shown that fresh, corrective evidence may work on people who feel unthreatened by it, but be resisted by those whose identities are in some way endorsed by the earlier false information. What's more, corrective evidence can backfire, causing people with deeply entrenched views to dig in further. Those with very strong views on the presence of weapons of mass destruction in Iraq have been shown to hold onto them even more powerfully when challenged by new, contrary evidence. Those convinced that President

Obama was not born in the US were only briefly prepared to reconsider when his long-form birth certificate was produced.[22] Part of the reason why people have this tendency to push back against unwelcome new information is that it causes them to seek more arguments to support their current view, and so ultimately fixes that view more firmly. You can see this at work at the extreme in conspiracy theories, where evidence that should disprove the belief is instead continually rebutted in such a way that it only goes to persuade 'believers' of the depth of dishonesty they are up against. Of course, the passing of time may cause certain beliefs to be held less fervently – the belief in the existence or otherwise of weapons of mass destruction, for example – but even then, people tend not to change their position on an underlying issue that divides their group from another.[23] Corrections in the media, too, can be unproductive, particularly when they touch on partisan politics, and again may do no more than reinforce earlier prejudice.[24] News organisations and fact-checking sites understandably call out misleading statements made by prominent political figures. The evidence suggests, though, that this is an ineffective way of reducing misperceptions.

The persuasive power of doubt and slowing down

So, if challenging false information doesn't work, what does? One approach which has been shown to work is to say, not that something *isn't* true, but that its opposite *is* true. Responding to a false claim with a negation (for example, 'John is not a criminal') causes people to remember the core of the sentence more easily ('John is a criminal').[25] That doesn't happen, though, when a corrective affirmation ('John is exonerated') is offered. Researchers have found that when people are presented with evidence that negates racial and gender stereotypes, they tend to double down. But if they're asked to affirm non-stereotypical information to counter their prejudices, they are more responsive.[26]

Another way to challenge false perceptions that doesn't involve an ineffective bombardment of contrary facts is to encourage people to re-examine the foundations on which their beliefs rest. Humans suffer from what is technically known as the illusion of explanatory depth (IOED).[27] In other words, we tend to believe that we understand things far more precisely and coherently than we actually do. We've all had that experience of being asked to explain something that we thought we knew all about, and finding ourselves floundering. We may think we know precisely how a fridge works, for example – until we're asked to explain its mechanism in detail. Or why an aeroplane is able to stay in the sky. Or why a policy we support or despise can definitively be shown to work or be hopelessly flawed. But if we're asked to explain the bases of our understanding or our beliefs, we may find ourselves forced to confront their fragility and moderate our stance accordingly. Just as the more confident we become about a view, the more extreme we tend to be (see Chapter 3), so the more uncertain we become, the more likely it is that we'll be receptive to an alternative view.

The process by which this is achieved is known as mechanistic reasoning, and involves getting ourselves or others to explain a particular belief or policy position and showing, step by step, how it works. Researchers have found that when people are brought face-to-face with the fact that they don't know as much as they thought they did in a mechanistic (step-by-step fashion), they tend to become less extreme. This was well demonstrated in one US study where participants – of various political affiliations – were asked to explain how different policies – such as instituting a system to cap and trade carbon emissions – would bring about specific outcomes, and a check was then made to see whether as a result their donations to relevant advocacy groups increased or decreased.[28] The money element in the study was key: it involved a financial commitment and a clearly measurable outcome. The results were clear-cut. Among those who had to explain policies in detail, donations to the advocacy groups declined. Among those who had simply been asked to provide a list of reasons why they supported a particular policy and who remained adamant about it, the pattern of donations did not change. Arguments that rely on values, hearsay and general principles do not require much knowledge, are hard to counter and are vigorously defended. Pierce the bubble of certainty and that misplaced confidence lessens; extreme views are weakened and, in the process, become less integral to who we are and how we regard ourselves. This then creates the opportunity for alternative perspectives to be considered. As the University of Toronto's Emeritus Professor of Applied Psychology Keith Stanovich puts it: 'When a conviction is held less like a possession, it is less likely to be projected on to new evidence inappropriately.'[29] It's a sentiment echoed by an academic at the University of Southern California, Jonas Kaplan, who points out further that a good way to make facts matter is to remind people that who they *are* and what they *believe* are two separate things.[30]

It's something that is worth trying for yourself. Before you commit yourself to a position or a policy, ask yourself to explain mechanistically how you think it will bring about its intended outcome. Pick a topic you feel strongly about: climate change, immigration, taxation, gun laws, euthanasia. Then don't simply justify it: write down or explain to someone else step-by-step how your thinking operates and why therefore it will succeed. If that seems too challenging, psychologists at Washington and Lee University in Virginia have shown that the same beneficial effect can be achieved simply by spending a few moments reflecting on your ability to explain a given issue to a true expert 'in a step-by-step, causally connected manner, with no gaps in your story'.[31]

Another way to achieve much the same result is to follow one question with carefully thought-through follow-up questions. It's an approach famously developed by the Greek philosopher Socrates more than 2,000 years ago. Unconvinced that the Oracle at Delphi was right to assert that he was the wisest man in the world, it is said he went off to question other wise men in Athens, only to discover that, when pressed on the details of their beliefs, they not only knew less than they claimed but also were unwilling to admit it. The forensic way in which he conducted his interrogations, known as the Socratic method, involved exposing contradictions and inconsistencies through a constant stream of questions, and, in exposing them, inviting those on the receiving end to moderate their stance or even adopt a new one. He demonstrated how wary we should all be of judging harshly people who say 'I do not know'. Instead, encouraging people to confront their own knowledge gaps before exposing them to new or contradictory information could make them more open to receive it, more able to change their views, and less likely to convert their ideological views into emotional (affective) responses.[32]

Such critical thinking forces us, of course, to slow down our mental processes. In so doing we move from what cognitive psychologists, most famously Daniel Kahneman and Amos Tversky, describe as system 1 thinking (fast, automatic, intuitive, and emotional), to the more reflective, slower and effortful system 2 thinking.[33] This transition is particularly important in the context of deliberate misinformation and fake news. Neither type of information is new. Misinformation has been around for as long as there have been humans. Fake news has always accompanied the written word, whether it's taken the form of the witch pamphlets of the seventeenth century or the claim by the *New York Sun* in 1835 that there was civilisation on the moon. But there's no doubt (as pointed out in Chapter 6) that the ease and speed of online communication have fuelled its intensity. The University of Regina's Gordon Pennycook and MIT's David Rand argue that people fall for fake news when they fail to engage in sufficient critical thinking.[34] It follows, therefore, that persuading or nudging them to slow down and think critically about everything they see on social media will reduce their propensity to fall for stories that to others are so obviously untrue. Certainly, in their study of nearly 3,500 people, Rand and Pennycook found consistent evidence to support their conjecture that those more willing to use analytical thinking are less likely to think fake news is accurate. Put another way, thoughtful people are more likely to discern the truth or otherwise of the news they encounter, regardless of whether or not it accords with their political ideology.

The idea of slowing people down from system 1 to system 2 thinking is something that social media organisations have started to engage with. Whereas usually one can retweet a message straightaway, during the US 2020 presidential election Twitter introduced a new protocol whereby users were prompted to read linked-to stories before sharing them. They also tested a second approach where users were encouraged to add their own comments rather than simply retweet. After the election, Twitter made the former change permanent. Such extra steps act as a buffer, introducing friction and encouraging a cooling-off period, albeit a brief one. In a similar way it's possible to imagine Facebook introducing a respect button rather than responses based on likes or finding a different approach to framing content that creates a less combative mindset. One promising study has explored adapting the principles of CAPTCHA images – whereby users have to click on a common element in a series of pictures (for example a lamp post), to prove they are not a robot – to serve as a more reflective way of interacting via online forums. The thesis is that by using more positive images to act as a built-in pause point in politically charged online forums, people's framing and approach to engagement will be altered and improved.[35]

Adopting an understanding mindset

If sowing a seed of doubt and slowing down can change our minds, so can activating a sense of shared humanity. This basic truth was famously explored by Frank Wesley, a psychology professor at Portland State University and mentor to Peter Boghossian, co-author of *How to Have Impossible Conversations*. Wesley had noticed that during the Korean War in the 1950s some US prisoners of war had defected to North Korea. It might be assumed that this was because they had been tortured or been unable to withstand interrogation. Or that they hadn't been sufficiently trained to hate the Koreans. But it wasn't. Instead, it turned out that in one particular US training camp they had been taught that Koreans were 'cruel and heartless' and trained to hate them deeply. So when they were shown unexpected kindness and compassion[36] by their Korean captors, which flew in the face of the barbarism they had been trained to expect, their prior beliefs crumbled.[37] In fact, soldiers who had been trained in this particular US camp were far more likely to defect than POWs who had not been given any training on the North Koreans or had been given more neutral information.

A more recent example of the surprising impact of kindness is that of the YouTube star Famke Louise, who shot to fame when her prank videos caught the attention of hundreds, then thousands, then tens of thousands of people. As her audience and profile grew, the young Dutch woman started to sing and model, before appearing on the Dutch/Belgian version of the reality TV adventure show *Survivor*. Within a few years she had a following in excess of one million on Instagram and 350,000 on YouTube and several gold and platinum records.[38] When the coronavirus pandemic hit in March 2020, and the Dutch government needed to get public health messages to every section of society at speed, it turned for help to social media influencers, knowing that their profile would guarantee their influence with the general public when it came to asking them to wear a face mask and accept restrictions on their daily lives. Famke was one of those with large followings the government recruited.[39]

By September, compliance with restrictions had started to reduce and the disease had taken hold again, leading to regional clamp-downs to slow the spread.[40] However, this in turn sparked a protest movement – Viruswaarheid ('Virus Truth'), formerly known as Viruswaanzin ('Virus Madness') – which staged protests in the Hague and then recruited several social media influencers to promote their hashtag #ikdoenietmeermee – 'I'm no longer participating.' Among the young people who had tired of the restrictions and wanted their old lives back was Famke. In a TV appearance, she and the campaign she now supported went further, calling for others to ignore the restrictions the government was placing on them.[41] Cries of frustration and accusations of hypocrisy swiftly followed. The science was clear: the virus was spreading and risked overloading the health system. Famke lost a contract at a music event and faced ridicule – from some fans as well as politicians – in a competing hashtag #ikdoewel-mee, 'I do participate.' Within days she had altered course, writing an Instagram post that it was 'all in all not my best day', and that she now 'realise[d] the seriousness of making unsubstantiated statements'.

Tales of YouTubers apologising for stances taken are hardly new. But what's interesting about Famke's story is how her Damascene moment occurred. When the backlash began, Diederik Gommers, a doctor based at a Rotterdam intensive care unit, and the chair of the Dutch Association for Intensive Care, tried repeatedly to reach out to her. 'I phoned her every day last week, initially to support Famke . . . the backlash she received was too strong,' he said.[42] Gommers then invited Famke to visit him at his hospital, to help her understand more about how the virus works and recognise her illusion of explanatory depth. The point is, though, that he did all this kindly, not critically or censoriously. Famke acknowledged that 'she just needed that': it was his kindness, it seems, that made the difference. Shortly afterwards Gommers joined Instagram, recognising that it was a channel he should be on. One of his first posts, somewhat grainier than Famke's usual poised style, was of the two of them in his office.

As she helped promote his work, Gommers became an influencer himself. Within days he had over 200,000 followers. He and Famke now work together to get messages to young people about the importance of compliance. 'Except for my son, I get positive and warm reactions from many people,' Gommers has confided.[43]

Kindness involves a mindset of understanding, not winning. A zero-sum, winner-takes-all mentality makes both sides think that if the other side wins, they lose. An understanding mentality ensures that because neither side loses, neither side puts winning beyond everything else. It's another lesson learnt by Jordan Blashek and Chris Haugh, the two political rivals who ended up going on road trips together (see Chapter 8). As Jordan observed:

First, . . . when you enter these kinds of conversations, if your intention is to win or to change the other person's mind, it's probably not going to go that well . . . We were just waiting for our chance to score the next point or bring our own facts or data to bear. And those usually spiralled out of control. So instead, we started having conversations where we entered with the intention just to learn from the other side. And we found that in doing so, it made our own positions better, and our own views stronger, more reasoned and nuanced. Second, we realised that a lot of our assumptions about the other side turned out to be wrong. And usually when we looked at someone as a Democrat or Republican and assumed that we knew what they would think on a given issue, our assumptions misled us and led us into arguments that we shouldn't have been having because we were defending our party as opposed to articulating our own genuine beliefs on the issue.[44]

The psychologists Katharina Kugler and Peter Coleman argue that complexity creates space for trade-offs and problem-solving, in a way that a simplistic winner-takes-all mentality can never do. They also point out just how intractable and involved 'them-and-us' conflicts can become: 'paradoxically, the conflict itself becomes increasingly more complex (involving new issues, circumstances, and disputants over time), but disputants' perceptions and experiences of the conflict become steadily more simplistic (us vs them, good vs evil), stable, and resistant to attempts at resolution.'[45] An experiment the two researchers conducted demonstrates this point well. It involved two groups, the same task, but two very different goals. Both groups were given a particular moral topic to discuss, the legal framework for it and a set of opposing opinions. But while one group was told it was important to consider different perspectives (high complexity), the other was informed that what mattered was to seek a clear perspective (low complexity). And while the high-complexity group was presented with differing opinions integrated into a discursive piece, their low-complexity peers were shown the two sets of ideas as arguments and counterarguments. The results spoke for themselves. All those in the high-complexity group were able to agree on a joint position statement at the end of the session. Under half (45.5 per cent) of those in the low-complexity group were able to do so. Moreover, those in the high-complexity group *felt* more positive about the experience than those in the low-complexity one.

For Maggie Neale, Stanford professor emerita of management, complex (as opposed to simplistic, win-or-lose) thinking is the key to the art of successful negotiation. In her view, 'rather than thinking about negotiation as a battle, you should think about negotiation as collaborative problem-solving.'[46] She argues that it is critical that you start by being prepared – and able – to frame your proposals as a solution to a problem your counterpart has. This in turn means that you need to understand what they are hoping to gain from the negotiation, which in turn requires that you listen, and that you consider outcomes that may not be the ones you first had in mind. If you can do all that, you are more likely to come up with a mutually acceptable solution. 'You are not trying to blast them out,' says Danny Finkelstein, the Conservative peer and former Executive Editor of *The Times* newspaper.

> You have got to make concessions. You have got to help them develop a story which allows them to integrate the position you want them to take from the position they have got. So, you are trying to tell them, 'You're right.' And the point that I believe fits with what you think already.[47]

All techniques to break down divides require us to be more open-minded. We need to be alive to new evidence. We have to allow ourselves to be prepared to be convinced by opposing arguments. We must revisit conclusions as we receive new and relevant information, actively look for reasons why we might be wrong, and focus on understanding rather than winning.

One final way to counter polarisation is to formulate a markedly different position from our usual one and come up with reasons for it. Can we understand why someone would hold such a view? It may be different from ours, but is it genuinely worse – or perhaps better? If we can see how we might change our mind on one thing, it can unlock flexibility in other areas. And of course, we are not alone – people can and do change their minds – and gradually making that a 'good' norm has its place in helping to encourage flexibility and responsiveness.

10

CHANGED MY MIND

Personal journeys

The Emperor Ashoka ruled over a huge Indian Empire, which included much of what is now Afghanistan, Bangladesh, India, and Pakistan, from around 268 to 232 BC. He is best known for becoming a religious convert and for rejecting military aggression, but before his change of mind he was a successful warrior, conquering Kalinga, an ancient territorial subdivision of central-east India, which now roughly maps to modern Orissa. It was a bitterly destructive war in which tens of thousands died. After witnessing the slaughter he had caused, and 'sickened by the loss of life', Ashoka embraced Buddhism and started to preach a new doctrine of non-violence. His 'Ashokan edicts' – inscriptions engraved on rocks and pillars – show a man concerned for justice, fairness and benevolence. When India gained independence from Britain in 1947, the new state chose as its emblem the lion capital from one of Ashoka's pillars to symbolise its commitment to tolerance within a secular state.[1]

For a leader to change their mind takes bravery and involves considerable risk. History is littered with the names of those who felt it imperative to alter course and who suffered as a result – regardless of the wisdom or otherwise of the move they made. Judged in narrow terms of personal political power, modern leaders Theresa May (a Remainer who tried to implement the UK public's wishes to leave the EU), Mikhail Gorbachev (who moved the Soviet Union away from Marxism-Leninism towards social democracy) and Anwar Sadat (who helped broker the peace accord between Egypt and Israel) all paid a price (in Sadat's case, a fatal one) for changing direction. At the same time, of course, the outcome for those who have stubbornly refused to shift their stance has not necessarily been better. For example, while Gorbachev ultimately fell from power for changing his mind, fellow leaders of Eastern bloc countries who resisted following suit were pushed from office rather sooner. In the UK, Margaret Thatcher's political demise was a direct consequence of an increasing inflexibility in outlook in general, digging her heels in on Europe and refusing to cancel the introduction of an unpopular tax (the community charge or 'poll tax') in particular.

There is accordingly no immutable rule as to the wisdom of either standing one's ground or altering one's view in any given situation. But the wisdom of displaying a willingness to *consider* a new perspective is unquestionable. Margaret Thatcher offers an interesting case study in this respect. Famous for her seeming inflexibility (not for nothing was she known as 'The Iron Lady'),[2] there was nevertheless one occasion at least when she adopted a more open-minded approach. And it paid dividends. Naturally hostile to the USSR, but unfamiliar with foreign policy and its new leader's character, she decided to invite specialists to Chequers, her country residence, in order to take stock of their advice about Mikhail Gorbachev. With her own Cabinet she could be dictatorial, dismissive, and abrasive (on the issue of Europe, her Minister Geoffrey Howe memorably likened her to a cricket captain who broke the team's bats before they walked out to the wicket).[3] But on this occasion, she intuitively followed a depolarising route: try to understand rather than win, slow down, and do not anchor to a view that you cannot update. Later in 1984, when Gorbachev visited the UK, she declared he was 'a man one could do business with' (US president Ronald Reagan was later to follow suit). She also triggered a sense of shared identity when she found that Gorbachev's wife was wearing something she would have chosen for herself.[4] Her shift in attitude presaged the softening of Western attitudes to the USSR, helped slow the arms race, and in so doing eased Gorbachev's path towards a more democratic system of government.

In the course of recording our podcast *Changed My Mind*, we talked to people who have changed political parties, changed sides in an ideological war, or renounced previously strongly held beliefs. The path each has taken is different, but there are common themes to many accounts of their journeys and those highlighted by academic studies: rethinking and/or getting to know the 'enemy' (in other words, who the 'them' is); seeking to establish a shared identity; moving from a winning to an understanding mindset; being presented with a route to change that made it less costly; rethinking a position in the face of kindness; identifying a common goal rather than a 'winning' position; listening to a trusted 'messenger'; letting go of a belief if a mechanistic attempt to justify it failed or if presented with overwhelming contrary evidence.

Take Leah Garcés, a vegan, and president of Mercy for Animals, and Craig Watts, a chicken factory farmer. When they first met, Leah assumed that because Craig ran precisely the sort of enterprise she was campaigning against, they would not find much common ground: 'I encountered a person who would normally be my arch enemy,' she recalled. 'And this was a chicken factory farmer. And through a mutual journalist friend, I was invited by this farmer to visit him and see what was going on inside of his chicken farms. So I went.'

Then the shift took place:

It was through conversations with him that I realised that he wasn't the enemy. It was the system that was an enemy to all of us ... It turned out he hated factory farming as much as I did. All of this came as a total shock to me, listening to this man in Fairmont, North Carolina, and hearing how he felt like an indentured servant, that he felt as trapped as the chickens in the system. He didn't see a way out. He was so indebted. He had hundreds of thousands of dollars of debt he couldn't get out of. And this was a big wake-up call for me. After working with him, we worked together. We exposed the industry.[5]

Leah and Craig became an unlikely partnership pushing for reform. But what was it about that encounter that made it possible for them to get to a place where they could hear each other out?

We both had three kids, and my oldest was the same age as his two youngest, who are twins. And I realised he had strong family values. He believed in paying for his kids' college and preparing a life for them the same way that I was doing. We started off as human beings [with] very similar objectives in life, which is to raise kids, to have them do well, to teach them basic values in life. [And] we were bothered by the fact that the American public were being lied to, essentially hoodwinked by what the industry was saying. From his perspective, the industry was saying, 'Farmers are treated great.' And from my perspective, it was, 'Animals are being treated great.' And it turns out neither are [true]. I think we figured out that that was a really powerful thing for a factory farmer and an animal rights activist to come together on that point.

Leah and Craig were able to activate their other identities – as parents, as people who valued education, as people who cared about sharing the reality of the situation with a wider group of people – which meant they could treat each other with kindness, explore each other's views in more depth and, in the process, move from a winning position to an understanding one in which they could establish a shared goal.

Leah summed up the challenge of getting to that point:

> You have to be comfortable with being uncomfortable. And I think the key takeaway there is that if we continue to only speak to people who agree with us, we won't make change. We won't change people's minds. So the first step is being comfortable with being uncomfortable: being willing to speak to people who don't agree with you. The second is that we have to recognise that the people that we're speaking to, that maybe we see as enemies or as adversaries, quite often have a lot more in common with us than we care to realise ... And finding those similar interests and values can really lead to a very productive conversation and understanding. And the third part is looking for win-wins. So, once you've entered that discomfort zone, once you've sat down with someone and recognised, hey, they're not so different than me, then [it's about] finding the places where you have common ground and building from there, finding the things that benefit both of you, both of your values, where you both can start from, where you're similar rather than you're different.

As the Stanford professor Maggie Neale has said, to negotiate you need to see the process as collaborative problem-solving rather than winner-takes-all. This was something that Leah and Craig were able, intuitively, to do.

The journey taken by Derek Black, whom we met at the beginning of this book, also has much to teach us. Born into a family deeply embedded in the white nationalist movement in Florida, with a father who had established the Internet's first significant white nationalist website and a godfather who had been a Klansman, Derek grew up very aware that his beliefs, and those of his family and friends, set him apart from the wider community in Florida. He was also aware that those beliefs were widely condemned. As a young man, he thought his family were right – that they must be because, to him, they were brilliant individuals. But he also possessed the curiosity to want to encounter and get to know a wide range of people. He worked hard to keep the two parts of his life – as a vocal member of a nationalist family and as a school student – completely separate, perhaps because the cognitive dissonance caused by acknowledging both simultaneously would have been too challenging.

At university, he initially continued to hide his involvement with white nationalism, but became increasingly aware that this was not going to be possible to sustain. He was right. His fellow students found out about his background and he was ostracised. Knowing how unwelcome he was, he moved into off-campus accommodation. But not everyone turned their back on him. Matthew, an Orthodox Jew, who was friends with Derek before his background was revealed, invited him to a Shabbat dinner, not to persuade him to change his mind but to bring him back into contact with others. His kindness was such that Derek started attending Shabbat dinners on a regular basis. At first some other guests shunned him, but then many engaged with him. One of them, Alison, asked him to explain in detail the foundations of his belief system. It turned out this was the first time Derek had ever tried to explain his position to someone who did not share his view or was not a journalist.[6] Previously, he had always shut such conversations down.

Over time, Derek came to realise that he could not both keep his new friends and maintain a view that some of them didn't belong to American society. Issues that had once seemed abstract had acquired faces and personalities. Now, as he grappled to understand why his transition from a family to a college community had involved such a challenge to his fundamental beliefs, he became interested in contact theory (see Chapter 8). White nationalism, for him, was no longer a given or an 'academic' debate.

Derek acknowledges that Matthew and Alison's generosity of spirit and their willingness to engage him in constructive debate was 'amazing'. It was also effective: Derek changed his views dramatically in a way that would have been unthinkable had the story ended with his ostracism. He went on to renounce the white nationalist movement, comparing his experience with that of someone rejecting membership of a religious community, and did so even though he could not be sure he would ever re-establish relations with his family. It's proved a difficult journey, but if divides are to be bridged, Derek told us, such journeys are essential. And it's something we all must do. As Derek puts it: 'There is no person who is unimportant to talk to . . . if you lead with your values and try to be understanding but also quite forceful when something is inhumane, that has an impact . . . we cannot be silent.'[7]

Postscript

We hope this book has given you hope that we do not have to be entrenched and divided, that if we want to change our societies for the better, we can. There are many steps we can all take as individuals to engage better with others, but this is particularly true if you hold a position of influence, as change at a system level is needed to increase the benefits and reduce the costs for all.

Here's a quick recap of what you can do as an individual:

- Try to rethink and/or get to know the 'enemy'; it isn't easy, but it can make it more possible to reach across a divide (see Chapter 8)
- Seek to establish a shared identity before discussing beliefs, as this can offset 'us-and-them' thinking (see Chapter 8)
- Identify a common goal rather than a 'winning' position, so that there is a shared reason to engage across the divide (see Chapter 8)

- Use a trusted 'messenger' to engage with other groups and frame messages in a way that will appeal to them (see Chapter 8)
- Rather than relying on facts to persuade/wear others down, try re-examining the foundations of your own beliefs and asking others to do the same (see Chapter 9)
- In the same vein, before you commit yourself to a position or a policy, ask yourself to explain mechanistically how you think it will bring about its intended outcome (see Chapter 9)
- Be prepared to let go of a belief if a mechanistic attempt to justify it fails or if presented with overwhelming contrary evidence (see Chapter 9)
- Move from a winning to an understanding mindset, as it changes the conversation and allows for greater exploration of ideas. A zero-sum, winner-takes-all mentality makes both sides think that if the other side wins, they lose (see Chapter 9)
- Offer others a route to changing their mind that makes it less costly for them personally, which may involve everyone making concessions (see Chapter 9)

There are also ways to work together that help to lessen 'us' and 'them' dynamics and support constructive debate:

- Explore shared activities that slow down thinking and enable a greater quality of discussion (see Chapter 8)
- Identify what is common rather than different as a way into a better-quality, inclusive discussion (see Chapter 8)
- Activate elements of shared identity – e.g. American rather than Democrat or Republican (see Chapter 8)
- Use messages that include rather than reprimand, so that those engaged are not pushed to double down on existing beliefs about the 'other' (see Chapter 8)

- Attach a shared goal to cross-group interactions which can make them more likely to succeed than contact alone (see Chapter 8)

Debate is good. Disagreement is good. Entrenching in our own beliefs to the extent that we can't tolerate either does us much harm. These are some approaches to making engagement across the divide more constructive. They've changed the way the authors think; maybe they will change your mind too.

If you would like to find out more about what you can do and download our free resources, please visit: www.depolarizationproject.com

AFTERWORD

It was an autumn afternoon, and we were busy promoting the hard-back edition of *Poles Apart*. On a radio phone-in with the genial but tough BBC host Nihal Arthanayake, we noticed that he started to laugh nervously. Apparently, a member of the public had just texted to ask one of our number, Alex, a former Conservative politician, 'Do you have a soul?'

The conditions that can amplify division have only grown since this book was first published. The pandemic has increased uncertainty. The gaps between rich and poor are widening and are likely to continue doing so as inflation sets in. A global supply chain under stress has served to make resources scarcer – a situation that will become worse as the effects of climate change continue to kick in. Commercial incentives to capitalise on division remain. Add to all that the fact that while polarisation ebbs and flows are normal, the longer people remain divided, the harder it is to return to normality, and there are causes for deep concern. It is an ominous sign, for example, that young people, who were especially hard hit in the pandemic, are losing faith in democracy at an even greater rate than we noted in Chapter 4.[1] So deep are political divisions that they spill over into other aspects of our lives: in the US, Boston College's Masha Krupenkin noted, pre-pandemic, that people were 6 per cent more likely to get their children vaccinated if the person they voted for became president.[2]

When feelings drown out facts, our view of the world becomes distorted. A furore involving Robert Unanue, the CEO of Goya Foods, comes to mind in this context. In the run-up to the 2020 presidential election, Unanue, who had overseen the brand beloved in the Latino community and beyond for fifteen years – growing it to a $2b-a-year business – announced the US is 'truly blessed' to have a leader like [President] Donald Trump.[3] When he was reminded that Trump had a history of insulting Latino voters (in the 2016 presidential election he had called Mexicans 'rapists' and 'drug runners'[4]), he doubled down on his position. Immediately, the battlelines were drawn. Those who opposed Trump called for a boycott. Alexandria Ocasio Cortez, the Democrat New York Congresswoman who leads a movement tens of millions strong, amplified the campaign. CNN ran the headline 'Goya was a staple in Latino households. It likely won't be anymore.'[5] Seventy-five per cent of the chat on Twitter was supportive of the boycott. It looked as though a movement was going to hold to account a CEO whose views were seen by many as unacceptable. The signs were that the campaigners had triumphed.

In fact, they hadn't. Trump encouraged his supporters to buy Goya, and as a result, sales actually increased 22 per cent in the three weeks the story dominated the papers. Increases were driven largely by new purchasers, their concentration 166 per cent higher in Republican counties.[6] The call to boycott may have dominated the social media conversation. However, it had backfired on the ground. The CEO remains in post, and even confirmed his support for Trump after the riots on Capitol Hill that came in the wake of the then-President's refusal to accept his election defeat. A political row caused a commercial campaign that was misinterpreted by its supporters as a success.

If this story involving Donald Trump shows how easily adherents of a cause can become blinded to the facts, the former president also exemplifies the way in which an important bulwark against polarisation, party apparatus, can become subsumed and captured by a single individual. So fused is he with the Republican Party that his supporters are openly hostile even to fellow Republicans who dare to criticise him. Senator Liz Cheney is a case in point. Daughter of George W. Bush's vice-president, Dick Cheney, her Republican credentials were so strong that they landed her a leadership role in the GOP caucus. But in the wake of the Capitol Hill riot of 6 January 2021, Cheney decided to break with the majority of her party and vote, alongside nine other GOP members of Congress, in favour of impeaching Donald Trump for his role in the riots. '[T]he integrity of our election system was being attacked and trust in it was being eroded – with disastrous consequences,' she argued.[7] Cheney did not stop there at her criticism of the former president, labelling Trump clearly unfit for future public office and declaring the GOP had a particular duty to make sure that Donald Trump is 'never anywhere close to the reins of power ever again'.[8] First, Cheney was deposed from her leadership role in the caucus. Now, an embittered Trump is both trying to get the rules tilted against Cheney and supporting a well-funded primary challenge against her.[9]

Liz Cheney's unpopularity among many Republicans exemplifies the tribalism of contemporary American politics – a tribalism that is replicated in many countries across the world. But the political journey that she has recently gone on also demonstrates a more encouraging aspect of polarisation, which we discuss in detail in the final chapter of the book: essentially, once you open your mind to an alternative point of view on one issue, you are more likely to change your mind on other questions as well. Cheney was prepared to listen to voices that went against Republican received wisdom. In the wake of that decision came a renunciation of her previous opposition to same-sex marriage.[10] For now, she is an ostracised voice on the

Republican benches, but her stance shows that a willingness to be open-minded is not dead. Polarisation may beget further polarisation, but changing your mind once also begets further openness. Moreover, while she may not have persuaded Republicans to join her (and it's hard not to see how Republican attacks on her can be anything but a disincentive for others to join her), she has helped moderate Democrat views of Republicans. Even a single voice can weaken the strength of polarisation.[11]

So, while it feels all too easy to be despondent about the current state of the world, there are reasons for optimism. Certainly, we have been greatly heartened by the response this book has received. Business leaders, movement builders, campaigners and others have all told us that they now consider that they could unwittingly have been part of the problem; that they can see they have a responsibility to be part of the solution; and that the book provides them with the tools they need to achieve that.

Promising new research suggests that one aspect of mindfulness – that focuses on befriending strangers and difficult people – can reduce hostility to political outgroups.[12] Led by Otto Simonsson,[13] researchers at Oxford University conducted an experiment in which, during the course of a ten-minute meditation, Democrats and Republicans were asked to bring to mind a loved one, a stranger and a difficult person, and to wish them and all living creatures to be 'happy and healthy'. What they found was that getting people to adopt this mindset resulted in a drop in polarised feelings towards every outgroup, including those who were strangers and those considered difficult. We should slow down, engage more thoughtfully, and take time to adopt a position. It's far easier and healthier to do that than to seize upon a view on the assumption that you can always change your mind later. A sense of humour can help, too: it's hard to dislike someone you share a joke with, as those who protested outside the New Zealand parliament building against strict lockdown measures found when they were greeted by the music of Barry Manilow and the Spanish dance tune, 'Macarena'. In fact, in as much as it's possible to characterise an entire country as embodying a particular quality or mindset, New Zealand, with its general good humour and low levels of inter-group political hostility – through successive changes of government and emotional debate about the country's history – should give us all hope.

Which brings us back to Alex's soul. Her anxious laugh as Nihal posed the question developed into widespread mirth amongst us all. As we highlighted our shared common bond – and our own certainty that yes, Alex does have a soul – you could feel a release of tension. It *is* possible to bridge divides and ride the storm ahead, and we *can* all do something about it.

ACKNOWLEDGEMENTS

This book would not have been possible without invaluable contributions from many generous and talented people.

Nigel Wilcockson, our Editor, whose feedback and challenge fostered a step change in the clarity of our thinking. Polarisation is a challenging and complex topic, with many strands to draw together. Our work would be immeasurably poorer without his guidance in shepherding a first draft into the text you have just read. Our formidable agent Caroline Michel and the supportive team at PFD, especially Rebecca Wearmouth, believed that Nigel would be a dream editor. They were right.

We are lucky to have many brilliant mentors who have proudly introduced us to contacts and friends. Steve Martin, who makes a habit of supporting younger generations, did precisely that when he connected us to Nigel. We are beyond grateful, for that, his title suggestion and candidness in telling us that, just sometimes, we should be open to changing our minds too.

Our relationship with Steve was deepened through our podcast *Changed My Mind*. This was inspired by a series Ali was involved in crafting as a student at Stanford: in the aftermath of Trump's victory some responded to his election by establishing resistance schools, but

Stanford walked another path, looking to see how it could understand, build bridges and maintain integrity. That response was supported by the late Dean Arjay Miller and a successor Dean Jonathan Levin. Professor Saumitra Jha and Bernadette Clavier were brilliant champions of that work. The development of the podcast, The Depolarization Project, this book and what may come in the future would have been impossible without them and their ongoing mentorship. It was in one of those sessions that Karen Warner asked a speaker, Trump supporting Katherine (Kat) Vasconez, what she had changed her mind on and why. Kat took a deep breath and explained that an out, gay housemate at university had made her realise that homosexuality was not a sin as she had previously thought. She went further, continuing to say she was now confident all sexualities should be treated equally. It was a response that fundamentally changed the tone of the discussion. Others too started talking about where they had had an experience that caused them to reflect and change their minds. Kat continues to be a valuable advisor, thought partner and friend.

That transformation into a podcast was enabled by Mary Fitzgerald and the team at Open Democracy, who positively leapt at the concept when it was shared over a quiet drink in an East London garden. Mary, alongside our producer, Caroline Crampton helped to sharpen and refine a raw product into one that reached a hugely engaged audience. But that engagement was dependent on the many wonderful guests to whom we posed the same question Karen asked Kat at Stanford. This book is really *our* book. We would not have started down the road without you sharing so candidly your stories on what you changed your mind on and why. Aimen Dean and Thomas Small; Carwyn Jones; Chris Hough and Jordan Blashek; Craig Beaumont; Danny Finkelstein; Deborah Mattison; Derek Bardowell; Derek Black; Helen Lewis; Jamie Susskind; Jeff Pfeffer; Jo Swinson; Jonathan Haidt; Joseph Marks; Julia Margo; Kajal Odedra; Leah Garcés; Maggie

Neale; Marcia Chatelain; Peter Gabriel; Peter Geoghegan; Sarah Soule; Shannon Downey; Sonia Sodha; Steve Martin and Tali Sharot.

Over the last three years we have supplemented these interviews, built on the projects and study we have been involved in at Stanford, University College London and the Universities of Bath, Cardiff and York. They had already given us a hearty respect for academics doing work in this nascent field. We hope that as we have brought together the many strands of thinking, based on years of research, we have done those academics justice. It brought us particular joy when we found lesser known work, or those from scholars at the start of their careers. Whatever their seniority we encountered significant support for our work. Any errors in interpretation are, of course, our own.

Finding those lesser known works could be a labour of love, one we were deeply assisted in by Lara Spirit. A formidable researcher whose curiosity and intellect meant we covered far more ground, in more interesting ways than we could have imagined. Maya Dusenbery for her first rate fact-checking, which helped us to sleep at night. And to Jason Hopper for turning our thoughts into images others can understand and at very short notice.

Alongside this were the many interviews and thought partners we developed in this project. Alana Conner, Alex Runswick, Alison Smith, Allison Rouse, Andrew Benbow, Antonia Bance, Ben Kohlman, Blair Glencorse, Bridget Harris, Carrie Keller Lynn, Charles Ewald, Charmian Love, Claire Yorke, David Broockman, David Garbett, David Stevens, David Wall, Debilyn Molineux, Duncan Hames, Ed Batista, Ellie Gellard, Eric Singler, Ezra Hewing, Giles Edwards and the team at BBC Four Thought, Glenn Kramon, Graeme Trayner, Graham Covington, Helen and Andy Mayer, Imran Ahmed, James Gurling, Nick Barron and the team at MHP, James Ravenscroft, Jasmine Compton, Jay Owens, Jess Day, Jo Warner, Jon Lu, Jon Neal, Jon Roozenbeek, John Ball, Joseph Marks, Juani Swart, Julian Huppert and The Intellectual Forum at Jesus College, Kate Archibald, Kate

Maltby, Katie Crocker Behroozi, Keith Hennessey, Kirsty McNeill, Kristin Hansen, Kyle Emilie, Laura Arrillaga-Andreessen, Lee de Witt, Lenny Mendonca, Leor Zmigrod, Linda Taylor, Linda Capello, Magda Osman, Mark Gerzon, Mat Morrison, Matt Muir, Michael Hayman, Michael Hollins, Miguel Head, Miriam Juan-Torres González, Nir Halevey, Noel and Vera Kenehan, Oli Barrett, Paddy Barwise, Paul Adams, Paul Drechsler, Paul Howie Roberts, Owen Tudor, Polly MacKenzie, Quintin Oliver, Rob Blackie, Rob Smith, Roger Harding, Salma Mousa, Sam Jeffers, Sarah Bonk, Scott Young, Shannon Fitzgerald, Shiv Malik, Sophia Wolpers, Stefan Hunt, Stewart Wood, Sunder Katwala, Tim Weir, Timur Kuran, Tony Curzon Price, Will Tanner, Lord William Waldegrave and many we can not name. And some friends and colleagues that we'd like to thank for their endless support and encouragement: Andrew Neal, Anne Keenan, Anya Bialeska, Beckie Murphy, Dan Freeman, Fiona Weir, Ian Taylor, Jenny Dixon, Katie Bebbington Moore, Lib Adams, Monique Rotik, Muniya Barua, Nicholas Crapp, Nicole Brigandi, Rebecca Zylberman, Safia Iman, Stephen Brooks, Sarah Otner and Will Brayne. As well as all our other friends, mentors and acquaintances with terrifyingly sharp minds, who provided first rate critique, challenge, warnings and insight on early drafts. Thank you to them for believing in us and helping us to keep open minds.

As authors the three of us would never have formed the bonds we have without being brought together by the senior leadership of Which? Richard Lloyd, Julia Margo, Alex Neill and Helen Parker were instrumental in creating the teams we came to lead and the spirit of co-operation we've relied on heavily.

Our approaches have been honed by many others whose involvement in our life predates this book. At work our colleagues at Chime, Deryn, Maitland, PPS, Leonard Cheshire, the Joseph Rowntree Reform Trust, the Department of Business, the CMA and FCA. At school Jane Walford, Katherine MacDonald, Felicity Evans and

Colin Grundy left lasting impressions that shaped us and inevitably the approach to the book.

But our greatest cheerleaders in this project, and in everything else, have been our families. When we signed up to do the book the world was a very different place. Over the course of writing, a global pandemic hit, meaning we set up impromptu home schools. We broke bones, gave birth, fought elections, changed jobs, got promoted and honoured commitments that meant the demands we had placed on them became greater. But they never wavered in their support, something that too often remains unusual for women. Cathy and Jeff Walton, Philippa Wiltshire; Peter, Anna, Winston and Nerissa Chesterfield; Sheila and Brian Stacey, Ruth and Prad Patel. Sheena, Michael and Emma Osborne, Ian and Anne Goldsworthy and Midge Gibbons. We reserve special thanks for our husbands. Will, Doug and Jimmy; and our children Evie, Teddy, Tomos, Anna and Ellie. Mummy can finally put down the laptop!

NOTES

Prologue

1 L. N. Diab, 'A Study of Intragroup and Intergroup Relations among Experimentally Produced Small Groups,' *Genetic Psychology Monograph*, vol. 82, 1970, pp. 49–82. Cited in *Us and Them: The Science of Identity*, David Berreby, University of Chicago Press, 2008, p. 178.

2 R. M. Shafranek, 'Political Considerations in Non-Political Decisions: A Conjoint Analysis of Roommate Choice', *Political Behaviour*, vol. 43, no. 1, 2021, pp. 271–300, www.doi.org.

3 Alex Chesterfield, Ali Goldsworthy and Laura Osborne interview Aimen Dean and Thomas Small, 'Changed My Mind: from Al-Qaeda bombmaker to MI6 spy', *Changed My Mind*, www.opendemocracy.net, 27 May 2020.

4 Murat Somer and Jennifer McCoy, 'Déjà vu? Polarization and Endangered Democracies in the 21st Century', *American Behavioral Scientist*, vol. 62, no. 1, 2018, p. 5.

5 M. Krupenkin, 'Does Partisanship Affect Compliance with Government Recommendations?', *Political Behaviour*, vol. 43, no. 1, 2021, www.doi.org.

6 Eitan D. Hersh and Matthew N. Goldenberg, 'Democratic and Republican Physicians Provide Different Care on Politicized Health Issue', *PNAS*, vol. 113, no. 42, 2016, pp. 11811–16.

7 K. Gift and T. Gift, 'Does Politics Influence Hiring? Evidence from a Randomized Experiment', *Political Behaviour*, vol. 37, no. 677, 2015, pp. 653–75, www.doi.org.

8 M. Levendusky, 'Review: *Changing Minds or Changing Channels? Partisan News in an Age of Choice By Kevin Arceneaux and Martin Johnson*', *Perspectives on Politics*, vol. 12, no. 2, 2014, pp. 474–5.

9 Shanto Iyengar, Gaurav Sood and Yphtach Lelkes, *Affect, Not Ideology: A Social Identity Perspective on Polarization*, Oxford University Press, 2012; John R. Alford, Peter K. Hatemi, John R. Hibbing et al., 'The Politics of Mate Choice', in *Journal of Politics*, vol. 73, no. 2, 2011, pp. 362–79.

10 Samara Klar and Alexandra McCoy, 'Partisan Motivated Evaluations of Sexual Misconduct and the Mitigating Role of the #MeToo Movement', *School of Government and Public Policy Works-In-Progress Series*, 2019.

11 Annie Murphy Paul, 'Where Bias Begins: The Truth About Stereotypes', www.psychologytoday.com, 1 May 1998.

12 Noam Gidron, James Adams and Will Horne, 'How Ideology, Economics and Institutions Shape Affective Polarization in Democratic Polities', *Annual Conference of the American Political Science Association,* 2018, www.ces.fas.harvard.edu.

13 Levi Boxell, Matthew Gentzkow and Jesse M. Shapiro, 'Cross-Country Trends in Affective Polarization', National Bureau of Economic Research, January 2020, in *Breaking the Social Media Prism*, Chris Bail, Princeton University Press, 2021, p.47.

14 *A Networked Age Guide to Communicating in a Polarised World*, MHP, 2021, www.mhpc.com.

15 Shanto Iyengar, Gaurav Sood and Yphtach Lelkes, *Affect, Not Ideology: A Social Identity Perspective on Polarization*; L. Mason, '"I Disrespectfully Agree": The Differential Effects of Partisan Sorting on Social and Issue Polarization', *American Journal of Political Science*, vol. 59, 2015, pp. 128–45, www.doi.org.

16 Bobby Duffy, *Why We're Wrong About Nearly Everything: A Theory of Human Misunderstanding*, Atlantic, US edition, 2019, p. 145.

17 Ibid., p. 95.

Chapter 1: Where Our Views Come From

1 Dominic Pulera, *Sharing the Dream: White Males in Multicultural America*, Continuum, 2004.

2 As we entered the twenty-first century the white nationalist movement became increasingly Islamophobic as well as anti-Semitic.

3 Derek changed his mind at university, leaving the white nationalist movement and strongly renouncing his previous views; Alex Chesterfield, Ali Goldsworthy and Laura Osborne, 'Leaving the white nationalist movement with Derek Black', *Changed My Mind*, www.opendemocracy.net, 10 January 2019.

4 *Biographical Memoirs: Volume 64*, National Academies Press, 1994, p. 321, www. doi.org.

5 The idea that humans are 'rational animals' is built into the name of our species, *Homo sapiens* (meaning wise), as well as the way we think about ourselves. See Patrick Rysiew, 'Rationality', www.oxfordbibliographies.com, 12 November 2012.

6 The term rationality is used in many different ways and can be interpreted differently according to the discipline involved, whether economics, philosophy, maths or psychology. Focusing on what is or isn't rational is beyond the bounds of this book. A good place to start reading more on the topic is Dan Sperber and Hugo Mercier, *The Enigma of Reason*, Penguin Random House, 2018 or Ralph Hertwig and Stefan M. Herzog, 'Fast and Frugal Heuristics: Tools of Social Rationality', *Social Cognition*, vol. 27, no. 5, 2009, pp. 661–98.

7 For more details, see Roy F. Baumeister and Kathleen D. Vohs, *Encyclopaedia of Social Psychology*, Sage, 2007.

8 For more details, see *The Handbook of Attitudes*, ed. Dolores Albarracin, Blair T. Johnson and Mark P. Zanna, Psychology Press, 2014.

9 S. H. Schwartz, 'Are There Universal Aspects in the Content and Structure of Values?', *Journal of Social Issues*, vol. 50, 1994, pp. 19–45.

10 Anja Neundorf and Kaat Smets, 'Political Socialization and the Making of Citizens', in *Oxford Handbooks Online in Political Science*, Oxford University Press, 2017, www.doi.org.

11 Richard G. Niemi and M. Kent Jennings, 'Issues and Inheritance in the Formation of Party Identification', *American Journal of Political Science*, vol. 35, no. 4, 1991, pp. 970–88, www.jstor.org.

12 For further reading on this, see Angus Campbell, Philip E. Converse, Warren E. Miller et al., *The American Voter*, University of Chicago Press, 1960; M. Kent Jennings and Richard G. Niemi, 'The Transmission of Political Values from Parent to Child', *The American Political Science Review*, vol. 62, no. 1, 1968, pp. 169–84; M. Kent Jennings, Laura Stoker and Jake Bowers, 'Politics Across Generations: Family Transmission Reexamined', *The Journal of Politics*, vol. 71, no. 3, July 2009, pp. 782–99.

13 David Easton and Jack Dennis, *Children in the Political System: Origins of Political Legitimacy*, Cambridge University Press, 1969.

14 Anja Neundorf and Kaat Smets, 'Political Socialization and the Making of Citizens'.

15 For more on this, see M. Kent Jennings and Richard G. Niemi, *Political Character of Adolescence: The Influence of Families and Schools*, Princeton University Press, 1974; Guillem Rico and M. Kent Jennings, 'The Formation of Left-Right Identification: Pathways and Correlates of Parental Influence', *Political Psychology*, vol. 37, no. 2, 2016, pp. 237–52.

16 Abdallah Fayyad, 'Are politics hereditary?', www.theatlantic.com, 1 June 2018; see J. Lyons, 'The Family and Partisan Socialization in Red and Blue America', *Political Psychology*, vol. 38, 2017, pp. 297–312, www.doi.org. Lyons' research highlights that parental influence is reduced by exposure to new environments and periods of turbulent politics.

17 Anja Neundorf and Kaat Smets, *Political Socialization and the Making of Citizens*, Oxford University Press, 2017.

18 Peter K. Hatemi and Rose McDermott, 'Give Me Attitudes', *Annual Review of Political Science*, vol. 19, 2016, pp. 331–50; C. L. Funk, K. B. Smith, J. R. Alford et al., 'Genetic and Environmental Transmission of Political Orientations', *Political Psychology*, vol. 34, no. 6, 2013, pp. 805–19, www.doi.org.

19 P. K. Hatemi, S. E. Medland, R. Klemmensen et al., 'Genetic Influences on Political Ideologies: Twin Analyses of 19 Measures of Political Ideologies from Five Democracies and Genome-Wide Findings from Three Populations', *Behavioural Genetics*, vol. 44, 2014, pp. 282–94, www.doi.org. For more on Alford's response to the critique of his research, see John R. Alford, C. L. Funk and J. R. Hibbing, 'Beyond Liberals and Conservatives to Political Genotypes and Phenotypes', *Perspectives on Politics*, vol. 6, no. 2, 2008, pp. 321–8, www.doi.org.

20 L. J. Eaves and H. J. Eysenck, 'Genetics and the Development of Social Attitudes', *Nature*, vol. 249, 1974, www.doi.org; N. G. Martin, L. J. Eaves, A. C. Heath et al., 'Transmission of Social Attitudes', *PNAS*, vol. 83, no. 12, 1986, pp. 4364–8, www.doi.org; L. J. Eaves, H. J. Eysenck and N. G. Martin, *Genes, Culture and Personality: An Empirical Approach*, Academic Press, 1989.

21 A. Tesser, 'The Importance of Heritability in Psychological Research: The Case of Attitudes', *Psychological Review*, vol. 100, no. 1, 1993, pp. 129–42, www.doi.org.

22 L. J. Eaves and H. J. Eysenck, 'Genetics and the Development of Social Attitudes'; N. G. Martin, L. J. Eaves, A. C. Heath et al., 'Transmission of Social Attitudes'; L. J. Eaves, H. J. Eysenck and N. G. Martin, *Genes, Culture and Personality: An Empirical Approach*.

23 Tom Gilovich, Dacher Keltner, Serena Chen et al., *Social Psychology*, W. W. Norton, 2006.

24 See P. K. Hatemi, L. Eaves and R. McDermott, 'It's the End of Ideology as We Know It', *Journal of Theoretical Politics*, vol. 24, no. 3, 2012, pp. 345–69; P. K, Hatemi, S. E. Medland, R. Klemmensen et al., 'Genetic Influences on Political Ideologies: Twin Analyses of 19 Measures of Political Ideologies from Five Democracies and Genome-Wide Findings from Three Populations', pp. 282–94.

25 Ibid.

26 Ibid.

27 For example, researchers were able to predict party affiliation with more than 80 per cent accuracy by viewing the participants' neural patterns while they played a simple card game designed to assess risk and reward strategies. The accuracy of this prediction is more than double what social or environmental models have produced. See D. Schreiber, G. Fonzo, A. N. Simmons et al., 'Red Brain, Blue Brain: Evaluative Processes Differ in Democrats and Republicans', *PloS One*, vol. 8, no. 2, 2013, www.doi.org.

28 The chart shows relative proportion of variance on each trait explained by the aggregate effect of all genetic influences and the combination of all environmental influences. Data derived from Hatemi and McDermott's 2012 research.

29 Epigenetics is the study of how behaviour and environment can cause changes that affect the way our genes work. See www.cdc.gov/genomics/disease/epigenetics.htm.

30 John R. Alford and John R. Hibbing, 'The Origin of Politics: An Evolutionary Theory of Political Behavior', *Perspectives on Politics*, vol. 2, no. 4, 2004, pp. 707–23, www.jstor.org; R. Plomin, M. J. Owen and P. McGuffin, 'The Genetic Basis of Complex Human Behaviors', *Science*, vol. 264, 1994, pp. 1733–9, www.doi.org.

31 Gary Marcus, 'Making the Mind', www.bostonreview.net, January 2004.

32 Bryce Donovan, 'The Science of Risk: How a Neuroscientist and Professional Climber Learned From One Another', www.web.musc.edu, 18 March 2019.

33 See Gary Marcus, 'Making the Mind'; Matt Ridley, *Nature via Nurture: Genes, Experience, and What Makes Us Human*, Harper Collins, 2003.

34 Peter K. Hatemi and Rose McDermott, 'Give Me Attitudes', *Annual Review of Political Science*, vol. 19, 2016, pp. 331–50.

35 Ibid.

36 Ibid. For a review of studies on the neurology of political attitudes and how the neural structures of people playing card games predicted their political orientation with over 80 per cent accuracy, see p. 333.

37 Ibid.

38 C. L. Funk, K. B. Smith, J. R. Alford et al., 'Genetic and Environmental Transmission of Political Orientations'.

39 Lemberg, which lay in Poland between 1919 and 1939, is now in Ukraine and called Lviv.

40 The methodology of Frenkel-Brunswik and her colleagues has susbsequently been criticised, and her original authoritarianism scale modified and relabelled right-wing authoritarianism (RWA). Despite its wide use in studies across a range of disciplines, the notion of right-wing authoritarianism (RWA) has generated considerable debate and criticism, particularly since it negatively stereotypes conservatism. See John Levi Marin, '*The Authoritarian Personality* 50 Years Later:

What Questions Are There for Political Psychology?', *Political Psychology,* vol. 22, no. 1, 2002, pp. 1–26; Stanley Feldman, 'Enforcing Social Conformity: A Theory of Authoritarianism', *Political Psychology*, vol. 24, no. 1, 2003, pp. 41–74.

41 Steven Ludeke, Wendy Johnson and Thomas J. Bouchard, '"Obedience to traditional authority": A Heritable Factor Underlying Authoritarianism, Conservatism and Religiousness', *Personality and Individual Differences*, vol. 55, no. 4, 2013, pp. 375–80. See also earlier Figure 3 on genetic and environmental explanations of the variance in attitudes to authoritarianism. Kathryn McCourt, Thomas J. Bouchard Jr., David T. Lykken et al., 'Authoritarianism Revisited: Genetic and Environmental Influences Examined in Twins Reared Apart and Together', *Personality and Individual Differences*, vol. 27, no. 5, 1999, pp. 985–1014.

42 Tom Jacobs, 'Authoritarianism: The Terrifying Trait That Trump Triggers', www. psmag.com, 26 March 2018; Karen Stenner and Jonathan Haidt, 'Authoritarianism Is Not a Momentary Madness, But an Eternal Dynamic Within Liberal Democracies', in *Can It Happen Here?*, ed. Cass Sunstein, Dey Street, 2018, pp.175–220.

43 D. R. Carney, J. T. Jost, S. D. Gosling et al., 'The Secret Lives of Liberals and Conservatives: Personality Profiles, Interaction Styles and the Things They Leave Behind', *Political Psychology*, vol. 29, 2008, pp. 807–40, www.doi.org; J. T. Jost, J. Glaser, A. W. Kruglanskiand et al., 'Political Conservatism as Motivated Social Cognition', *Psychological Bulletin*, vol. 129, no. 3, 2003, pp. 339–75, www.doi.org.

44 Alan S. Gerber, Gregory A. Huber, David Doherty et al., 'Personality and Political Attitudes: Relationships across Issue Domains and Political Contexts', *American Political Science Review*, vol. 104, no. 1, 2010, pp. 111–33, www.jstor.org; Jeffery J. Mondak, *Personality and the Foundations of Political Behaviour*, Cambridge University Press, 2008.

45 As with all theories of personality, the Big Five is influenced by nature and nurture. Twin studies (e.g. Kerry L. Jang, W. John Livesley and Philip A. Vernon, 'Heritability of the Big Five Personality Dimensions and Their Facets: A Twin Study', *Journal of Personality,* vol. 64, no. 3, 1996) find the 'heritability' (the amount of variance attributed to genes) of the Big Five traits is 40–60 per cent.

46 A. H. Sinclair, M. L. Stanley and P. Seli, 'Closed-Minded Cognition: Right-Wing Authoritarianism is Negatively Related to Belief Updating Following Prediction Error', *Psychonomic Bulletin and Review*, vol. 27, 2020, pp. 1348–61, www.doi.org.

47 For more, see L. R. Goldberg, 'An Alternative "Description of Personality": The Big-Five Factor Structure', *Journal of Personality and Social Psychology*, vol. 59, 1990, pp. 1216–29, www.doi.org; R. R. McCrae and P. T. Costa Jr, *Personality in Adulthood: A Five-Factor Theory Perspective*, second edition, Guilford Press, 2003, www.doi.org.

48 D. R. Carney, J. T. Jost, S. D. Gosling et al., 'The Secret Lives of Liberals and Conservatives: Personality Profiles, Interaction Styles, and the Things They Leave

Behind', *Political Psychology*, vol. 29, 2008, pp. 807–40, www.doi.org; J. T. Jost, J. Glaser, A. W. Kruglanski et al., 'Political Conservatism as Motivated Social Cognition', *Psychological Bulletin*, vol. 129, no. 3, 2003, pp. 339–75, www.doi.org.

49 J. Graham, J. Haidt and B. A. Nosek, 'Liberals and Conservatives Rely on Different Sets of Moral Foundations', *Journal of Personality and Social Psychology*, vol. 96, no. 5, 2009, pp. 1029–46; J. Haidt and J. Graham, 'When Morality Opposes Justice: Conservatives Have Moral Intuitions that Liberals May Not Recognize', *Social Justice Research*, vol. 20, 2007, pp. 98–116; J. Haidt and C. Joseph, 'Intuitive Ethics: How Innately Prepared Intuitions Generate Culturally Variable Virtues', *Daedalus*, vol. 133, no. 4, 2004, pp. 55–66.

50 Haidt's approach is not without its criticisms. See Oliver Scott Curry, 'What's Wrong with Moral Foundations Theory, and How to get Moral Psychology Right', www.behavioralscientist.org, 26 March 2019.

51 Haidt and Joseph, 'Intuitive Ethics: How Innately Prepared Intuitions Generate Culturally Variable Virtues'.

52 Jonathan Haidt, www.moralfoundations.org, October 2019.

53 Haidt defines this in terms of liberal or conservative. In a British context, 'progressive' equates reasonably well with 'liberal'.

54 Philip E. Converse, 'The Nature of Belief Systems in Mass Publics', *Critical Review*, vol. 18, nos. 1–3, 1964, pp. 1–74, www.doi.org.

55 C. L. Funk, K. B. Smith, J. R. Alford et al., 'Genetic and Environmental Transmission of Political Orientations'.

56 K. B. Smith, D. Oxley, M. V. Hibbing et al., 'Disgust Sensitivity and the Neurophysiology of Left-Right Political Orientations', *PloS ONE*, vol. 6, no. 10, www.doi.org; L. Sagiv, S. Roccas, J. Cieciuch et al., 'Personal Values in Human Life', *Nature Human Behaviour*, vol. 1, 2017, pp. 630–9, www.doi.org.

57 S. H. Schwartz, 'An Overview of the Schwartz Theory of Basic Values', *Online Readings in Psychology and Culture*, vol. 2, no. 1, 2012, www.doi.org; Y. Piurko, S. H. Schwartz and E. Davidov, 'Basic Personal Values and the Meaning of Left-Right Political Orientations in 20 Countries', *Political Psychology*, vol. 32, 2011, pp. 537–61, www.doi.org. Further research in over 82 different countries has validated Schwartz's 10 values.

58 The four dimensions illustrate the relationships between the values themselves. For example, openness to change (which includes values 3, 4 and 5) contrasts with conversation (which includes 8, 9 and 10).

59 A. Knafo and L. Sagiv, 'Values and Work Environment: Mapping 32 Occupations', *European Journal of Psychology of Education*, vol. 19, no. 3, 2004, pp. 255–73.

60 S. H. Schwartz, G. Caprara and M. Vecchione, 'Basic Personal Values, Core Political Values, and Voting: A Longitudinal Analysis', *Political Psychology*, vol. 31, no. 3, pp. 421–52.

61 B. C. Rathbun, J. D. Kertzer, J. Reifler et al., 'Taking Foreign Policy Personally: Personal Values and Foreign Policy Attitudes', *International Studies Quarterly*, vol. 60, no. 1, 2016, pp. 124–37.

62 These cultural world views – (a) hierarchic and egalitarian (grid) and (b) individualistic and solidarity (group) – originally developed by Mary Douglas, are broadly comparable to Schwartz's basic value dimensions. A 'low group' world view coheres with an individualistic social order, in which individuals are expected to secure their own needs without collective assistance, and in which individual interests enjoy immunity from regulation aimed at securing collective interests. A 'high group' world view, in contrast, supports a solidaristic or communitarian social order, in which collective needs trump individual initiative, and in which society is expected to secure the conditions of individual flourishing. A 'high grid' world view favours a hierarchical society, in which resources, opportunities, duties, rights, political offices and the like are distributed on the basis of conspicuous and largely fixed social characteristics – gender, race, class, lineage. A 'low grid' world view favours an egalitarian society, one that emphatically denies that social characteristics should matter in how resources, opportunities, duties, and the like are distributed.

63 For example, see P. C. Stern, T. Dietz, T. D. Abel et al., 'A Value-Belief-Norm Theory of Support for Social Movements: The Case of Environmentalism', *Human Ecology Review*, vol. 6, no. 2, 1999, pp. 81–97; S. H. Schwartz and W. Bilsky, 'Toward A Universal Psychological Structure of Human Values', *Journal of Personality and Social Psychology*, vol. 53, no. 3, 1987, pp. 550–62; S. van der Linden, 'The Social-Psychological Determinants of Climate Change Risk Perceptions: Towards a Comprehensive Model', *Journal of Environmental Psychology*, vol. 41, 2015, pp. 112–24.

64 Karen Stenner and Jonathan Haidt, 'Authoritarianism Is Not a Momentary Madness, But an Eternal Dynamic Within Liberal Democracies', in *Can It Happen Here?*, ed. Cass Sunstein, Dey Street, 2018, pp. 175–220.

65 Leor Zmigrod, 'The Role of Cognitive Rigidity in Political Ideologies: Theory, Evidence, and Future Directions', *Current Opinion in Behavioral Sciences*, vol. 34, 2020, pp. 34–39.

66 Leor Zmigrod, 'A Psychology of Ideology: Unpacking the Psychological Structure of Ideological Thinking', *PsyArXiv*, 2020, www.doi.org.

67 Leor Zmigrod, P. J. Rentfrow and T. W. Robbins, 'Cognitive Underpinnings of Nationalistic Ideology in the Context of Brexit', *PNAS*, vol. 115, no. 19, 2018.

68 When it came to Brexit their model accounted for a very significant proportion of the outcome (amounting to 47.6 per cent of the variance in support of Brexit). Many behaviours can only be explained to a small degree (low variance) so being able to account for a large proportion of the variance reflects a model that includes relevant and predictive variables.

69 Leor Zmigrod, P. J. Rentfrow and T. W. Robbins, 'The Partisan Mind: Is Extreme Political Partisanship Related to Cognitive Inflexibility?', *Journal of Experimental Psychology: General*, vol. 149, no. 3, 2020, pp. 407–18, www.doi.org.

70 Leor Zmigrod, S. Zmigrod, P. J. Rentfrow et al., 'Cognitive Flexibility and Religious Disbelief', *Psychological Research*, vol. 83, no. 3, 2018, pp. 1–11.

71 Leor Zmigrod, P. J. Rentfrow and T.W. Robbins, 'Cognitive Inflexibility Predicts Extremist Attitudes', *Frontiers in Psychology*, vol. 10, 2019, p. 989.

72 Leor Zmigrod, S. Zmigrod, P. J. Rentfrow et al., 'The Psychological Roots of Intellectual Humility: The Role of Intelligence and Cognitive Flexibility', *Personality and Individual Differences*, vol. 141, 2019, pp. 200–8.

73 Peter Wason, 'On the Failure to Eliminate Hypotheses in a Conceptual Task', *Quarterly Journal of Experimental Psychology*, vol. 12, no. 3, pp. 129–40.

74 As described in Ulrike Hahn and Adam J. L. Harris, 'What Does It Mean to be Biased: Motivated Reasoning and Rationality', *Psychology of Learning and Motivation*, Volume 61, ed. Brian H. Ross, Academic Press, 2014, pp. 41–102.

75 Raymond Nickerson, 'Confirmation Bias: A Ubiquitous Phenomenon in Many Guises', *Review of General Psychology*, vol. 2, no. 2, 1998, pp. 175–220.

76 Ibid. Confirmation bias is not about the deliberate suppression of particular content (e.g. looking at colour as opposed to shape), but about *strategy* (i.e. deciding where to look): what kinds of questions should we ask of the world in order to determine the accuracy of our beliefs? Nor does it mean that we necessarily have any actual psychological desire to confirm the hypothesis for which we seek evidence.

77 Gary Marcus, *Kluge: The Haphazard Construction of the Human Mind*, Faber & Faber, 2008, p. 56.

78 H. Mercier and D. Sperber, 'Why Do Humans Reason? Arguments for an Argumentative Theory', *Behavioral and Brain Sciences*, vol. 34, no. 2, 2010, pp. 57–74.

79 For a recent review, see D. Molden and E. Higgins, 'Motivated Thinking', in *The Cambridge Handbook of Thinking and Reasoning*, Cambridge University Press, 2005. Motivated reasoning has been studied in many areas. For example, participants can dig in and occasionally alter their memories to preserve a positive view of themselves (D. Dunning, J. Meyerowitz and A. Holzberg, 'Ambiguity and Self-Evaluation: The Role of Idiosyncratic Trait Definitions in Self-Serving Assessments

of Ability', *Journal of Personality and Social Psychology*', vol. 57, no. 6, 1989; B. H. Ross and G. H. Bower, 'Comparisons of Models of Associative Recall', *Memory and Cognition,* vol. 9, 1981; R. Sanitioso, Z. Kunda and G. T. Fong, 'Motivated Recruitment of Autobiographical Memories', *Journal of Personality and Social Psychology,* vol. 59, no. 2, 1990). They modify their causal theories to defend a favoured belief (Ziva Kunda, 'Motivated Inference: Self-Serving Generation and Evaluation of Causal Theories', *Journal of Personality and Social Psychology,* vol. 53, no. 4, 1987). When they are told the outcome of a game on which they had made a bet, they use events in the game to explain why they should have won when they lost (Tom Gilovich, 'Biased Evaluation and Persistence in Gambling', *Journal of Personality and Social Psychology,* vol. 44, no. 6, 1983). Political experts use similar strategies to explain away failed predictions and bolster their theories (Philip E. Tetlock, 'Sober Second Thought: The Effects of Accountability, Anger, and Authoritarianism on Attributions of Responsibility', *Personality and Social Psychology Bulletin,* vol. 24, no. 6, 1998). Reviewers fall prey to motivated reasoning and look for flaws in a paper in order to justify its rejection when they don't agree with its conclusions (Jonathan Koehler, 'The Influence of Prior Beliefs on Scientific Judgements of Evidence Quality', *Organizational Behavior and Human Decision Processes,* vol. 56, 1993; Michael Mahoney, 'Publication Prejudices: An Experimental Study of Confirmatory Bias in the Peer Review System', *Cognitive Therapy and Research,* vol. 1, 1977). In economic settings, people use information flexibly so as to be able to justify their preferred conclusions or arrive at the decision they favour (L. G. Boiney, J. Kennedy and P. Nye, 'Instrumental Bias in Motivated Reasoning: More When More is Needed', *Organizational Behavior and Human Decision Processes,* vol. 72, 1997; Christopher K. Hsee, 'Elastic Justification: How Tempting but Task-Irrelevant Factors Influence Decision', *Organizational Behavior and Human Decision Processes,* vol. 62, no. 3, 1995; M. E. Schweitzer and C. K. Hsee, 'Stretching the Truth: Elastic Justification and Motivated Communication of Uncertain Information', *Journal of Risk and Uncertainty,* vol. 25, 2002).

80 Ziva Kunda, 'The Case for Motivated Reasoning', *Psychological Bulletin,* vol. 108, no. 3, 1990, pp. 480–98; Ziva Kunda and R. Sanitioso, 'Motivated Changes in the Self-Concept', *Journal of Experimental Social Psychology,* vol. 25, 1989, pp. 272–85.

81 See Charles S. Taber and Milton Lodge, 'Motivated Skepticism in the Evaluation of Political Beliefs', *American Journal of Political Science,* vol. 50, no. 3, 2006, pp. 755–69, www.doi.org.

82   C. G. Lord, L. Ross and M. R. Lepper, 'Biased Assimilation and Attitude Polarization: The Effects of Prior Theories on Subsequently Considered Evidence', *Journal of Personality and Social Psychology*, vol. 37, no. 11, 1979, pp. 2098–109, www.doi.org.

83   'Biased evaluation' is actually a bit misleading (H. Mercier and D. Sperber, 'Why Do Humans Reason? Arguments for an Argumentative Theory', pp. 57–74). In this and many related experiments, despite being asked to evaluate the evidence, most participants produced arguments to support or rebut the argument depending on whether they agreed with its conclusion or not. Participants do not try to form an opinion: they already have one!

84   H. J. Greenwald, 'Dissonance and Relative Versus Absolute Attractiveness of Decision Alternatives', *Journal of Personality and Social Psychology*, vol. 11, no. 4, 1969, pp. 328–33, www.doi.org; E. M. Pomerantz, S. Chaiken and R. S. Tordesillas, 'Attitude Strength and Resistance Processes', *Journal of Personality and Social Psychology*, vol. 69, no. 3, 1995, pp. 408–19.

85   C. W. Korn, L. La Rosée, H. R. Heekeren et al., 'Processing of Information About Future Life Events in Borderline Personality Disorder', *Psychiatry Research*, vol. 245, 2016, pp. 719–24; C. W. Korn, K. Prehn, S. Q. Park et al., 'Positively Biased Processing of Self-Relevant Social Feedback', *The Journal of Neuroscience*, vol. 32, 2012.

86   See, for example, David Eil and Justin M. Rao, 'The Good News-Bad News Effect: Asymmetric Processing of Objective Information about Yourself', *American Economic Journal: Microeconomics*, vol. 3, no. 2, 2011, pp. 114–38.

87   C. Moutsiana, P. Fearon, L. Murray et al., 'Making an Effort to Feel Positive: Insecure Attachment in Infancy Predicts the Neural Underpinnings of Emotion Regulation in Adulthood', *Journal of Child Psychology and Psychiatry and Allied Disciplines*, vol. 55, no. 9, 2014, pp. 999–1008, www.doi.org; T. Sharot, C. W. Korn and R. Dolan, 'How Unrealistic Optimism is Maintained in the Face of Reality', *Nature Neuroscience*, vol. 14, 2011, pp. 1475–79, www.doi.org. For a counter view, see P. Shah, A. J. Harris, G. Bird et al., 'A Pessimistic View of Optimistic Belief Updating', *Cognitive Psychology*, vol. 90, 2016, pp. 71–127.

88   Charles S. Taber and Milton Lodge, 'Motivated Skepticism in the Evaluation of Political Beliefs', *American Journal of Political Science*, vol. 50, 2006, pp. 755–69, www.doi.org; Charles S. Taber, D. Cann and S. Kucsova, 'The Motivated Processing of Political Arguments', *Political Behavior*, vol. 31, no. 2, 2009, pp. 137–55, www.doi.org.

89   What if information is desirable in terms of outcome, but inconsistent with prior beliefs? In a recent experiment conducted in the wider context of the US presidential

election, a robust desirability bias was observed – individuals updated their beliefs more if the evidence was consistent with their desired outcome. This bias was independent of whether the evidence was consistent or inconsistent with their prior beliefs. See B. M. Tappin, L. van der Leer and R. T. McKay, 'The Heart Trumps the Head: Desirability Bias in Political Belief Revision', *Journal of Experimental Psychology: General*, vol. 146, no. 8, 2017, pp. 1143–9, www.ncbi.nlm.nih.gov.

90 C. L. Guenther and M. D. Alicke, 'Self-Enhancement and Belief Perseverance', *Journal of Experimental Social Psychology*, vol. 44, no. 3, 2017, pp. 706–12, www.doi.org. For an early demonstration, see Dale T. Miller and Michael Ross, 'Self-Serving Biases in the Attribution of Causality: Fact or Fiction?', *Psychological Bulletin*, vol. 82, no. 2, 1975, pp. 213–25.

91 J. Kaplan, S. Gimbel and S. Harris, 'Neural Correlates of Maintaining One's Political Beliefs in the Face of Counterevidence', *Scientific Reports*, vol. 6, 2016, www.doi.org.

92 Given that all participants were strong liberals, it is not clear how well these results would describe conservatives, or people with less polarised beliefs.

93 Tali Sharot, 'Intelligent People Have Greater Difficulty Changing Their Beliefs', World Economic Forum, June 2018, www.youtube.com/watch?v=UkdrZ9d3j6g.

94 Caitlin Drummond and Baruch Fischhoff, 'Science Knowledge and Polarization', Proceedings of the National Academy of Sciences, August 2017, www.doi.org.

95 See earlier footnote on caveats around rationality.

96 Elliot Aronson, 'Dissonance, Hypocrisy and the Self-Concept', in E. Harmon-Jones (ed.) *Cognitive Dissonance: Reexamining a Pivotal Theory in Psychology*, American Psychological Association, 2019, pp. 141–57, www.doi.org.

97 Arnaud D'Argembeau, 'On the Role of the Ventromedial Prefrontal Cortex in Self-Processing: The Valuation Hypothesis', *Frontiers in Human Neuroscience*, vol. 7, 2013.

98 Leon Festinger, Henry W. Riecken and Stanley Schachter, *When Prophecy Fails*, University of Minnesota Press, 1956.

99 Ibid., p. 3.

Chapter 2: From Individual Beliefs to Group Identities

1 Donelson R. Forsyth, *Group Dynamics*, Wadsworth Cengage Learning, sixth edition, 2014, p. 2.

2 Ibid.

3 C. E. Alexander, 'You Are What You Do', *Journal of Relational Child and Youth Care Practice*, vol. 20, no. 3, 2007, pp. 17–21; F. de Waal, *Primates and Philosophers: How Morality Evolved*, ed. S. Macedo and J. Ober, Princeton University Press, 2006.

4 L. M. Stennes, M. M. Burch, M. G. Sen et al., 'A Longitudinal Study of Gendered Vocabulary and Communicative Action in Young Children', *Developmental Psychology*, vol. 41, no. 1, 2005, pp. 75–88.

5 M. Kircher and L. Furby, 'Racial Preferences in Young Children', *Child Development*, vol. 42, no. 6, 1971, pp. 2076–8.

6 K. M. Zosuls, C. L. Martin, D. N. Ruble et al., '"It's Not That We Hate You": Understanding Children's Gender Attitudes and Expectancies About Peer Relationships', *British Journal of Developmental Psychology*, vol. 29, no. 2, pp. 288–304, 2011.

7 S. R. Waxman, 'Names Will Never Hurt Me? Naming and the Development of Racial and Gender Categories in Preschool-Aged Children', *European Journal of Social Psychology*, vol. 40, no. 2, 2010, pp. 593–610, www.doi.org; G. Diesendruck and H. HaLevi, 'The Role of Language, Appearance, and Culture in Children's Social Category-Based Induction', *Child Development*, vol. 77, no. 3, 2006, pp. 539–53, www.doi.org; H. McGlothlin and M. Killen, 'Intergroup Attitudes of European American Children Attending Ethnically Homogeneous Schools', *Child Development*, vol. 77, no. 5, 2006, pp. 1375–86, www.doi.org.

8 M. Plötner, H. Over, M. Carpenter et al., 'What Is a Group? Young Children's Perceptions of Different Types of Groups and Group Entitativity', *PloS ONE*, vol. 11, no. 3, 2016.

9 R. F. Baumeister and M. R. Leary, 'The Need to Belong: Desire For Interpersonal Attachments as a Fundamental Human Motivation', *Psychological Bulletin*, vol. 117, no. 3, 1995, pp. 497–529.

10 G. W. Allport, *The Nature of Prejudice*, Addison-Wesley, 1954; R. Kurzban and S. Neuberg, 'Managing Ingroup and Outgroup Relationships', in *The Handbook of Evolutionary Psychology*, ed. D. M. Buss, Wiley, 2005, pp. 653–75; D. S. Wilson and E. O Wilson, 'Rethinking the Theoretical Foundation of Sociobiology', *The Quarterly Review of Biology*, vol. 82, no. 4, 2007, pp. 327–48.

11 Henri Tajfel, 'Experiments in Intergroup Discrimination', *Scientific American*, vol. 223, 1970, pp. 96–102; Henri Tajfel and John C. Turner, 'An Integrative Theory of Intergroup Conflict', in *The Social Psychology of Intergroup Relations*, ed. W. G. Austin and S. Worchel, Brookes-Cole, 1979, pp. 33–7; Henri Tajfel, 'Social Psychology of Intergroup Relations', *Annual Review of Psychology*, vol. 33, 1982, pp. 1–39, www.doi.org; Michael A. Hogg and S. A. Reid, 'Social Identity, Self Categorization, and the Communication of Group Norms', *Communication Theory*, vol. 16, 2006, pp. 7–30, www.doi.org.

12 Michael A. Hogg and Graham Vaughan, *Social Psychology*, Pearson, seventh edition, 2014, p. 278.

13 Nick O'Shea, *Covid-19 and the Nation's Mental Health*, Centre for Mental Health, October 2020, www.centreformentalhealth.org.uk.

14 United Nations Standard Minimum Rules for The Treatment of Prisoners (the Nelson Mandela Rules), http://undocs.org/A/RES/70/175.

15 N. I. Eisenberger, M. D. Lieberman and K. D. Williams, 'Does Rejection Hurt? An FMRI Study of Social Exclusion', *Science*, vol. 302, 2003, pp. 290–2.

16 P. R. Kunz and M. Woolcott, 'Season's Greetings: From My Status to Yours', *Social Science Research*, vol. 5, no. 3, 1976, pp. 269–78.

17 For an excellent summary, see Donelson R. Forsyth, *Group Dynamics*.

18 D. Cartwright and A. Zander, 'Power and Influence in Groups: Introduction', *Group Dynamics: Research and Theory*, vol. 3, 1968, pp. 215–35; Kurt Lewin, *Field Theory of Social Science: Selected Theoretical Papers*, ed. Dorwin Cartwright, Harper & Brothers, 1951.

19 Roey Rosenbilth, 'Over Detroit Skies', *Huffpost*, 25 May 2011.

20 Donelson R. Forsyth, *Group Dynamics*.

21 Robert K. Merton, 'The Thomas Theorem and the Matthew Effect', *Social Forces*, vol. 74, no. 2, 1995, pp. 379–422.

22 D. S. Thomas and W. I. Thomas, *The Child in America*, Knopf, 1928, quoted in Robert K Merton, 'The Thomas Theorem and the Matthew Effect'.

23 D. T. Campbell, 'Common Fate, Similarity, and Other Indices of the Status of Aggregates of Persons as Social Entities', *Behavioral Science*, vol. 3, no. 1, 1958, pp. 14–25, www.doi.org.

24 Taken, with permission, from B. Lickel, D. L. Hamilton, G. Wieczorkowska, A. Lewis, S. J. Sherman and A. N. Uhles, (2000), 'Varieties of groups and the perception of group entitativity', *Journal of Personality and Social Psychology*, vol. 78, no. 2), pp. 223–246, www.doi.org.

25 Henri Tajfel and John C. Turner, 'An Integrative Theory of Intergroup Conflict'; John C. Turner, 'Social Categorization and the Self-Concept: A Social Cognitive Theory of Group Behavior', *Advances in Group Processes: Theory and Research Volume 2*, ed. E. J. Lawler, JAI Press, 1985, pp. 72–121; John C. Turner, *Rediscovering the Social Group: A Self-Categorization Theory*, Blackwell, 1987.

26 P. J. Oakes, 'The Salience of Social Categories', in *Rediscovering the Social Group*, ed. John C. Turner, M. A. Hogg, P. J. Oakes et al., Blackwell, 1987, pp. 117–41); P. J. Oakes and J. C. Turner, 'Is Limited Information Processing Capacity the Cause of Social Stereotyping?', in *European Review of Social Psychology*, ed. W. Stroebe and M. Hewstone, vol. 1, Wiley, 1990, pp. 111–35.

27 D. T. Campbell, 'Common Fate, Similarity, and Other Indices of the Status of Aggregates of Persons as Social Entities'.

28 R. J. Rydell, K. Hugenberg, D. Ray, D. M. Mackie, 'Implicit Theories About Groups and Stereotyping: The Role of Group Entitativity', *Personality and Social Psychology Bulletin,* vol. 33, no. 4, 2007, pp. 549–58.

29 M. T. Crawford, S. J. Sherman and D. L. Hamilton, 'Perceived Entitativity, Stereotype Formation, and the Interchangeability of Group Members', *Journal of Personality and Social Psychology,* vol. 83, no. 5, 2002, pp. 1076–94, www.doi.org.

30 N. Dasgupta, M. R. Banaji and R. P. Abelson, 'Group Entitativity and Group Perception: Associations Between Physical Features and Psychological Judgment', *Journal of Personality and Social Psychology,* vol. 77, no. 5, 1999, pp. 991–1003, www.doi.org.

31 A. Zander, E. Stotland and D. Wolfe, 'Unity of Group, Identification with Group, and Self-Esteem of Members', *Journal of Personality,* vol. 28, 1960, pp. 463–78, www.doi.org.

32 A. L. Alter and J. M. Darley, 'When the Association Between Appearance and Outcome Contaminates Social Judgment: A Bidirectional Model Linking Group Homogeneity and Collective Treatment', *Journal of Personality and Social Psychology,* vol. 97, no. 5, 2009, pp. 776–95.

33 This term 'groupishness' was popularised by Jonathan Haidt to illustrate how humans fundamentally like to be a part of something bigger than themselves; Jonathan Haidt, *The Righteous Mind,* Penguin Random House, 2012.

34 Donelson R. Forsyth, *Group Dynamics.*

35 These are kumi, han, gurupu, shudan, kyudan, renchuu, dojo, nakama, kurabu, saakuru, renshukai, kenkyukai, keikokai and shugyoaki.

36 Michael A. Hogg, 'Subjective Uncertainty Reduction Through Self-Categorization: A Motivational Theory of Social Identity Processes', *European Review of Social Psychology,* vol. 11, 2000, pp. 223–55.

37 Henri Tajfel, 'Experiments in Intergroup Discrimination'; Henri Tajfel and John C. Turner, 'An Integrative Theory of Intergroup Conflict'; Henri Tajfel, 'Social Psychology of Intergroup Relations'. Turner's self-categorization theory was developed as a companion theory to Tajfel's social identity theory, and the two theories are together known as the social identity approach.

38 V. L. Vignoles, C. Regalia, C. Manzi et al., 'Beyond Self-Esteem: Influence of Multiple Motives on Identity Construction', *Journal of Personality and Social Psychology,* vol. 90, no. 2, 2006, pp. 308–33.

39 This is an area that merits further research to establish the interplay between group hierarchies and polarisation.

40 R. B. Cialdini, R. J. Borden, A. Thorne et al., 'Basking in Reflected Glory: Three (Football) Field Studies', *Journal of Personality and Social Psychology*, vol. 34, no. 3, 1976, pp. 366–75.

41 B. Major, C. R. Kaiser and S. K. McCoy, 'It's Not My Fault: When and Why Attributions to Prejudice Protect Self-Esteem', *Personality and Social Psychology Bulletin*, vol. 29, no. 6, 2003, pp. 772–81.

42 S. J. Stanton, J. C. Beehner, E. K. Saini et al., 'Dominance, Politics, and Physiology: Voters' Testosterone Changes on the Night of the 2008 United States Presidential Election', *PloS ONE*, vol. 4, no. 10, 2009, www.doi.org.

43 A. Mazur and A. Booth, 'Testosterone and Dominance in Men', *Behavioral and Brain Sciences*, vol. 21, 1998, pp. 353–63, www.doi.org.

44 P. C. Bernhardt, J. M. Dabbs Jr, J. A. Fielden et al., 'Testosterone Changes During Vicarious Experiences of Winning and Losing Among Fans at Sporting Events', *Physiology & Behavior*, vol. 65, no. 1, 1998, pp. 59–62. Bernhardt measured football fans' testosterone changes after the outcome of a World Cup match. They found that even vicariously experiencing competition (i.e. watching one's favourite sports teams win or lose) increases testosterone in winners and decreases it in losers.

45 S. J. Stanton, J. C. Beehner, E. K. Saini et al., 'Dominance, Politics, and Physiology: Voters' Testosterone Changes on the Night of the 2008 United States Presidential Election', *PloS ONE*, vol. 4, no. 10, 2009, www.doi.org.

46 See B. A. Bettencourt and D. Hume, 'The Cognitive Contents of Social Group Identity: Values, Emotions, and Relationships', *European Journal of Social Psychology*, vol. 29, 1999, pp. 113–21; Daniel C. Feldman, 'The Development and Enforcement of Group Norms', *The Academy of Management Review*, vol. 9, no. 1, 1984, pp. 47–53, www.doi.org; Carolyn W. Sherif, Muzafer Sherif and Roger E. Nebergall, *Attitude and Attitude Change: The Social Judgment-Involvement Approach*, W. B. Saunders, 1965.

47 'Social Identity Theory', www.psychology.iresearchnet.com, 2021.

48 Muzafer Sherif, 'A Study of Some Social Factors in Perception: Chapter 2', *Archives of Psychology*, no. 187, 1935, pp. 17–22.

49 Mark K. MacNeil and Muzafer Sherif, 'Norm Change Over Subject Generations as a Function of Arbitrariness of Prescribed Norms', *Journal of Personality and Social Psychology*, vol. 34, 1976, pp. 762–73; and D. Abrams and J. M. Levine, 'Norm Formation: Revisiting Sherif's Autokinetic Illusion Study', in J. R. Smith and S. A. Haslam (eds), *Psychology: Revisiting the Classic Studies*, Sage Publications Ltd, 2012, pp. 57–75.

50 John C. Turner, 'Social Identification and Psychological Group Formation', in *The Social Dimension: European Developments in Social Psychology*, ed. Henri Tajfel, Cambridge University Press, 1984, p. 528, www.doi.org.

51 D. Abrams, M. Wetherell, S. Cochrane et al., 'Knowing What to Think by Knowing Who You Are: Self-Categorization and the Nature of Norm Formation, Conformity and Group Polarization', *British Journal of Social Psychology*, vol. 29, 1990, pp. 97–119, www.doi.org.

52 T. Newcomb, *Personality and Social Change: Attitude Formation in a Student Community*, Dryden, 1943.

53 D. F. Alwin, R. L. Cohen and T. Newcomb, *Political Attitudes Over the Life Span: The Bennington Women After Fifty Years*, University of Wisconsin Press, 1991; Charles E. Bidwell, 'Review of *Persistence and Change: Bennington College and Its Students After Twenty-Five Years* by Theodore M. Newcomb, Kathryn E. Koenig, Richard Flacks, and Donald P. Warwick', *Social Forces*, vol. 46, no. 4, 1968, pp. 566–7, www.doi.org.; Theodore M. Newcomb 'Attitude development as a function of reference groups: The Bennington Study' in Eleanor E. Maccoby, Theodore M. Newcomb, & Eugene L. Hartley, *Readings in Social Psychology*, New York, Academic Press, 1958.

54 Anja Neundorf and Kaat Smets, 'Political Socialization and the Making of Citizens'.

55 Logan Strother, Spencer Piston, Ezra Golberstein et al., 'College roommates have a modest but significant influence on each other's political ideology', *PNAS*, vol. 118, no. 2, 2021, www.doi.org.

56 Donald M. Taylor and Janet R. Doria, 'Self-Serving and Group-Serving Bias in Attribution', *The Journal of Social Psychology*, vol. 113, no. 2, 1981, pp. 201–11.

57 N. Ellemers, R. Spears, B. Doosje, 'Sticking Together or Falling Apart: In-Group Identification as a Psychological Determinant of Group Commitment Versus Individual Mobility', *Journal of Personality and Social Psychology*, vol. 72, no. 3, 1997, pp. 617–26.

58 Leah A. Fredman, Michael D. Buhrmester, Angel Gomez, William T. Fraser, Sanaz Talaifar, Skylar M. Brannon and William B. Swann, Jr, 'Identity Fusion, Extreme Pro-Group Behavior, and the Path to Defusion', *Social and Personality Psychology Compass* 9/9, 2015, pp. 468–80.

59 Ibid.

60 W. B. Swann and M. D. Buhrmester, 'Identity Fusion', *Current Directions in Psychological Science*, vol. 24, no. 1, 2015, pp. 52–7; W. B. Swann, J. Jetton Jr., A. Gomez et al., 'When Group Membership Gets Personal: A Theory of Identity Fusion', *Psychological Review*, vol. 119, no. 3, 2012, pp. 441–56.

61 W. B. Swann, M. D. Buhrmester, A. Gomez et al., 'What Makes a Group Worth Dying for? Identity Fusion Fosters Perception of Familial Ties, Promoting Self-Sacrifice', *Journal of Personality and Social Psychology*, vol. 106, no. 6, 2014, pp. 912–26.

62 Joseph Marks, Eloise Copland, Eleanor Loh et al., 'Epistemic Spillovers: Learning Others' Political Views Reduces the Ability to Assess and Use Their Expertise in Nonpolitical Domains', *Cognition*, vol. 188, 2019, pp. 74–84, www.doi.org.

63 Dan M. Kahan, Hank Jenkins-Smith and Donald Braman, 'Cultural Cognition of Scientific Consensus', *Journal of Risk Research*, vol. 14, 2010, pp. 147–74.

64 Ibid.

65 T. J. Leeper and R. Slothuus, 'Political Parties, Motivated Reasoning, and Public Opinion Formation', *Political Psychology*, vol. 35, 2014, pp. 129–56.

66 L. M. Bartels, 'Beyond the Running Tally: Partisan Bias in Political Perceptions', *Political Behavior*, vol. 24, 2002, pp. 117–50.

67 B. J. Gaines, J. H. Kuklinski, P. J. Quirk et al., 'Same Facts, Different Interpretations: Partisan Motivation and Opinion on Iraq', *Journal of Politics*, vol. 69, no. 4, 2007, pp. 957–74.

68 Dan M. Kahan, David A. Hoffman, Donald Braman et al., ' "They Saw a Protest": Cognitive Illiberalism and the Speech-Conduct Distinction', *Stanford Law Review*, vol. 64, no. 4, 2012, pp. 851–906.

69 Cohen was at Yale when the research was conducted in 2003.

70 G. L. Cohen, 'Party Over Policy: The Dominating Impact of Group Influence on Political Beliefs', *Journal of Personality and Social Psychology*, vol. 85, 2003, pp. 808–22; M. C. Schwalbe, G. L. Cohen and L. D. Ross, 'The Objectivity Illusion and Voter Polarization in the 2016 Presidential Election', *PNAS*, vol. 117, no. 35, 2020, pp. 21218–29.

71 Ibid.

72 Ibid.

73 Cass Sunstein, Sebastian Bobadilla-Suarez, Stephanie C. Lazzaro et al., 'How People Update Beliefs about Climate Change: Good News and Bad News', *Cornell Law Review*, vol. 102, no. 6, 2017, pp. 1431–43.

74 P. C. Ellsworth and S. R. Gross, 'Hardening of the Attitudes: Americans' Views on the Death Penalty', *Journal of Social Issues*, vol. 50, 1994, p. 23.

75 See interview with Christoper Achen and Larry Bartels in Sean Illing, 'Two Eminent Political Scientists: The Problem With Democracy is Voters', www.vox.com, 24 June 2017; see also M. Barber and J. C. Pope, 'Does Party Trump Ideology? Disentangling Party and Ideology in America', *American Political Science Review*, vol. 113, no. 1, 2019, pp. 38–54.

76 Russell J. Dalton, 'Party Identification and Its Implications', www.oxfordre.com, 9 May 2016.

77 Angus Campbell, Philip E. Converse, Warren E. Miller, and Donald E. Stokes, *The American Voter*.

78 According to analysis from the Kaiser Family Foundation (in collaboration with the Cook Political Report), in 2019 around 30 per cent of US voters didn't know how they planned to vote the following year; Ashley Kirzinger, Audrey Kearney, Mollyann Brodie et al., 'Data Note: A Look at Swing Voters Leading Up to the 2020 Election', www.kff.org, 5 September 2019. In contrast, a New York Times article published just before the US election noted: 'In a Times/Siena Poll of the country released last week, 9 percent of likely voters said they were still torn or they planned to support a third-party candidate. When including voters who said they were supporting Mr. Biden or Mr. Trump but only when pushed, that climbed to 13 percent'; Giovanni Russonello, 'Undecided Voters Could Still Decide the Election: They Tend to Dislike Trump', www.nytimes.com, 4 November 2020. UK elections have seen a greater level of volatility. In 2010, 32 per cent of voters picked a different party than the one they voted for in 2005. Between 2010 and 2015, 43 per cent of voters switched. In 2017, the figure dropped back down to 33 per cent. The pollster Lord Ashcroft said: 'More than half of voters said they made up their minds within the last month, with a quarter saying they did so within the last few days, including 16% saying they decided on election day or the day they filled in their postal ballot'; Lord Ashcroft, 'How Britain Voted and Why: My 2019 General Election Post-Vote Poll', www.lordashcroftpolls.com, 13 December 2019.

79 P. Molenberghs, V. Halász, J. B. Mattingley et al., 'Seeing is Believing: Neural Mechanisms of Action-Perceptions are Biased by Team Membership', *Human Brain Mapping,* vol. 34, no. 9, 2013, pp. 2055–68; Dan M. Kahan, David A. Hoffman, Donald Braman et al., '"They Saw a Protest": Cognitive Illiberalism and the Speech-Conduct Distinction'; E. M. Caruso, N. Mead and E. Balcetis, 'Political Partisanship Influences Perception of Biracial Candidates' Skin Tone', *PNAS,* vol. 106, no. 48, 2009, pp. 20168–73; Y. Granot, E. Balcetis, K. E. Schneider et al., 'Justice is Not Blind: Visual Attention Exaggerates Effects of Group Identification on Legal Punishment', *Journal of Experimental Psychology General,* vol. 143, no. 6, 2014, pp. 2196–208.

80 J. J. Van Bavel and A. Pereira, 'The Partisan Brain: An Identity-Based Model of Political Belief', *Trends in Cognitive Sciences,* vol. 22, no. 3, 2018, pp. 213–24, www.doi.org.

81 S. J. Frenda, Eric D. Knowles, William Saletan et al., 'False Memories of Fabricated Political Events', *Journal of Experimental Social Psychology,* vol. 49, no. 2, 2013,

pp. 280–6; see also L. Castelli and L. Carraro, 'Ideology is Related to Basic Cognitive Processes Involved in Attitude Formation', *Journal of Experimental Social Psychology*, vol. 47, no. 5, 2011, pp. 1013–6.

82 Steve Liesman, 'Optimism on economy, stocks surges since Trump election: CNBC survey', www.cnbc.com, 9 December 2016.

83 B. J. Gaines, J. H. Kuklinski, P. J. Quirk et al., 'Same Facts, Different Interpretations: Partisan Motivation and Opinion on Iraq'.

84 'The Perils of Perception 2018', www.ipsos.com, 6 December 2018, cited in 'The Public's Brexit Misconceptions', King's College London/Ipsos MORI, 2018, www.kcl.ac.uk.

85 Deborah Mattinson, 'Die-hard or devastated, they've stuck to their guns', www.thetimes.co.uk, 13 December 2020.

86 See also J. N. Druckman and T. Bolsen, 'Framing, Motivated Reasoning, and Opinions About Emergent Technologies', *Journal of Communication*, vol. 61, 2011, pp. 659–88, www.doi.org; Dan M. Kahan, Donald Braman, Paul Slovic et al., 'Cultural Cognition of the Risks and Benefits of Nanotechnology', *Nature Nanotechnology*, vol. 4, no. 2, 2009, pp. 87–91.

87 H. Allcott, L. Boxell, J. Conway et al., 'Polarization and Public Health: Partisan Differences in Social Distancing During the Coronavirus Pandemic', *Journal of Public Economics*, vol. 191, 2020.

88 J. J. Van Bavel and A. Pereira, 'The Partisan Brain: An Identity-Based Model of Political Belief'.

89 Ibid.

90 D. J. Flynn, B. Nyhan and J. Reifler, 'The Nature and Origins of Misperceptions: Understanding False and Supported Beliefs about Politics', *Political Psychology*, vol. 28, no. 51, 2017, pp. 127–50; J. N. Druckman and M. C. McGrath, 'The Evidence for Motivated Reasoning in Climate Change Preference Formation', *Nature Climate Change*, vol. 9, no. 2, 2019, pp. 111–9, www.doi.org.

91 The Bill – which became the Act – was discussed in 1975. It was the third of its kind; the first two were in 1965 and 1968.

92 See the example given in Henri Tajfel, *Human Groups and Social Categories*, Cambridge University Press, p. 228. It was also reported in *The Times*, 2 December 1975.

93 Born into a Jewish family in Poland as Hersz Mordche, Tajfel was studying at the Sorbonne in France when his homeland was invaded by Germany. Fluent in French, Tajfel went on to serve in the French army but was captured and became a prisoner of war. Identified as Jewish, all his immediate family and many of his

friends were killed in the Holocaust. Tajfel hid his Polish Jewish heritage and survived the prisoner of war camp by adopting a French identity. In his academic career at the universities of Oxford and Bristol, Tajfel's ambition was to understand how group identity can cause so much harm.

Chapter 3: Us and Them

1 Muzafer Sherif, *Experimental Study of Positive and Negative Intergroup Attitudes Between Experimentally Produced Groups: Robbers Cave Study,* Norman, 1954.

2 G. Andreeva, 'Cognitive Processes in Developing Groups', in *Directions in Soviet Social Psychology,* ed. L. H. Strickland, Springer, 1984, pp. 67–82.

3 L. N. Diab, 'A Study of Intragroup and Intergroup Relations among Experimentally Produced Small Groups', *Genetic Psychology Monograph,* vol. 82, 1970, pp. 49–82. in *Us and Them: The Science of Identity,* David Berreby, University of Chicago Press, 2008, p. 178.

4 In 1954, Allport published *The Nature of Prejudice* based on his research. The book was widely read and cited, not only by other psychologists but also by civil rights leaders such as Martin Luther King, Jr., and Malcolm X.

5 M. B. Brewer and D. T. Campbell, *Ethnocentrism and Intergroup Attitudes: East African Evidence,* Sage, 1976.

6 R. D. Vanneman and T. F. Pettigrew, 'Race and Relative Deprivation in the Urban United States', *Race,* vol. 13, no. 4, 1972, pp. 461–86, www.doi.org.

7 See Tom Gilovich, Dacher Keltner, Serena Chen et al., *Social Psychology,* p. 443.

8 Henri Tajfel, M. G. Billig, R. P. Bundy et al., 'Social Categorization and Intergroup Behaviour', *European Journal of Social Psychology,* vol. 1, no. 2, 1971, pp. 149–77.

9 Tajfel wanted to ascertain which of the three payoffs would have the biggest influence on the participants' choices: 1. Maximum joint profit (giving the largest reward to members of both groups); 2. Largest possible reward to the ingroup (giving the largest reward to the member of the ingroup regardless of the reward to the boy from the other group); or 3. Maximum difference (giving the largest possible difference in rewards between members of the different groups, i.e., 'ingroup' favouritism).

10 Henri Tajfel, M. G. Billig, R. P. Bundy et al., 'Social Categorization and Intergroup Behaviour', p. 173.

11 M. B. Brewer and R. J. Brown, 'Intergroup Relations', in *The Handbook of Social Psychology,* ed. D. T. Gilbert, S. T. Fiske and G. Lindzey, McGraw-Hill, fourth edition, 1998, pp. 554–94; M. A. Hogg, D. Abrams, S. Otten et al., 'The Social Identity

Perspective: Intergroup Relations, Self-Conception, and Small Groups', *Small Group Research*, vol. 35, no. 3, 2004, pp. 246–76; V. Yzerbyt and S. Demoulin, 'Intergroup Relations', in *The Handbook of Social Psychology*, ed. D. T. Gilbert, S. T. Fiske and G. Lindzey, Wiley, fifth edition, 2010, pp. 1024–83, www.doi.org.

12 D. Abrams, A. Rutland, J. M. Ferrell et al., 'Children's Judgments of Disloyal and Immoral Peer Behavior: Subjective Group Dynamics in Minimal Intergroup Contexts', *Child Development*, vol. 79, no. 2, 2008, pp. 444–61; Y. Dunham, A. S. Baron and S. Carey, 'Consequences of "Minimal" Group Affiliations in Children', *Child Development*, vol. 82, no. 3, 2011, pp. 793–811; M. G. Schug, A. Shusterman, H. Barth et al., 'Minimal-Group Membership Influences Children's Responses to Novel Experience with Group Members', *Developmental Science*, vol. 16, no. 1, 2013, pp. 47–55; M. D. Yee and R. Brown, 'Self-Evaluations and Intergroup Attitudes in Children Aged Three to Nine', *Child Development*, vol. 63, no. 3, 1992, pp. 619–29.

13 M. B. Brewer, 'The Psychology of Prejudice: Ingroup Love and Outgroup Hate?', *Journal of Social Issues*, vol. 55, 1999, pp. 429–44, www.doi.org; Miles Hewstone, Mark Rubin and Hazel Willis, 'Intergroup Bias', *Annual Review of Psychology*, vol. 53, no. 1, 2002, pp. 575–604; B. Mullen, R. Brown and C. Smith, 'Ingroup Bias as a Function of Salience, Relevance, and Status: An integration', *European Journal of Social Psychology*, vol. 22, no. 2, 1992, pp. 103–22, www.doi.org.

14 Seven-year-old children in one town were asked, 'Which are better, the children in this town or in Smithfield [a neighbouring town]?' Almost all replied, 'The children in this town.' When asked why, the children usually replied, 'I don't know the kids in Smithfield'. What is alien is regarded as less good, even inferior (but there is not necessarily hostility). See Allport, *Nature of Prejudice*.

15 Henri Tajfel and John C. Turner, 'An Integrative Theory of Intergroup Conflict'.

16 J. Krueger, 'Psychology of Social Categorization', in *International Encyclopedia of the Social and Behavioral Sciences*, ed. Neil J. Smelser and Paul B. Baltes, Pergamon, 2001, pp. 14219–23; M.B. Brewer, 'Social Psychology of Intergroup Relations', in *International Encyclopedia of the Social and Behavioral Sciences*, ed. Neil J. Smelser and Paul B. Baltes, Pergamon, 2001, pp. 7728–33.

17 Self-categorisation is a particular kind of social categorisation developed by Turner as an extension of Social Identity Theory.

18 A. P. Fiske, N. Haslam and S. T. Fiske, 'Confusing One Person With Another: What Errors Reveal About the Elementary Forms of Social Relations', *Journal of Personality and Social Psychology*, vol. 60, no. 5, 1991, pp. 656–74, www.doi.org; C. Stangor, L. Lynch, C. Duan et al., 'Categorization of Individuals on the Basis of

Multiple Social Features', *Journal of Personality and Social Psychology,* vol. 62, no. 2, 1992, pp. 207–18, www.doi.org.

19 We define partisan as a strong supporter of a party, cause, or person.

20 Sara Holbolt's research at LSE suggests that opinion-based groups and identities emerge in situations where people are compelled to take sides on an issue or in response to dramatic events, such as Brexit. Later in this chapter, we return to how people categorise themselves and others in a political context – when not restricted to identification with a particular political party. Sara Hobolt, Thomas J. Leeper and James Tilley, 'Divided by the Vote: Affective Polarization in the Wake of the Brexit Referendum', *British Journal of Political Science,* 2020, pp. 1–18, www.eprints.lse.ac.uk; M. T. Parker and R. Janoff-Bulman, 'Lessons from Morality-Based Social Identity: The Power of Outgroup "Hate," Not Just Ingroup "Love"', *Social Justice Research,* vol. 26, no. 1, 2013, pp. 81–96.

21 C. McGarty, A. M. Bliuc, E. F. Thomas et al., 'Collective Action as the Material Expression of Opinion-Based Group Membership', *Journal of Social Issues,* vol. 65, no. 4, 2009, pp. 839–57.

22 Story taken from Tom Gilovich, Dacher Keltner, Serena Chen et al., *Social Psychology,* p. 239.

23 See earlier caveats in Chapter 1 around the concept of rationality.

24 For example, Robert E. Lane, *Political Life: Why People Get Involved in Politics,* The Free Press, 1959; Philip E. Converse, 'The Nature of Belief Systems in Mass Publics'; D. F. Alwin, R. L. Cohen and T. Newcomb, *Political Attitudes Over the Life Span: The Bennington Women After Fifty Years,* p. 159; Donald Green, Bradley Palmquist and Eric Schickler, *Partisan Hearts and Minds: Political Parties and the Social Identities of Voters,* Yale University Press, 2002; Herbert Hyman, *Political Socialization: A Study in the Psychology of Political Behaviour,* The Free Press, 1959; D. O. Sears and C. L. Funk, 'Evidence of the Long-Term Persistence of Adults' Political Predispositions', *The Journal of Politics,* vol. 61, no. 1, 1999; M. Kent Jennings, Laura Stoker and Jake Bowers, 'Politics across Generations: Family Transmission Re-examined'.

25 Quoted in L. Huddy, 'From Group Identity to Political Cohesion and Commitment', in *The Oxford Handbook of Political Psychology,* ed. D. O. Sears, J. S. Levy and L. Huddy, Oxford University Press, second edition, 2013.

26 Sara Hobolt, Thomas J. Leeper and James Tilley, 'Divided By the Vote: Affective Polarization in the Wake of the Brexit Referendum'.

27 Ibid., p. 8: 'During the 2015 General Election, only a year ahead of the Brexit referendum vote, less than 10 per cent of British people identified membership of

the EU as being among the two most important issues facing Britain (see IPSOS Mori, 2018, for time series data on the question: "What would you say is the most important issue facing Britain today? What do you see as other important issues facing Britain today?") and debates about the EU played a minimal role in the election campaign. Prior to the referendum Britain's role in the EU was not a highly salient political issue, never mind a matter of identity politics. There were no labels for sides in the Brexit debate until the campaign itself'. Over a year after the referendum, 75 per cent of the UK population had a Brexit identity, in that they could come up with a single answer to the question 'Since the EU referendum last year, some people now think of themselves as Leavers and Remainers, do you think of yourself as a Leaver, a Remainer, or neither a Leaver or Remainer?' Respondents demonstrated that they had developed strong emotional attachments to their new identities – indeed attachments that were slightly stronger than the ones they felt to a particular political party (see p. 13 of Holbolt paper for detailed surveys). Five statements were used to measure emotional attachment, for example: 'When people criticise the [respondent identity] it feels like a personal insult'.

28 Research into what determined the outcome of the Brexit vote indicates that the referendum mobilised an underlying fault line between social liberals with weak national identities, who tend to be younger and have more educational qualifications, and social conservatives with stronger national identities, who tend to be older with fewer educational qualifications (Sara B. Hobolt and James Tilley, 'Fleeing the Centre: The Rise of Challenger Parties in the Aftermath of the Euro Crisis', *West European Politics*, vol. 39, no. 5, 2016, pp. 971–91; Harold D. Clarke, Matthew Goodwin and Paul Whiteley, *Brexit: Why Britain Voted to Leave the European Union*, University of Essex, 2017; Geoffrey Evans and James Tilley, *The New Politics of Class: The Political Exclusion of the British Working Class*, Oxford University Press, 2017; Will Jennings and Gerry Stoker, 'Tilting Towards the Cosmopolitan Axis? Political Change in England and the 2017 General Election', *The Political Quarterly*, vol. 88, no. 3, 2017; John Curtice, 'General Election 2017: A New Two-Party Politics?', *Political Insight*, vol. 8, no. 2, 2017); 'Daniel Hannan, The Man Who Brought You Brexit', *Guardian*, www.theguardian.com, 29 September 2016.

29 Laura G. E. Smith, Emma F. Thomas and Craig McGarty, '"We Must Be the Change We Want to See in the World": Integrating Norms and Identities Through Social Interaction', *Political Psychology*, vol. 36, no. 5, 2015, pp. 543–57.

30 L. Huddy, 'From Social to Political Identity: A Critical Examination of Social Identity Theory', *Political Psychology*, vol. 22, no. 1, 2001, pp. 127–56; L. Huddy, 'From Group Identity to Political Cohesion and Commitment', pp. 737–73.

31 Cass R. Sunstein, 'Partyism', *University of Chicago Legal Forum*, vol. 2015, www.chicagounbound.uchicago.edu.

32 In Chapter 2 we described the way humans 'see' groups to maximise entitativity (which Turner described as 'metacontrast') by emphasising the differences between groups and the similarities within groups.

33 P. W. Linville, P. Salovey and G. W. Fischer, 'Stereotyping and Perceived Distributions of Social Characteristics: An Application to Ingroup-Outgroup Perception', in *Prejudice, Discrimination and Racism*, ed. J. F. Dovidio and S. L. Gaertner, Academic Press, pp. 165–208; T. M. Ostrom and C. Sedikides, 'Out-Group Homogeneity Effects in Natural and Minimal Groups', *Psychological Bulletin*, vol. 112, no. 3, 1992, pp. 536–552; C. A. Meissner and J. C. Brigham, 'Thirty Years of Investigating the Own-Race Bias in Memory for Faces: A Meta-Analytic Review', *Psychology, Public Policy, and Law*, vol. 7, 2001, pp. 3–35.

34 P. W. Linville, G. W. Fischer and P. Salovey, 'Perceived Distributions of Characteristics of Ingroup and Outgroup Members: Empirical Evidence and a Computer Simulation', *Journal of Personality and Social Psychology*, vol. 57, 1989, pp. 165–88; B. Mullen and L. Hu, 'Perceptions of Ingroup and Outgroup Variability: A Meta-Analytic Integration', *Basic and Applied Social Psychology*, vol. 10, pp. 233–52; D. M. Messick and D. M. Mackie, 'Intergroup Relations', *Annual Review of Psychology*, vol. 40, 1989, pp. 45–81, www.doi.org.

35 For more detail, see M. B. Brewer and R. J. Brown, 'Intergroup Relations'; R. Brown, 'Social Identity Theory: Past Achievements, Current Problems and Future Challenges', *European Journal of Social Psychology*, vol. 30, 2000; Thierry Devos, Loraine Devos-Comby and J. C. Deschamps, 'Asymmetries in Judgements of Ingroup and Outgroup Variability', *European Review of Social Psychology*, vol. 7, no. 1, 1996; P. W. Linville, G. W. Fischer and P. Salovey, 'Perceived Distributions of Characteristics of Ingroup and Outgroup Members: Empirical Evidence and a Computer Simulation'; B. Park, C. S. Ryan and C. M. Judd, 'Role of Meaningful Subgroups in Explaining Differences in Perceived Variability for Ingroups and Outgroups', *Journal of Personality and Social Psychology*, vol. 63, no. 4, 1992, pp. 553–67.

36 P. W. Linville and E. E. Jones, 'Polarized Appraisals of Outgroup Members', *Journal of Personality and Social Psychology*, vol. 38, no. 5, 1980, pp. 689–703, www.doi.org.

37 Z. Richards and M. Hewstone, 'Subtyping and Subgrouping: Processes for the Prevention and Promotion of Stereotype Change', *Personality and Social Psychology Review*, vol. 5, no. 1, 2001, pp. 52–73.

38 S. A. Haslam, P. J. Oakes and J. C. Turner, 'Social Identity, Self-Categorization, and the Perceived Homogeneity of Ingroups and Outgroups: The Interaction Between

Social Motivation and Cognition', in *Handbook of Motivation and Cognition: The Interpersonal Context Volume 3*, Guilford Press, 1996, pp. 182–222.

39 M. Schalle and L. G. Conway III, 'Influence of Impression-Management Goals on the Emerging Contents of Group Stereotypes: Support for a Social-Evolutionary Process', *Personality and Social Psychology Bulletin*, vol. 25, no. 7, 1999, pp. 819–33, www.doi.org.

40 S. Guimond, 'Group Socialization and Prejudice: The Social Transmission of Intergroup Attitudes and Beliefs', *European Journal of Social Psychology*, vol. 30, no. 3, 2000, pp. 335–54, www.doi.org.

41 C. M. Judd and B. Park, 'Definition and Assessment of Accuracy in Social Stereotypes', *Psychological Review*, vol. 100, no. 1, 1993, pp. 109–28, www.doi.org.

42 Douglas J. Ahler and G. Sood, 'The Parties in Our Heads: Misperceptions about Party Composition and Their Consequences', *The Journal of Politics*, vol. 80, 2018, pp. 964–81.

43 Alex Chesterfield, Ali Goldsworthy and Laura Osborne, 'Interview with Danny Finkelstein', *Changed My Mind*, www.opendemocracy.net, 6 March 2019.

44 J. A. Bargh, 'The Cognitive Monster: The Case Against the Controllability of Automatic Stereotype Effects', in *Dual-Process Theories in Social Psychology*, ed. S. Chaiken and Y. Trope, Guilford Press, 1999, pp. 361–82.

45 Annie Murphy Paul, 'Where Bias Begins: The Truth About Stereotypes'.

46 Walter Lippmann, *The World Outside and the Pictures in Our Heads*, Macmillan, 1922, pp. 3–32.

47 L. Hirschfeld, *Race in the Making: Cognition, Culture and the Child's Construction of Human Kinds*, MIT Press, 1996; V. Yzerbyt, G. Schadron, J. Leyens et al., 'Social Judgeability: The Impact of Meta-Informational Cues on the Use of Stereotypes', *Journal of Personality and Social Psychology*, vol. 66, 1994, pp. 48–55.

48 J. E. Rothschild, A. J. Howat, R. M. Shafranek et al., 'Pigeonholing Partisans: Stereotypes of Party Supporters and Partisan Polarization', *Political Behavior*, vol. 41, 2019, p. 423–43, www.doi.org.

49 Yaacov Trope and Erik P. Thompson, 'Looking for Truth in All the Wrong Places? Asymmetric Search of Individuating Information About Stereotyped Group Members', *Journal of Personality and Social Psychology*, vol. 73, no. 2, 1997, pp. 229–41.

50 L. Lepore and R. Brown, 'Category and Stereotype Activation: Is Prejudice Inevitable?', *Journal of Personality and Social Psychology*, vol. 72, no. 2, 1997, pp. 275–87, www.doi.org.

51 J. Fyock and C. Stangor, 'The Role of Memory Biases in Stereotype Maintenance', *British Journal of Social Psychology*, vol. 33, no. 3, 1994, pp. 331–43, www.doi.org.

52 M. Snyder, E. D. Tanke and E. Berscheid, 'Social Perception and Interpersonal Behavior: On the Self-Fulfilling Nature of Social Stereotypes', *Journal of Personality and Social Psychology,* vol. 35, no. 9, 1977, pp. 656–66, www.doi.org; C. O. Word, M. P. Zanna and J. Cooper, 'The Nonverbal Mediation of Self-Fulfilling Prophecies in Interracial Interaction', *Journal of Experimental Social Psychology,* vol. 10, no. 2, 1974, pp. 109–20, www.doi.org.

53 L. A. Rudman and J. E. Phelan, 'The Effect of Priming Gender Roles on Women's Implicit Gender Beliefs and Career Aspirations', *Social Psychology,* vol. 41, no. 3, 2010, pp. 192–202, www.doi.org.

54 Coffey Bentley and Patrick A. McLaughlin, 'Do Masculine Names Help Female Lawyers Become Judges? Evidence from South Carolina', *American Law and Economics Review,* vol. 11, no. 1, 2009, pp. 112–33, www.doi.org.

55 L. von Stockhausen, S. Koeser and S. Sczesny, 'The Gender Typicality of Faces and its Impact on Visual Processing and on Hiring Decisions', *Experimental Psychology,* vol. 60, no. 6, pp. 444–52, www.doi.org.

56 L. Jussim, S. L. Robustelli, and T. R. Cain, 'Teacher Expectations and Self-Fulfilling Prophecies', in *Handbook of Motivation at School,* ed. K. R. Wenzel and A. Wigfield, Routledge, 2009, pp. 349–80.

57 C. M. Steele and J. Aronson, 'Stereotype Threat and the Intellectual Test Performance of African Americans', *Journal of Personality and Social Psychology,* vol. 69, no. 5, 1995, pp. 797–811; Steve Stroessner and Catherine Good, 'Stereotype Threat: An Overview', www.studymode.com, 24 June 2013.

58 M. Chen and J. A. Bargh, 'Consequences of Automatic Evaluation: Immediate Behavioral Predispositions to Approach or Avoid the Stimulus', *Personality and Social Psychology Bulletin,* vol. 25, no. 2, 1999, pp. 215–24, www.doi.org.

59 C. Stangor and C. Duan, 'Effects of Multiple Task Demands Upon Memory for Information About Social Groups', *Journal of Experimental Social Psychology,* vol. 27, no. 4, 1991, pp. 357–78, www.doi.org.

60 E. A. Plant and D. A. Butz, 'The Causes and Consequences of an Avoidance-Focus for Interracial Interactions', *Personality and Social Psychology Bulletin,* vol. 32, no. 6, 2006, pp. 833–46, www.doi.org; J. N. Shelton, 'Interpersonal Concerns in Social Encounters Between Majority and Minority Group Members', *Group Processes and Intergroup Relations,* vol. 6, 2003, pp. 171–85.

61 C. N. Macrae, G. V. Bodenhausen and A. B. Milne et al., 'Out of Mind but Back in Sight: Stereotypes on the Rebound', *Journal of Personality and Social Psychology,* vol. 67, no. 5, 1994, pp. 808–17, www.doi.org.

62 S. T. Fiske, 'Warmth and Competence: Stereotype Content Issues for Clinicians and Researchers', *Canadian Psychology,* vol. 53, no. 1, pp. 14–20, www.doi.org.

63 S. T. Fiske, 'Stereotype Content: Warmth and Competence Endure', *Current Directions in Psychological Science*, vol. 27, no. 2, 2018, pp. 67–73.

64 Ibid.

65 S. Hinkle and R. J. Brown, 'Intergroup Comparisons and Social Identity', in *Social Identity Theory: Constructive and Critical Advances*, Springer, 1990, pp. 48–70.

66 Naomi Ellemers, Russell Spears and Bertjan Doosje, 'Self and Social Identity', *Annual Review of Psychology*, vol. 53, no. 1, 2002, pp. 161–86.

67 Naomi Ellemers, Russell Spears and Bertjan Doosje, 'Self-Stereotyping in the Face of Threats to Group Status and Distinctiveness: The Role of Group Identification', *Personality and Social Psychology Bulletin*, vol. 23, 1997, pp. 538–53.

68 What happens if the outgroup 'wins'? Our self-esteem is now threatened, hurting us and leading to 'negative social identity'. How do we respond? To help us feel better about ourselves and increase our sense of self-esteem we may leave our ingroup and join another group that has higher value or status. However, this is not always practical, particularly if our group is defined by social categories such as gender, class, ethnic background, and so on. Alternatively we may opt to exaggerate the ingroup's strengths or deny the positive aspects of the outgroup or simply avoid comparing our ingroup to a relevant outgroup altogether. A more creative strategy, known technically as 'disidentification', is to minimise our personal connection with our group, perhaps by referring to it as 'they' rather than 'we' (compare Cialdini's football fan story in Chapter 2).

69 Mark Levine, Amy Prosser, David Evans et al., 'Identity and Emergency Intervention: How Social Group Membership and Inclusiveness of Group Boundaries Shape Helping Behavior', *Personality and Social Psychology Bulletin*, vol. 31, 2005, pp. 443–53.

70 A. H. Hastorf and H. Cantril, 'They Saw a Game: A Case Study', *Journal of Abnormal Psychology*, vol. 49, no. 1, 1954, pp. 129–34.

71 T. J. Leeper and R. Slothuus, 'Political Parties, Motivated Reasoning, and Public Opinion Formation', *Political Psychology*, vol. 35, 2014, pp. 129–56.

72 Milton Lodge and Charles S. Taber, *The Rationalizing Voter*, Cambridge University Press, 2013, p. 281.

73 D. J. O'Keefe, *Persuasion Theory and Research*, Sage, second edition, 2002.

74 Keith Stanovich and Richard West first used these terms to describe dual-process models of thinking. Kahneman then popularised them in his 2011 book *Thinking Fast and Slow*; K. E. Stanovich and R. F. West, 'Individual Difference in Reasoning: Implications for the Rationality Debate?', *Behavioral and Brain Sciences*, vol. 23, no. 5, 2001; Daniel Kahneman, *Thinking Fast and Slow*, Farrar, Straus and Giroux, 2011.

75 Dan M. Kahan, 'The Expressive Rationality of Inaccurate Perceptions', *Behavioral Brain Sciences*, vol. 40, no. 6, 2017.

76 M. B. Petersen, M. Skov, S. Serritzlew et al., 'Motivated Reasoning and Political Parties: Evidence for Increased Processing in the Face of Party Cues', *Political Behavior*, vol. 35, no. 4, 2013, pp. 831–54.

77 Charles S. Taber and Milton Lodge, 'Motivated Skepticism in the Evaluation of Political Beliefs'; see also Dan M. Kahan, Donald Braman, Paul Slovic et al., 'Cultural Cognition of the Risks and Benefits of Nanotechnology'; David P. Redlawsk, 'Hot Cognition or Cool Consideration? Testing the Effects of Motivated Reasoning on Political Decision Making', *Journal of Politics*, vol. 64, no. 4, 2002.

78 Dan M. Kahan, 'Ideology, Motivated Reasoning, and Cognitive Reflection', *Judgment and Decision Making*, vol. 8, 2013, pp. 407–24.

79 Milton Lodge and Charles S. Taber, 'The Illusion of Choice in Democratic Politics: The Unconscious Impact of Motivated Political Reasoning', *Political Psychology*, vol. 37, 2016, pp. 61–85.

80 C. Drummond and B. Fischhoff, 'Individuals with Greater Science Literacy and Education Have More Polarized Beliefs on Controversial Science Topics', *PNAS*, vol. 114, 2017, pp. 9587–92.

81 Dan M. Kahan, E. Peters, M. Wittlin et al., 'The Polarizing Impact of Science Literacy and Numeracy on Perceived Climate Change Risks', *Nature Climate Change*, vol. 2, 2012, pp. 732–5. For more on this, see T. Bolsen, J. N. Druckman and F. L. Cook, 'Citizens', Scientists', and Policy Advisors' Beliefs About Global Warming', *Annals of the American Academy of Political and Social Science*, vol. 658, no. 1, 2015, pp. 271–95; Dan M. Kahan, 'Climate-Science Communication and the Measurement Problem', *Political Psychology*, vol. 36, no. 1, 2015, pp. 1–43; L. C. Hamilton, M. J. Cutler and A. P. Schaefer, 'Public Knowledge and Concern About Polar-Region Warming', *Polar Geography*, vol. 35, no. 2, 2012, pp. 155–68.

82 Dan M. Kahan, E. Peters, M. Wittlin et al., 'The Polarizing Impact of Science Literacy and Numeracy on Perceived Climate Change Risks'.

83 J. J. Van Bavel and A. Pereira, 'The Partisan Brain: An Identity-Based Model of Political Belief'.

84 David Schkade, Cass Sunstein and Reid Hastie, 'When Deliberation Produces Extremism', *Critical Review: A Journal of Politics and Society*, vol. 22, no. 2, 2010, pp. 227–52.

85 Timur Kuran, *Private Truths, Public Lies: The Social Consequences of Preference Falsification*, Harvard University Press, 1997.

86 A. Edmondson, 'Psychological Safety and Learning Behavior in Work Teams', *Administrative Science Quarterly*, vol. 44, no. 2, 1999, pp. 350–83, www.doi.org.

87 Timur Kuran, 'Another Road to Serfdom: Cascading Intolerance' in *Can It Happen Here?*, ed. Cass Sunstein, Dey Street, 2018, pp. 233–276.

88 Note that this is not just a group-size issue. Minorities can polarise, too. See S. Moscovici and C. Faucheux, 'Social Influence, Conformity Bias, and the Study of Active Minorities', in *Advances in Experimental Social Psychology Volume 6*, Academic Press, 1972, pp. 149–202.

89 M. Rollwage, R. J. Dolan and S. M. Fleming, 'Metacognitive Failure as a Feature of Those Holding Radical Beliefs', *Current Biology*, vol. 28, no. 24, 2018, pp. 4014–21; H. Fischer, D. Amelung and N. Said, 'The Accuracy of German Citizens' Confidence in Their Climate Change Knowledge', *Nature Climate Change*, vol. 9, no. 10, 2019, pp. 776–80.

90 A. Lerman, M. Sadin and S. Trachtman, 'Policy Uptake as Political Behavior: Evidence from the Affordable Care Act', *American Political Science Review*, vol. 111, no. 4, 2017, pp. 755–70.

91 Simon Maloy, 'This is what ripping holes in Obamacare looks like: The horrific human cost of the GOP's anti-reform crusade', www.salon.com, 14 May 2015.

92 For more on this, see S. J. Westwood, S. Iyengar, S. Walgrave et al., 'The Tie That Divides: Cross-National Evidence of the Primacy of Partyism', *European Journal of Political Research*, vol. 57, no. 2, 2015; Markus Wagner and D. Bischof, 'Do Voters Polarize When Radical Parties Enter Parliament?', *American Journal of Political Studies,* vol. 63, no. 4, 2019; Noam Gidron, J. Adams and W. Horne, 'Toward a Comparative Research Agenda on Affective Polarization in Mass Publics', *APSA Comparative Politics Newsletter,* vol. 29, 2019; Andres Reiljan, ' "Fear and Loathing Across Party Lines" (also) in Europe: Affective Polarisation in European Party Systems', *European Journal of Political Research,* vol. 59, no. 2, 2019; A. Lauka, J. McCoy, R. B. Firat, 'Mass Partisan Polarization: Measuring a Relational Concept', *American Behavioral Scientist,* vol. 62, no. 1, 2018; Eelco Harteveld, 'Ticking All the Boxes: A Comparative Study of Social Sorting and Affective Polarization', www.eelcoharteveld.nl, 2020.

93 Quoted in Shanto Iyengar, Gaurav Sood and Yphtach Lelkes, *Affect, Not Ideology: A Social Identity Perspective on Polarization.*

94 Ibid.

95 Ibid.

96 John R. Alford, Peter K. Hatemi, John R. Hibbing et al., 'The Politics of Mate Choice'.

97 Stephen Nicholson, Chelsea Coe, Jason Emory et al., 'The Politics of Beauty: The Effects of Partisan Bias on Physical Attractiveness', *Political Behavior*, vol. 38, 2016.

98 R. M. Shafranek, 'Political Considerations in Non-Political Decisions: A Conjoint Analysis of Roommate Choice'.

99 Sharon Barnhardt, 'Near and Dear? Evaluating the Impact of Neighbor Diversity on Inter-Religious Attitude', 2009.

100 S. Banet-Weiser, *Authentic™: The Politics of Ambivalence in a Brand Culture*, New York University Press, 2012, www.doi.org.

101 Daniel Della Posta, Yongren Shi and Michael Macy, 'Why Do Liberals Drink Lattes?', *American Journal of Sociology*, 2015, pp. 1473–1511.

102 Cleopatra Veloutsou and Luiz Moutinho, 'Brand Relationships Through Brand Reputation and Brand Tribalism', *Journal of Business Research*, vol. 62, no. 3, 2009, pp. 314–22.

103 Deborah Mattinson and Max Templer, 'How we uncovered Labour's quinoa quandry', www.totalpolitics.com, 14 September 2018.

104 'My Dear Countrymen', *The Boston Post-Boy and Advertiser*, 16 November 1767, www.masshist.org.

105 'Address to the Ladies', *The Boston Post-Boy and Advertiser*, 16 November 1767, www.masshist.org.

106 Thomas Roulet, *The Power of Being Divisive*, Stanford University Press, 2020.

107 Brent Hannify, 'Nine Line Will Not Apologize for a Damn Thing', GOVx, September 2016, www.govx.com.

108 Christopher McConnell, Yotam Margalit, Neil Malhotra et al., 'The Economic Consequences of Partisanship in a Polarized Era', *American Journal of Political Science*, vol. 64, no. 4, 2020, pp. 1047–9.

109 K. Michelitch, 'Does Electoral Competition Exacerbate Interethnic or Interpartisan Economic Discrimination? Evidence from a Field Experiment in Market Price Bargaining', *American Political Science Review*, vol. 109, no. 1, 2015, pp. 43–61.

110 Xueming Luo, Michael Wiles and Sascha Raithel, 'Make the Most of a Polarizing Brand', www.hbr.org, November 2013.

111 Gary Coombe, 'Should Brands Take a Stand?', www.britishbrandsgroup.org.uk, July 2019.

112 Kim Elsesser, 'Will Gillette's Ad Campaign On Sexual Harassment And Toxic Masculinity Bring Change?', www.forbes.com, 14 January 2019.

113 Steve Wyche, 'Colin Kaepernick explains why he sat during the national anthem', www.nfl.com, 27 August 2016.

114 'The State of Moral Marketing', www.brandwatch.com.

115 Kacey Culliney, 'P&G 2019 sales strong but Gillette write-down drags down profits', 7 August 2019, www.cosmeticsdesign-europe.com.

116 Helen Lewis, 'How Capitalism Drives Cancel Culture. Beware splashy corporate gestures when they leave existing power structures intact', *The Atlantic*, July 2020, www.theatlantic.com.

117 'Edelman UK Trust Barometer 2020', www.edelman.co.uk, 28 January 2020.

118 'The Deloitte Global Millennial Survey 2020: Millennials and Gen Zs hold the key to creating a "better normal"', www2.deloitte.com, 25 June 2020.

119 'CEO Activism in 2018: The Purposeful CEO', www.webershandwick.com, March 2019.

Chapter 4: The Economic Factor

1 Noam Gidron, J. Adams and W. Horne, 'Toward a Comparative Research Agenda on Affective Polarization in Mass Publics'.

2 Ricardo Reis, 'The Portugese Slump and Crash and the Euro Crisis', *Brookings Papers on Economic Activity*, vol. 46, no. 1, 2013, pp. 143–210.

3 'Eurozone crisis: Portugal protests against austerity', www.bbc.co.uk, 2 March 2013.

4 Helena Smith, 'Greece erupts in violent protest as citizens face a future of harsh austerity', www.theguardian.com, 2 May 2010.

5 Tim Alberta, *American Carnage: On the Front Lines of the Republican Civil War and the Rise of President Trump*, Harper Collins, 2019, p. 30.

6 R. D. Vanneman and T. F. Pettigrew, 'Race and Relative Deprivation in the Urban United States'.

7 'Affective polarisation is defined as the difference between survey respondents' thermometer ratings of their in-party vs the average of out-parties. Higher values denote higher levels of polarisation', Noam Gidron, J. Adams and W. Horne, *American Affective Polarization in Comparative Perspective*, Cambridge University Press, 2020, p. 27. We are grateful to the authors for sharing the original data with us.

8 *Under Pressure: The Squeezed Middle Class*, OECD Publishing, 2019.

9 Colombia joined in 2020, taking the OECD to 37 countries.

10 This doesn't mean that the presence of a middle class prevents polarisation, just that it reduces the chances of polarisation reaching pernicious levels.

11 Adam Przeworski and Fernando Limongi, 'Modernization: Theories and Facts', *World Politics*, vol. 49, no. 2, 1997, pp. 155–83.

12 Dambisa Moyo, 'Why the survival of democracy depends on a strong middle-class', *The Globe and Mail*, 20 April 2018.

13 'Growth and the middle class', www.democracyjournal.org, Spring 2011.

14 Benedict Anderson, *Imagined Communities, Reflections on the Origin and Spread of Nationalism*, Verso, 2016, p. 18.

15 Some interpret the American Dream as financial success, others as personal freedom and the ability to enjoy a good life.

16 Noam Gidron, J. Adams and W. Horne, *American Affective Polarization in Comparative Perspective*, p. 27.

17 Ezra Klein, 'You have a better chance of achieving "the American dream" in Canada than in America', www.vox.com, 15 August 2019.

18 Jack Citrin and Laura Stoker, 'Political Trust in a Cynical Age', *Annual Review of Political Science*, vol. 21, no. 1, 2018, pp. 49–70.

19 Ibid.

20 Ibid.

21 'Financial crisis eroded trust in government, OECD says', www.cbc.ca, 5 November 2013.

22 R. S. Foa, A. Klassen, D. Wenger et al., 'Youth and Satisfaction with Democracy: Reversing the Democratic Disconnect?', Centre for the Future of Democracy, 2020.

23 Fred Lewsey, 'Faith in democracy: millennials are the most disillusioned generation 'in living memory', www.cam.ac.uk, October 2020.

24 Manuel Funke, Moritz Schularick and Christoph Trebesch, 'Going to Extremes: Politics After Financial Crises, 1870–2014', *European Economic Review*, vol. 88, 2016.

25 Economic stress and fear are excellent predictors for the success of a number of populist movements, including those in Ukraine (Yuri M. Zhukov, 'Trading Hard Hats for Combat Helmets: The Economics of Rebellion in Eastern Ukraine', *Journal of Comparative Economics*, vol. 44, no. 1, 2016) as well as the United States and United Kingdom (Martin Obschonka, Michael Stuetzer, Peter Rentfrow et al., 'In the Shadow of Coal: How Large-Scale Industries Contributed to Present-Day Regional Differences in Personality and Well-Being', *Journal of Personality and Social Psychology*, vol. 115, 2018; Sascha O. Becker, Thiemo Fetze and Dennis Novy, 'Who Voted for Brexit? A Comprehensive District-Level Analysis', *Economic Policy*, vol. 32, no. 92, 2017, pp. 601–50).

26 They did not find the same pattern for normal recessions or macroeconomic shocks that are not financial in nature.

27 Keith Hennessey, 'Memorandum for a member of Congress', www.keithhennessey.com, 25 February 2017.

28 Sara B. Hobolt and James Tilley, 'Fleeing the Centre: The Rise of Challenger Parties in the Aftermath of the Euro Crisis'.

29 See H. Winkler, 'The Effect of Income Inequality on Political Polarization: Evidence from European Regions 2002–2014', *Economics and Politics*, vol. 31, no. 2, 2019, pp. 137–62.

30 R. S. Foa, A. Klassen, D. Wenger et al., 'Youth and Satisfaction with Democracy: Reversing the Democratic Disconnect?', Centre for the Future of Democracy, 2020.

31 M. Azzimonti, 'Barriers to Investment in Polarized Societies', *American Economic Review*, vol. 101, 2011, pp. 2182–204.

32 Vicky Pryce, 'Want to see the economic damage already done by Brexit? Look to lost business investment', www.prospectmagazine.co.uk, 10 September 2019.

33 'Climate change: 11 facts you need to know', www.conservation.org, June 2020.

34 https://blogs.worldbank.org/climatechange/covid-climate-change-and-poverty-avoiding-worst-impacts.

35 Sam Mednick, 'Caught between climate crisis and armed violence in Burkina Faso', www.aljazeera.com, 27 July 2020.

36 Alexander J. Stewart, Nolan McCarty and Joanna J. Bryson, 'Polarization Under Rising Inequality and Economic Decline', *Science Advances*, vol. 6, no. 50, 11 December 2020, https://advances.sciencemag.org.

37 A study of millions of edits on Wikipedia showed that teams that drew contributions both from liberals and conservatives produced better articles, not just on politics but non-political issues too. Discussion that led to these finished products was more substantive, constructive, and unsurprisingly, longer.

38 Tjaša Redek, Andrej Sušjan and Črt Kostevc, 'Unemployment and Self-Concept', *Economic Research-Ekonomska Istraživanja*, vol. 26, no. 1, 2013, pp. 185–200.

39 J. Smári, E. Arason, H. Hafsteinsson et al., 'Unemployment, Coping and Psychological Distress', *Scandinavian Journal of Psychology*, vol. 38, no. 2, 1997, pp. 151–6; G. Grossi, 'Coping and Emotional Distress in a Sample of Swedish Unemployed', *Scandinavian Journal of Psychology*, vol. 40, 1999, pp. 157–65.

40 A. O. de Berker, R. B. Rutledge, C. Mathys et al., 'Computations of Uncertainty Mediate Acute Stress Responses in Humans', *Nature Communications*, vol. 7, 2016.

41 John Dewey (1929), *The Quest for Certainty: A Study of the Relation of Knowledge and Action*, Kessinger, reprint, 2005; also referenced in Michael A. Hogg, 'From Uncertainty to Extremism: Social Categorization and Identity Processes', *Current Directions in Psychological Science*, vol. 23, no. 5, 2014, pp. 338–42.

42 Michael A. Hogg, 'The Search for Social Identity Leads to "Us" versus "Them"', www.scientificamerican.com, 1 September 2019.

43 For a summary of research effects in meta-analysis, see E. U. Choi, Michael A. Hogg, 'Self-Uncertainty and Group Identification: A Meta-Analysis', *Group Processes and Intergroup Relations*, vol. 23, no. 4, 2020, pp. 483–501.

44 Michael A. Hogg and J. Adelman, 'Uncertainty–Identity Theory: Extreme Groups, Radical Behavior, and Authoritarian Leadership', *Journal of Social Issues*, vol. 69,

no. 3, 2013, pp. 436–54. Note these studies were part of a larger study over a two-year period in Israel and Palestine. There were over 1,600 self-identified Israeli and Palestinian participants of all major religious affiliations.

45 Ibid., p. 44. The researchers note 'the intergroup context in Israel/Palestine is one that casts Israeli Jews as the dominant high status numerical majority, and Palestinian Muslims as the lower status subordinate numerical minority. The two groups have starkly different positions of material power, and associated with this they have ready access to quite different resources to promote and protect their identities. Each group will have different beliefs about what actions are realistically likely to be effective for them as a group. Israeli Jews have substantially greater resources, including a large, well-equipped modern conventional military, than do Palestinian Muslims. Thus the two groups are constrained to resort to different tactics to promote their respective agendas – if they turn to extremism and resort to violence they are likely to employ and support different forms of violence that they believe have the greatest collective efficacy (Martjin Van Zomeren, Tom Postmes and Russell Spears, 'Toward an Integrative Social Identity Model of Collective Action: A Quantitative Research Synthesis of Three Socio-Psychological Perspectives', *Psychological Bulletin*, vol. 134, 2008, pp. 504–35). Israelis will resort to conventional military actions rather than suicide bombings, as they do not need to do the latter; whereas Palestinians will resort to suicide bombing rather than military actions, as they cannot do the latter.'

46 Z. P. Hohman, Michael A. Hogg and M. C. Bligh, 'Identity and Intergroup Leadership: Asymmetrical Political and National Identification in Response to Uncertainty', *Self and Identity*, vol. 9, no. 2, 2010, pp. 113–28.

47 Ibid., the researchers note: 'the speech itself was carefully chosen to ensure that the narrative could be read equally well as raising uncertainty or as lowering uncertainty, and that it did not invoke fear or anxiety. So, for example, a speech focusing on terrorism or the US military presence in Iraq would have been too fear-oriented. A number of alternatives were informally piloted. The best match to our criteria was a short (one page, single-spaced) speech about the environment given by President George W. Bush during one of his weekly radio addresses on 16 April 2005'. See the Appendix of the research paper for more detail.

48 D. K. Sherman, Michael A. Hogg and A. T. Maitner, 'Perceived Polarization: Reconciling Ingroup and Intergroup Perceptions Under Uncertainty', *Group Processes and Intergroup Relations*, vol. 12, no. 1, 2009, pp. 95–109.

49 L. Greenberg, 'Emotion-Focused Therapy', *Clinical Psychology and Psychotherapy*, vol. 11, no. 1, 2004, pp. 3–16. Cited in D. K. Sherman, Michael A. Hogg and

A. T. Maitner, 'Perceived Polarization: Reconciling Ingroup and Intergroup Perceptions Under Uncertainty'.

50 They experimentally manipulated feelings of uncertainty to look at their role in the relation between ingroup entitativity and perceptions of intergroup polarisation. Because the study was designed as an experiment, the researchers were able to look at causation as well as correlation.

51 Geert Hofstede's seminal study of culture defined uncertainty avoidance as the extent to which individuals within societies are socialised to avoid uncertain situations by establishing formal rules and structures; Geert Hofstede (1980), *Culture's Consequences: Comparing Values, Behaviors, Institutions and Organizations Across Nations*, Sage, second edition, 2001. See also www.hi.hofstede-insights.com.

52 Examples cited from Thomas Snitker, 'The Impact of Culture on User Research', in *Handbook of Global User Research*, Elsevier, 2010, p. 266, table 9.2.

53 For all explanations see this interactive tool: www.hofstede-insights.com.

54 Ronald Fischer and Crysta Derham, 'Is Ingroup Bias Culture-Dependent? A Meta-Analysis Across 18 Societies', *SpringerPlus*, vol. 5, 2016.

55 The IMF's World Uncertainty Index is a quarterly measure of uncertainty related to economic and political events. It covers 143 countries – all countries in the world with a population of at least two million – and provides data for the past 60 years.

56 Hites Ahir, Nicholas Bloom and Davide Fuceri, '60 Years of Uncertainty', IMF, March 2020, www.imf.org.

57 Kristalina Georgieva, 'The Financial Sector in the 2020s: Building a More Inclusive System in the New Decade', www.imf.org, 17 January 2020.

58 There are two caveats about uncertainty reduction. The first is that you cannot feel completely certain, only less uncertain (Henry N. Pollack, *Uncertain Science . . . Uncertain World*, Cambridge University Press, 2010). Living in an entirely certain world would probably be very boring (T. D. Wilson, D. B. Centerbar, D. A. Kermer et al., 'The Pleasures of Uncertainty: Prolonging Positive Moods in Ways People Do Not Anticipate', *Journal of Personality and Social Psychology*, vol. 88, no. 1, 2005, pp. 5–21), and people who claim complete certainty are often viewed with suspicion as dangerously deluded narcissists, zealots or ideologues. Typically, people work to reduce uncertainty until they feel 'sufficiently' certain about something to desist from dedicating further cognitive effort to uncertainty reduction – this provides closure (K. Koffka, *Principles of Gestalt Psychology*, Harcourt Brace, 1935) and allows cognitive effort to be directed elsewhere. Hence uncertainty-identity theory is about reducing uncertainty rather than achieving

certainty (Michael A. Hogg, Janice Adelman and Robert Blagg, 'Religion in the Face of Uncertainty: An Uncertainty-Identity Theory Account of Religiousness', *Personality and Social Psychology Review*, vol. 14, 2009, pp. 72–83).

59 A. Voci, 'The Link Between Identification and Ingroup Favouritism: Effects of Threat to Social Identity and Trust-Related Emotions', *British Journal of Social Psychology*, vol. 45, 2006, pp. 265–84.

60 Walter Stephan, Oscar Ybarra and Kimberly Rios, 'Intergroup Threat Theory', in *Handbook of Prejudice, Stereotyping, and Discrimination*, Routledge, 2009, pp. 43–59.

61 The theory also differentiates between threats felt individually vs felt at a group level. For example, a person could feel as though immigrants pose a threat to their nation's economy (realistic group threat), to their own ability to secure a job (realistic individual threat), to their nation's fundamental values (symbolic group threat), or to their own sense that they are valued and respected by others (symbolic individual threat).

62 Cicero Roberto Pereira, Jorge Vala, Jacques Philippe Leyens et al., 'From Infra-Humanization to Discrimination: Mediation of Symbolic Threat Needs Egalitarian Norms', *Journal of Experimental Social Psychology*, vol. 45, 2009, pp. 336–45.

63 Marta C. Gonzalez, Cesat Hidalgo and Albert-Laszlo Barabasi, 'Understanding Individual Human Mobility Patterns', *Nature*, 2008, p. 453.

64 Walter Stephan, Oscar Ybarra and Kimberly Rios, 'Intergroup Threat Theory'; Ute Stephan, Lorraine Uhlaner and Chris Stride, 'Institutions and Social Entrepreneurship: The Role of Institutional Voids, Institutional Support and Institutional Configurations', *Journal of International Business Studies*, vol. 46, 2015, pp. 308–31.

65 Kimberly Rios, Nicholas Sosa and Hannah Osborn, 'An Experimental Approach to Intergroup Threat Theory: Manipulations, Moderators, and Consequences of Realistic vs. Symbolic Threat', *European Review of Social Psychology*, vol. 29, no. 1, 2018.

66 Rita Guerra, Agnieszka Golec de Zavala and Claudia Simao, 'The Relationship between the Brexit Vote and Individual Predictors of Prejudice: Collective Narcissism, Right Wing Authoritarianism, Social Dominance Orientation', *Frontiers in Psychology*, vol. 8, 2017.

67 'Britain's immigration paradox: Areas with lots of migrants voted mainly to Remain. Or did they?', www.economist.com, 8 July 2016.

68 Jill Rutter and Rosie Carter, 'National Conversation on Immigration', www.nationalconversation.uk, September 2018.

69 Amy Leach, 'Public attitudes towards immigration and immigrants: what people think, why, and how to influence them', www.odi.org, 14 September 2020.

70 Moshe Semyonov, Rebeca Raijman, Anat Yom Tov et al., 'Population Size, Perceived Threat, and Exclusion: A Multiple-Indicators Analysis of Attitudes Toward Foreigners in Germany', *Social Science Research*, vol. 33, no. 4, 2004.

71 Irina Mosel, Christopher Smart, Marta Foresti et al., 'Public narratives and attitudes towards refugees and other migrants, Germany country profile', www.odi.org, 1 November 2019.

72 Amy Leach, 'Public attitudes towards immigration and immigrants: what people think, why, and how to influence them', www.odi.org, 14 September 2020.

73 J. T. Jost, I. Liviatan, J. van der Toorn et al., 'System Justification: A Motivational Process with Implications for Social Conflict', in *Justice and Conflicts*, ed. E. Kals and J. Maes, Springer, 2011.

74 'Stanford Professor Jeffrey Pfeffer on Why Flattery Changes Minds', Open Democracy, 8 August 2020, www.opendemocracy.net.

75 Archie Brown, *The Myth of the Strong Leader: Political Leadership in the Modern Age*, Basic Books, 2014, p. 368. Brown credits his Oxford colleague Stephen Whitefield for sharing the data that allowed him to draw these conclusions.

Chapter 5: The Political Factor

1 Timothy Tackett, *Becoming a Revolutionary: The Deputies of the French National Assembly and the Emergence of a Revolutionary Culture 1789–1790*, Pennsylvania University Press, 2006.

2 Anthony Downs, 'An Economic Theory of Political Action in a Democracy', *Journal of Political Economy*, vol. 65, no. 2, 1957, pp. 135–50.

3 Downs does acknowledge that this is a time and labour exhaustive process, so people are likely to take shortcuts and search for ideologies and use a sample to see if they agree.

4 Marcus Roberts, 'Do manifestos matter?', www.yougov.co.uk, 12 May 2017.

5 Alison F. Smith, *Political Party Membership in New Democracies: Electoral Rules in Central and East Europe*, Palgrave MacMillan, 2020, p. 124.

6 King's College London, '120 Years of the Labour Party: In conversation with Tony Blair', www.youtube.com, 20 February 2020.

7 'Wahl-o-mat: Interactive voting tool', www.bpd.de, 2 May 2021.

8 E. Rainsford, N. Randall, A. Dobson et al., 'Evaluating Verto: Bite the Ballot's youth voter advice app for the 2015 General Election', www.eprint.ac.uk, 2016 and

Cristina Burack, 'Undecided French voter? There's an app for that!', www.dw.com, 15 April 2017.

9 Simon Munzert, Pablo Barberá, Andrew Guess, JungHwan Yang, 'Do Online Voter Guides Empower Citizens? Evidence from a Field Experiment with Digital Trace Data', *Public Opinion Quarterly*, vol. 84, no. 3, 2020, pp. 675–698.

10 P. Goren, 'Party Identification and Core Political Values', *American Journal of Political Science*, vol. 49, no. 4, 2005, pp. 881–96.

11 L. M. Bartels, 'Beyond the Running Tally: Partisan Bias in Political Perceptions'.

12 B. J. Gaines, J. H. Kuklinski, P. J. Quirk et al., 'Same Facts, Different Interpretations: Partisan Motivation and Opinion on Iraq'.

13 L. M. Bartels, 'Partisanship and Voting Behaviour 1952–1996', *American Journal of Political Science*, vol. 44, no. 1, 2000; M. P. Fiorina, 'Parties and Partisanship: A 40-Year Retrospective', *Political Behavior*, vol. 24, no. 2, 2002; Christoper Achen and Larry Bartels in Sean Illing, 'Two Eminent Political Scientists: The Problem With Democracy is Voters'; M. Barber and J. C. Pope, 'Does Party Trump Ideology? Disentangling Party and Ideology in America'.

14 Russell J. Dalton, 'Party Identification and Its Implications'.

15 Nolan McCarty, 'The Polarization of Congressional Parties', www.legacy.voteview.com, 21 March 2015.

16 Douglas J. Ahler and David E. Broockman, 'The Delegate Paradox: Why Polarized Politicians Can Represent Citizens Best', *The Journal of Politics*, vol. 80, no. 4, 2018, pp. 1117–33.

17 Isabel Hardman, *Why We Get the Wrong Politicians*, Atlantic, 2019, p. 143.

18 'Political Polarization in the American Public, Section 5: Political Engagement and Activism', www.pewresearch.org, 12 June 2014.

19 Joshua Kalla and David Broockman, 'Campaign Contributions Facilitate Access to Congressional Officials: A Randomized Field Experiment', *American Journal of Political Science*, vol. 60, no. 3, 2016.

20 S. Radford, A. Mell, S. A. Thevoz, ' "Lordy Me!" Can Donations Buy You a British Peerage? A Study in the Link Between Party Political Funding and Peerage Nominations 2005–2014', *British Politics*, vol. 15, 2020, pp. 135–59.

21 '2020 election to cost $14 billion, blowing away spending records', www.opensecrets.org, 28 October 2020.

22 'Peter Geoghegan on dark money and returning home to Ireland', www.opendemocracy.net, 30 July 2020.

23 Ibid.

24 Laurent Bouton, Micael Castanheira, Allan Drazen, 'A Theory of Small Campaign Contributions', *National Bureau of Economic Research: Working Paper Series*, 2018.

25 'Labour Party Financial Statements for the Year Ended 31 December 2015', www.electoralcommission.org.uk.

26 Germany, in keeping with many European countries, has state funding support for political parties.

27 Meredith Kavanagh, 'Why small donations are worth more than you think', www.classy.org.

28 Alex Chesterfield, Ali Goldsworthy and Laura Osborne, 'Eric Singler, CEO and founder of BVA Nudge Unit, on driving successful behaviour change', *Changed My Mind*, www.opendemocracy.net, 28 February 2020.

29 Ingrid van Biezen and Thomas Poguntke, 'The Decline of Membership-Based Politics', *Party Politics*, vol. 20, no. 2, 2014, pp. 206–8.

30 Paul Whiteley, 'Is the Party Over? The Decline of Party Activism and Membership across the Democratic World', *Party Politics*, vol. 17, no. 1, 2010, pp. 21–44.

31 Adam Edelman, 'Hillary Clinton turns 68, asks supporters to sign "birthday card" and donate to campaign', www.nydailynews.com, 26 October 2015.

32 Hatty Collier, 'Corbyn Run: Computer game backing Labour leader is invented by his supporters', www.standard.co.uk, 30 May 2017.

33 Some organisations, such as Greenpeace, maintain charitable and non-charitable vehicles to keep a clear distinction between partisan and non-partisan campaigning and make sure they do not breach regulations.

34 There are notable occasions when this has not been the case. Nigel Farage, through the UKIP/Brexit Party, and Pim Fortyn in the Netherlands, caused a substantial shift in debate on membership of the European Union and immigration respectively.

35 David Segal, 'How Bell Pottinger, P.R. Firm for Despots and Rogues, Met It's End in South Africa', *New York Times*, 4 Feb 2018. We should declare that Alex, one of the authors, once worked for another part of Bell Pottinger's parent company Chime leading on market research. She left a decade before the events discussed.

36 Amanda Strydom, 'Manufacturing Divides: The Gupta-Linked RET Media Network', www.dc.sourceafrica.net.

37 Bell Pottinger was expelled from the public affairs industry's regulatory body for this behaviour.

38 D. M. Butler and M. M. Pereira, 'Trends: How Does Partisanship Influence Policy Diffusion?', *Political Research Quarterly*, vol. 71, no. 4, 2018, pp. 801–12.

39 Sinisa Sikman, 'What can NGO campaigners learn from non-violent pro-democracy movements?', www.europe.ecampaigningforum.com, 8 November 2017. Discussed as part of a keynote presentation. For further information see canvasopedia.org.

40 'How party activists, not voters in general, drive political polarization', www.brown.edu, 1 December 2016.

41 Giovanni Sartori, *Parties and Party Systems – a framework for analysis*, Cambridge University Press, 2016, p. 295. Nixon benefited from splits in the Democrat party as their Southern Wing splintered in protest of their position in favour of civil rights reform. George Wallace, a staunch segregationist, won in several states under the banner 'Segregation now, segregation tomorrow, segregation forever'. Nixon however still carried the majority of electoral college votes.

42 'The Federalist Papers No. 49: Method of Guarding Against the Encroachments of Any One Department of Government by Appealing to the People Through a Convention (1788)', www.avalon.law.yale.edu.

43 Douglass North, 'The New Institutional Economics and Third World Development', in *What is Politics,* ed. Adrian Leftwich, Polity Press, 2004, p. 23.

44 Ibid., p. 10.

45 In Chapter 7 we will consider how these rules and institutions, formal and informal, can help depolarise us.

46 Steven Levitsky and Daniel Ziblatt, *How Democracies Die*, Penguin Random House, 2019, pp. 79–83.

47 'C-Span Releases Third Historians Survey of Presidential Leadership', www.c-span.org, 17 February 2017.

48 Seymour Martin Lipset and Earl Raab, *The Politics of Unreason*. Cited in Steven Levitsky and Daniel Ziblatt, *How Democracies Die*, pp. 47–8.

49 Yoni Applebaum, 'Donald Trump IS Just Like . . . Henry Ford?' *The Atlantic*, 27 August 2015. In 1938 Ford was awarded the German Eagle, the highest honour that Nazi Germany could bestow on a foreign national. By then, 400 discriminatory decrees had been passed against Jews in Germany.

50 Steven Levitsky and Daniel Ziblatt, *How Democracies Die,* p. 45.

51 Julia Cagé, Anna Dagorret, Pauline Grosjean et al., 'Heroes and villains: How networks of influential individuals helped destroy one of the world's more durable democracies and legitimise a racist, authoritarian state', www.voxeu.org, 17 January 2021.

52 We will delve deeper into the role of the media and influencers in Chapter 6.

53 Tim Alberta, *American Carnage: On the Front Lines of the Republican Civil War and the Rise of President Trump*, pp. 11–12.

54 US Department of the Treasury, Treasury Notes, 11 September 2012, www.treasury.gov/connect/blog/Pages/aig-182-billion.aspx. Support for AIG came from both the Federal Reserve Bank of New York and the Federal Government.

55 'Barack Obama's Remarks to the Democratic National Convention', www.nytimes.com, 27 July 2004.

56 'Transcript of John McCain's Concession Speech', www.npr.org, 5 November 2008.

57 Tim Alberta, *American Carnage: On the Front Lines of the Republican Civil War and the Rise of President Trump*, p. 41.

58 D. M. Frankford, 'The Remarkable Staying Power of "Death Panels"', *Journal of Health Politics, Policy and Law*, vol. 40, no. 5, 2015, pp. 1087–101.

59 Tim Alberta, *American Carnage: On the Front Lines of the Republican Civil War and the Rise of President Trump*, p. 69.

60 Ibid. p.170. The Kochs, who were ambivalent on many social issues, did not become concerned about this until much later. Too late. Other large donors such as the Mercer family were all too happy to help though.

61 Ian Urbina, 'Beyond Beltway, Health Debate Turns Hostile', www.nytimes.com, 8 August 2009.

62 Jonathan Allen, 'You lie!' worth $2.7M for Wilson', www.politico.com, 15 October 2009.

63 John Doorman, 'Obama said his first instinct was to "walk down and smack" GOP Rep. Joe Wilson on the head after he shouted "you lie" at him during a joint session of Congress', www.businessinsider.com, 15 November 2020.

64 M. Beckel, 'Joe Wilson's "You Lie" Outburst Helps Bring South Carolina Candidates More Than $4 Million During Third Quarter', www.opensecrets.org, 19 October 2009.

65 Tim Alberta, *American Carnage: On the Front Lines of the Republican Civil War and the Rise of President Trump*, p. 66.

66 Robert Costa, 'Trump's $1 trillion stimulus is a gamble for re-election—and a sea change for Republicans once opposed to bailouts', www.washingtonpost.com, 18 March 2020.

67 Murkowski went on to run the second successful write-in campaign in more than 50 years to regain her seat; Yereth Rosen, 'Senator Lisa Murkowski wins Alaska write-in campaign', www.reuters.com, 18 November 2010.

68 Michael Patrick Leahy, 'Laura Ingraham: We Should Have Traded Cantor for Bergdahl', www.breitbart.com, 4 June 2014.

69 Tim Alberta, *American Carnage: On the Front Lines of the Republican Civil War and the Rise of President Trump*, p. 76.

70 'Before 2016, Donald Trump had a history of toying with a presidential run', www.pbs.org, 20 July 2016.

71 Gregory Kreig, '14 of Trump's most outrageous "birther" claims – half from after 2011', www.edition.cnn.com, 16 September 2016.

72 Molly Ball, 'The Final Humiliation of Reince Priebus', www.theatlantic.com, 30 July 2017.

73 Katie Bo Williams, 'Trump – Khan feud: A timeline', www.thehill.com, 1 August 2016.

Chapter 6: The Messages of Division

1   F. Heider and M. Simmel, 'An Experimental Study of Apparent Behavior', *The American Journal of Psychology*, vol. 57, 1944, pp. 243–59, www.doi.org.

2   Martin Weigel, 'Reconciling The Tension Between Code and Story', www.martin-weigel.org, 7 June 2011; originally from Robert McKee, *Story: Substance, Structure, Style, and the Principles of Screenwriting*, Harper Collins, 1997.

3   S. Sloane, R. Baillargeon and D. Premack, 'Do Infants Have a Sense of Fairness?', *Psychological Science*, vol. 23, no. 2, 2012, pp. 196–204.

4   P. J. Zak, 'Why Inspiring Stories Make Us React: The Neuroscience of Narrative', *Cerebrum*, 2015.

5   Christopher Orr, 'The Movie Review: Million Dollar Baby', www.theatlantic.com, 11 July 2005.

6   'How Hollywood Became the Unofficial Propaganda Arm of the U.S. Military', www.cbc.ca, 11 May 2020.

7   Laurence Zuckerman, 'How the CIA Played Dirty Tricks with Culture', www.nytimes.com, 18 March 2000.

8   Amanda Foreman, *Georgiana: Duchess of Devonshire*, Penguin Random House, 2021.

9   Whilst Britain was still a long way from being a democracy at this time, the campaigning involved must have been exhausting for the poor duchess.

10   Robert Mann, 'How the "Daisy" Ad Changed Everything About Political Advertising', www.smithsonianmag.com, 13 April 2016.

11   The North American Free Trade Agreement reduced trade barriers between Canada, Mexico and the USA.

12   Stephen Ansolabehere and Shanto Iyengar, 'Going Negative: How Political Advertisements Shrink and Polarize the Electorate', *Quill Magazine*, May 1996, www.uvm.edu.

13   'Presidential Candidates' Television Ads: Most Negative in History', www.sciencedaily.com, 1 November 2008.

14   Jonathan Tonge and Andrew Geddes, 'Conclusions: Economic Narratives and Party Leaders', *Parliamentary Affairs*, vol. 68, no. 1, 2015, pp. 255–62, www.doi.org.

15   Stephen Ansolabehere and Shanto Iyengar, 'Going Negative: How Political Advertisements Shrink and Polarize the Electorate'.

16   Josh Sanburn, 'The Ad That Changed Super Bowl Commercials Forever', www.time.com, May 2016.

17   Alan Gray, Brian Parkinson and Robin Dunbar, 'Laughter's Influence on the Intimacy of Self-Disclosure', *Human Nature*, vol. 26, no. 1, 2015. This interpretation

and application to storytelling was from Jennifer Aaker and Naomi Bagdonas's Stanford class, 'Humor: Serious Business'.

18 Quoted in Timur Kuran, *Private Truths Public Lies: The Social Consequences of Preference Falsification*.

19 The personal cost, however, can be high. On a resignation from Goldsmiths, see 'Resignation', www.feministkilljoys.com, 30 May 2016.

20 It is now agreed by all US intelligence agencies that these emails were hacked by a Kremlin-associated group named – wait for it – Fancy Bear.

21 Diana Gonimah, 'What is 4Chan?', www.storyful.com, 29 November 2018.

22 Polls show that 1 in 10 Bernie Sanders supporters went on to vote for Donald Trump; Danielle Kurtzleben, 'Here's How Many Bernie Sanders Supporters Ultimately Voted For Trump', www.npr.org, 24 August 2017. The battle in the primaries was acrimonious enough that when asked if she would support him in his 2020 bid Clinton wouldn't commit citing 'his online Bernie Bros and their relentless attacks on lots of his competitors, particularly the women'; Anthony L Fisher, 'Hillary Clinton keeps blaming Bernie Sanders, but he's not the reason she lost to Trump in 2016', www.businessinsider.com, 21 January 2020.

23 After the election Hillary Clinton embarked on a pizza-buying spree to support the restaurant. She then sent the pizzas anonymously to a local literacy club. Lissa Muscatine, 'Hilary Clinton Addresses That Pizzagate Hoax', www.youtube.com, 19 September 2017.

24 Camila Domonoske, 'Man Fires Rifle Inside D.C. Pizzeria, Cites Fictitious Conspiracy Theories', www.npr.org, 5 December 2016.

25 Merrit Kennedy, ' "Pizzagate" Gunman Sentenced to 4 Years in Prison', www.npr.org, 22 June 2017.

26 Amanda Robb, 'Anatomy of a Fake News Scandal', www.rollingstone.com, 16 November 2017.

27 Kathy Frankovic, 'Belief in conspiracies largely depends on political identity', www.today.yougov.com, 27 December 2016.

28 Amanda Robb, 'Anatomy of a Fake News Scandal'.

29 Jordan Harbinger, '16: Tali Sharot, Unpacking the Science of the Influential Mind', www.jordanharbinger.com.

30 For more on this research, see www.alisonledgerwood.com. See also M. Trussler and S. Soroka, 'Consumer Demand for Cynical and Negative News Frames', *The International Journal of Press/Politics*, vol. 19, no. 3, 2014, pp. 360–79; R. F. Baumeister, E. Bratslavsky, C. Finkenauer et al., 'Bad is Stronger than Good', *Review of General Psychology*, vol. 5, no. 4, 2001, pp. 323–70; Paul Rozin and

Edward B. Royzman, 'Negativity Bias, Negativity Dominance, and Contagion', *Personality and Social Psychology Review*, vol. 5, no. 4, 2001, pp. 296–320; S. Soroka and Stephen McAdams, 'News, Politics and Negativity', *Political Communication*, vol. 32, no. 1, 2015.

31 Richard Hofstadter, 'The Paranoid Style in American Politics', *Harper's Magazine*, November 1964.

32 Soroush Vosoughi, Deb Roy and Sinan Aral, 'The spread of true and false news online', www.ide.mit.edu, 2017.

33 Ibid.

34 M. Prasad, A. J. Perrin, K. Bezila et al., '"There Must Be a Reason": Osama, Saddam, and Inferred Justification', *Sociological Inquiry*, vol. 79, 2009, pp. 142–62, www.doi. org.

35 Underlying this explanation is the psychological model of information processing known as 'Bayesian updating' whereby people incrementally and rationally change their opinions as new information comes along.

36 'Estonia to hold first national Internet election', www.reuters.com, 21 February 2007.

37 'Republic of Estonia', www.electionguide.org.

38 Alison F. Smith, *Political Party Membership in New Democracies: Electoral Rules in Central and East Europe*, Palgrave MacMillan, 2020, p. 94.

39 Kate Maltby, 'Victor Orbán's masterplan to make Hungary great again', www. nybooks.com, 3 June 2020.

40 Ali Goldsworthy and Rob Blackie, 'Single Issue Campaigning and the Polarisation Problem', www.quillette.com, 9 October 2018.

41 S. Soroka and Stephen McAdams, 'News, Politics and Negativity'.

42 Interview with Timur Kuran conducted by the authors in June 2020.

43 Karen Hao, 'How Facebook got addicted to spreading misinformation', www.technologyreview.com, 11 March 2021.

44 For a personalised, black-and-white print letter sent through USPS (the US national postal service). In most countries the differences in cost are similar.

45 Based on sending a seven-figure list on a negotiated contract. Prices rise as list size shrinks, but to send an email to 50,000–250,000 addresses is still less than $0.008 per email sent; www.emailvendorselection.com.

46 Data taken from interview with Sam Jeffers (co-founder of Who Targets Me) conducted by the authors, August 2020; verified in Ad Library.

47 'Case Study: Rainforest Action Network', www.accessibleintelligence.io, 2020.

48 Dan Siroker, 'How Obama Raised $60 Million by Running a Simple Experiment', www.blog.optimizely.com, 29 November 2010.

49 'Obama for America's Digital Fundraising Machine'. www.optimizely.com, 2021.

50 Robert M. Faris, Hal Roberts, Bruce Etling et al., 'Partisanship, Propaganda, and Disinformation: Online Media and the 2016 U.S. Presidential Election', *Berkman Klein Center for Internet and Society Scholarly Articles*, 2017.

51 'Did social media help elect Donald Trump?', www.purdue.edu, 21 November 2016.

52 Arielle Pardes, 'The Facebook Defectors Turning Trump's Strategy Against Him', www.wired.com, 15 September 2020.

53 Rebecca Lewis, 'Alternative Influence: Broadcasting the Reactionary Right on You-Tube', www.datasociety.net, 18 September 2018.

54 'Twitter creator Jack Dorsey illuminates the site's founding document', www.latimesblogs.latimes.com, 18 February 2009.

55 It was originally a comedy and film festival but now the three weeks run one after the other.

56 Claudine Beaumont, 'Twitter users send 50 million tweets per day', www.telegraph.co.uk, 23 February 2010.

57 'Twitter useage statistics', www.internetlivestats.com/twitter-statistics/.

58 Twitter's series A funding has not been disclosed but it is thought to have been between $1- and $5 million. Its B and C funding rounds garnered $22 million and $35 million respectively.

59 'Twitter shares jump 73% in market debut', www.bbc.co.uk, 7 November 2013.

60 Interview conducted by the authors in summer 2020.

61 Ali Goldsworthy and Rob Blackie, 'Single Issue Campaigning and the Polarisation Problem'.

62 'Online Nation: 2020 report', www.ofcom.org.uk, 24 June 2020.

63 Diagnostic and Statistical Manual of Mental Disorders, American Psychiatric Publishing, 2013; A. A. Alhassan, E. M. Alqadhib, N. W. Taha et al., 'The Relationship Between Addiction to Smartphone Usage and Depression Among Adults: A Cross-Sectional Study', *BMC Psychiatry*, vol. 18, 2018, www.doi.org. Victoria L. Dunckley M.D., 'Gray Matters: Too Much Screen Time Damages the Brain', *Psychology Today*, 27 February 2014.

64 K. Z. Zhang, C. Chen and M. K. Lee, 'Understanding the Role of Motives in Smartphone Addiction', in *PACIS*, 2014, p. 131.

65 'Germany's AfD: How right-wing is nationalist Alternative for Germany?', www.bbc.co.uk, 11 February 2020.

66 Katharina Brunner and Sabrina Ebitsch, 'In der rechten Echokammer', www.sued-deutsche.de, 1 May 2017.

67 Kiran Garimella, Gianmarco Morales, Aristides Gionis et al., 'Political Discourse on Social Media: Echo Chambers, Gatekeepers, and the Price of Bipartisanship', *Proceedings of the 2018 World Wide Web Conference*, 2018.

68 Ibid., pp. 913–22.

69 Christopher A. Bail, Lisa P. Argyle, Taylor W. Brown et al., 'Exposure to Opposing Views on Social Media Can Increase Political Polarization', *PNAS*, vol. 115, no. 37, 2018, pp. 9216–21.

70 Johnny Lieu, 'Facebook admits it didn't do enough to prevent "offline violence" in Myanmar', www.uk.news.yahoo.com.

71 Eli Pariser, *The Filter Bubble*, Penguin Random House, 2021.

72 Cass R. Sunstein, *Republic.com 2.0*, Princeton University Press, 2009.

73 Axel Bruns, *Are Filter Bubbles Real?*, Polity, 2019.

74 Ben Page, CEO of Ipsos Mori, interviewed by the authors in September 2020.

75 Axel Bruns, *Are Filter Bubbles Real?*

76 Elizabeth Dubois and Grant Blank, 'The Echo Chamber is Overstated: The Moderating Effect of Political Interest and Diverse Media', *Information, Communication and Society*, vol. 21, no. 5, 2018, pp. 729–45.

77 Harry Enten, 'Less than 10% of Americans like QAnon', www.edition.cnn.com, 7 February 2021.

78 Levi Boxell, Matthew Gentzkow and Jesse M. Shapiro, 'Cross-Country Trends in Affective Polarization', www.brown.edu, 2020.

79 While academics tend to agree that affective polarisation has increased most in the US, some studies (e.g. Noam Gidron, J. Adams and W. Horne, *American Affective Polarization in Comparative Perspective*) suggest the increases in countries such as Greece have been higher.

80 Levi Boxell, Matthew Gentzkow and Jesse M. Shapiro, 'Internet Use and Political Polarization', *PNAS*, vol. 114, no. 40, 2017, pp. 10612–7.

81 Palihapitiya later tempered these comments after criticism from Facebook. He acknowledged that in general he believed the company to be a force for good.

82 Julia Carrie Wong, 'Former Facebook executive: social media is ripping society apart', www.theguardian.com, 11 December 2017.

83 Ryan Mac and Craig Silverman, 'Facebook Created an Employee "Playbook" to Respond to Accusations of Polarization', www.buzzfeednews.com, 21 March 2021.

84 Elizabeth Grieco, 'U.S. newspapers have shed half of their newsroom employees since 2008', www.pewresearch.org, 20 April 2020.

85 'New research reveals how Australian journalists are faring four years after redundancy', www.theconversation.com, 4 December 2018.

86 Amanda Meade, 'More than 150 Australian newsrooms shut since January 2019 as Covid-19 deepens media crisis', www.theguardian.com, 17 May 2020.

87 Davey Alba and Jack Nicas, 'As Local News Dies, a Pay-for-Play Network Rises in Its Place', www.nytimes.com, 20 October 2020.

88 'Protect Jobs, protect democracy, protect print media: Global unions launch campaign to ensure journalism's future', www.ifj.org, 18 September 2020.

89 Anthony Ha, 'Google Unveils its $300M News Initiative', www.techcrunch.com, 20 March 2020.

90 Hunt Allcott and Matthew Gentzkow, 'Social Media and Fake News in the 2016 Election', *Journal of Economic Perspectives*, vol. 31, no. 2, 2017, pp. 211–36.

91 The app is also available through other outlets so these figures are an underestimate. The other principal platform is the Google Play store.

92 'Narendra Modi: Latest News, Videos and Speeches', www.apptrace.com.

Chapter 7: Reshaping Institutions

1 The politics of recognising Kosovo as a sovereign state are complex. For the purposes of this book, we have assumed its status in line with the United States, most members of the European Union and many other countries.

2 Murat Somer, 'Cascades of Ethnic Polarization: Lessons from Yugoslavia', *AAPSS*, vol. 573, 2001, p. 139.

3 Nikolai Botev, 'Where East Meets West: Ethnic Intermarriage in the Former Yugoslavia, 1962 to 1989', *American Sociological Review*, vol. 59, no. 3, 1994, pp. 461–80.

4 J. Smits, 'Ethnic Intermarriage and Social Cohesion: What Can We Learn from Yugoslavia?' Social Indicators Research, vol. 96, no. 3, 2010, pp. 417–32.

5 Murat Somer, 'Cascades of Ethnic Polarization: Lessons from Yugoslavia'; Nikolai Botev, 'Where East Meets West: Ethnic Intermarriage in the Former Yugoslavia, 1962 to 1989'.

6 Adam LeBor, *Milosevic: A Biography*, Yale University Press, 2004.

7 Murat Somer, based at Koc University in Istanbul, put forward this explanation.

8 Timur Kuran, 'Ethnic Norms And Their Transformation Through Reputational Cascades', *The Journal of Legal Studies*, vol. 27, no. S2, 1998, pp. 623–659. JSTOR, www.jstor.org/stable/10.1086/468038.

9 Timur Kuran, 'Sparks and Prairie Fires: A Theory of Unanticipated Political Revolution', *Public Choice*, vol. 61, no. 1, 1989, pp. 41–74.

10 Ibid.

11 Ibid.

12 Philip N. Howard, Aiden Duffy, Deen Freelon et al., 'Opening Closed Regimes: What Was the Role of Social Media During the Arab Spring?', *Project on Information Technology and Political Islam*, 2011.

13 For more on Đurić, see Marie-Janine Calic, *A History of Yugoslavia*, Purdue University Press, 2019, p. 239.

14 Martin Bell, 'The legacy of Yugoslavia's Marshal Tito', www.news.bbc.co.uk, 26 April 2010.

15 Christopher C. Liu and Sameer B. Srivastava, 'Pulling Closer and Moving Apart: Interaction, Identity, and Influence in the U.S. Senate, 1973 to 2009', *American Sociological Review*, vol. 80, no. 1, 2015, pp. 192–217.

16 David S. Reynolds, 'Congressional Bloodshed: The Run-Up to the Civil War', www.nytimes.com, 24 September 2018.

17 Sartori is insistent that this is not the only explanation. J. McCoy, Murat Somer, 'Toward a Theory of Pernicious Polarization and How It Harms Democracies: Comparative Evidence and Possible Remedies', *AAPSS*, vol. 681, 2019, pp. 234–71.

18 Brussels Bureau, 'Divided Belgium: Greens, socialists and nationalist parties struggle to form government', www.euronews.com, 26 July 2019.

19 Elliot Gotkine, 'Israel's government collapses, not with a bang but a whimper, triggering fourth election in 2 years', www.edition.cnn.com, 22 December 2020.

20 'Russia report: New intelligence committee chair loses Tory whip', www.bbc.com, 16 July 2020.

21 'Parliamentary Committees as windows into the world of Covid-19 legislation and its impacts', www.wfd.org, 19 October 2020.

22 'The Elders call for urgent action to address multilateral failings exposed by COVID-19', www.theelders.org, 22 October 2020.

23 Giles Edwards, *The Ex Men: How Our Former Presidents and Prime Ministers Are Still Changing the World*, BBC Books, 2021, p. 49.

24 Giles Edwards, *The Ex Men*, p. 112.

25 Giles Edwards, *The Ex Men*, pp. 110–1.

26 Y. Schreuder, 'The Polder Model in Dutch Economic and Environmental Planning', *Bulletin of Science, Technology and Society*, vol. 21, no. 4, 2001, pp. 237–45.

27 R. Koopmans and J. C. Muis, 'The Rise of Right-Wing Populist Pim Fortuyn in The Netherlands: A Discursive Opportunity Approach', *European Journal of Political Research*, vol. 48, no. 5, pp. 642–64.

28 J. McCoy, Murat Somer, 'Toward a Theory of Pernicious Polarization and How It Harms Democracies: Comparative Evidence and Possible Remedies'.

29 Steven Levitsky and Daniel Ziblatt, *How Democracies Die*, Crown, 2019, pp. 97–117.

30 Richard L. Hasen, 'Polarization and the Judiciary', *Annual Review of Political Science*, vol. 22, 2019, pp. 261–76.

31 The Head of the General Services Administration did not officially acknowledge this until 23 November 2020, delaying the transition process.

32 Phillip Inman, 'City watchdog chief quits after George Osborne vote of no confidence', www.theguardian.com, 17 July 2015.

33 Phil Knight, *Shoe Dog*, Simon & Schuster, 2006, p. 56.

34 Juliet Bourke, 'The diversity and inclusion revolution: Eight powerful truths', www2.deloitte.com, 22 January 2018.

35 Ibid.

36 Katherine W. Phillips, 'How Diversity Makes Us Smarter', www.greatergood.berkeley.edu, 1 October 2014.

37 Stuart R. Levine, 'Diversity Confirmed to Boost Innovation and Financial Results', www.forbes.com, 15 January 2020.

38 Alex Chesterfield, Ali Goldsworthy and Laura Osborne, 'Negotiations expert Margaret Neale on changing her mind about conflict', *Changed My Mind*, www.opendemocracy.net, 6 March 2019.

39 Robert Kovach, 'How Tribalism Hurts Companies, and What to Do About It', www.hbr.org, 26 July 2017.

40 Jongsub Lee, Kwang J. Lee and Nandu J. Nagarajan, 'Birds of a Feather: Value Implications of Political Alignment Between Top Management and Directors', *Journal of Financial Economics*, vol. 112, no. 2, 2014, pp. 232–50.

41 Y. Bonaparte, A. Kumar and J. K. Page, 'Political Climate, Optimism, and Investment Decisions', *Journal of Financial Markets*, vol. 34, 2017, pp 69–94.

42 Syndicated loans bring together multiple lenders to grant credit to a borrower, typically a large multinational company or country.

43 Ramona Dagostino, Janet Gao, Janet and Pengfei Ma, 'Partisanship in Loan Pricing', www.ssrn.com, 28 September 2020.

44 Misaligned means someone who is affiliated with a different party from the one represented by the president in government. In this case a Democrat when a Republican President was elected.

45 M. B. Wintoki and Y. Xi, 'Political Partisan Bias in Mutual Fund Portfolios', *Journal of Financial and Quantitative Analysis*, vol. 55, no. 5, 2019.

46 K. Gift and T. Gift, 'Does Politics Influence Hiring? Evidence from a Randomized Experiment'.

47 Richard Feloni, 'Salesforce CEO Marc Benioff explains why a Hindu guru and Colin Powell were critical mentors', www.businessinsider.com, 3 March 2016.

48 R. S. Bigler and L. S. Liben, 'A Developmental Intergroup Theory of Social Stereotypes and Prejudice', *Advances in Child Development and Behavior*, ed. R. V. Kail, vol. 34, pp. 39–89; Miles Hewstone, Mark Rubin and Hazel Willis, 'Intergroup Bias', *Annual Review of Psychology*, vol. 53, 2002, p. 575.

49 Alex Chesterfield, Ali Goldsworthy and Laura Osborne, 'Jonathan Haidt: Why I changed my mind about the value of school tests', *Changed My Mind*, www.opendemocracy.net, 20 November 2018.

50 Karen Stenner and Jonathan Haidt, 'Authoritarianism Is Not a Momentary Madness, But an Eternal Dynamic Within Liberal Democracies', in *Can It Happen Here?*, ed. Cass Sunstein, Dey Street, 2018, p. 211.

Chapter 8: Reshaping Groups

1 Thomas F. Pettigrew and Linda R. Tropp, 'Allport's Intergroup Contact Hypothesis: Its History and Influence', in *On the Nature of Prejudice: Fifty Years After Allport*, ed. J. F. Dovidio, P. Glick and L. A. Rudman, Blackwell, 2005, pp. 262–77; citing Thomas F. Pettigrew, Linda R. Tropp, Ulrich Wagner et al., 'Recent Advances in Intergroup Contact Theory', *International Journal of Intercultural Relations*, vol. 35, no. 3, 2011, pp. 271–80.

2 Thomas F. Pettigrew and Linda R. Tropp, 'A Meta-Analytic Test of Intergroup Contact Theory', *Journal of Personality and Social Psychology*, vol. 90, no. 5, 2006, pp. 751–83.

3 David Broockman and Joshua Kalla, 'Durably Reducing Transphobia: A Field Experiment on Door-To-Door Canvassing', *Science*, vol. 352, 2016, pp. 220–4.

4 Florida is a swing state; south Florida, with a larger black population than north Florida, tends to swing more to the Democrats. For more, see David Weigel, 'The six political states of Florida', www.washingtonpost.com, 8 September 2020.

5 Christie Aschwanden and Maggie Koerth, 'How Two Grad Students Uncovered an Apparent Fraud—And a Way to Change Opinions on Transgender Rights', www.fivethirtyeight.com, 7 April 2016.

6 Susan Gilbert, 'A conversation with Elliot Aronson: No One Left to Hate, Averting Columbines', www.nytimes.com, 27 March 2001.

7 The Jigsaw Classroom, www.jigsaw.org.

8 E. Aronson, N. Blaney, C. Stephan et al., *The Jigsaw Classroom*, Sage, 1978.

9 I. Walker and M. Crogan, 'Academic Performance, Prejudice, and the Jigsaw Classroom: New Pieces to the Puzzle', *Journal of Community and Applied Social Psychology*, vol. 8, no. 6, 1998.

10 The studies also leverage perspective taking – understanding someone else's thoughts and viewpoints (perspective taking is a *cognitive* process and different from empathy which is understanding how someone else *feels*).

11 E. L. Paluck, 'Reducing Intergroup Prejudice and Conflict Using the Media: A Field Experiment in Rwanda', *Journal of Personality and Social Psychology*, vol. 96, no. 3, 2009, pp. 574–87.

12 E. L. Paluck, 'Is It Better Not to Talk? Group Polarization, Extended Contact, and Perspective Taking in Eastern Democratic Republic of Congo', *Personality and Social Psychology Bulletin*, vol. 36, no. 9, 2010, pp. 1170–85.

13 Salma Mousa, 'Building Social Cohesion Between Christians and Muslims Through Soccer in Post-ISIS Iraq', *Science*, vol. 369, 2009, pp. 866–70.

14 Ed Vulliamy, 'Bridging the gap', www.theguardian.com, 13 July 2008.

15 Howard Reich, 'Daniel Barenboim reflects on his return to CSO, 12 years later', www.chicagotribune.com, 23 October 2018.

16 Norman Lebrecht, 'Daniel Barenboim admits West-East Diwan's failure', www.slippedisc.com, 23 October 2019.

17 Steve Rathje, Leor Hackel and Jamil Zaki, 'Attending live theatre improves empathy, changes attitudes, and leads to pro-social behavior', *Journal of Experimental Social Psychology*, vol. 95, 2021.

18 Joshua P. Darr, Matthew P. Hitt, Johanna L. Dunaway, 'Newspaper Closures Polarize Voting Behavior', *Journal of Communication*, vol. 68, issue 6, December 2018, pp. 1007–28, www.doi.org; Diane Bolet, 'Drinking Alone: Local Socio-Cultural Degradation and Radical Right Support – The Case of British Pub Closures', *Journal of Comparative Political Studies*, March 2021, www.doi.org.

19 'BBC Radio 4 Four Thought: Full Script', www.craftivist-collective.com, 1 November 2020.

20 Dr Clodagh Harris, 'Bridging representative and direct democracy? Ireland's Citizens' Assemblies', www.hansardsociety.org.uk, 24 May 2018.

21 Stanford Center for Deliberative Democracy, www.cdd.stanford.edu. This is an example of deliberative polling, developed by Jim Fishkin at Stanford, which had

been conducted in 28 countries with 109 cases as of 2018; 'Revitalising our Politics through Public Deliberation', www.thersa.org, 6 December 2018.

22 Grainne Healy, Brian Sheehan and Noel Whelan, 'How the Yes was won: the inside story of the marriage referendum', www.irishtimes.com, 6 November 2015.

23 Lucy Parry, *Analysing the Foxhunting Debate: Implications for Animal Protection*, Centre for Animals and Social Justice, 2017.

24 Philip Faigle, 'How to Connect People in Polarized Communities?', www.constructiveinstitute.org, 2019.

25 Rev. Linda Taylor, 'What Do We Do on November 9th?', www.huffpost.com, 27 October 2017. Supplemented by interview with Rev. Linda Taylor, September 2020.

26 Gina Perry, *The Lost Boys: Inside Muzafer Sherif's Robbers Cave Experiment*, Scribe, 2018.

27 David Shariatmadari, 'A real-life Lord of the Flies: the troubling legacy of the robbers cave experiment', www.theguardian.com, 16 April 2018.

28 Tom Gilovich, Dacher Keltner, Serena Chen et al., *Social Psychology*.

29 Anecdote from Jon Hanson, *Ideology, Psychology, and Law*, Oxford University Press, 2012.

30 'The assassination of Egypt's President Sadat', www.bbc.com, 7 October 2015.

31 Mark Levine, Amy Prosser, David Evans et al., 'Identity and Emergency Intervention: How Social Group Membership and Inclusiveness of Group Boundaries Shape Helping Behavior'.

32 Matthew Levendusky, 'Americans, Not Partisans: Can Priming American National Identity Reduce Affective Polarization?', *The Journal of Politics*, vol. 80, 2017.

33 K. R. Binning, D. K. Sherman, G. L. Cohen et al., 'Seeing the Other Side: Reducing Political Partisanship via Self-Affirmation in the 2008 Presidential Election', *Analyses of Social Issues and Public Policy*, vol. 10, 2010, pp. 276–92; G. L. Cohen, A. Bastardi, D. K. Sherman et al., 'Bridging the Partisan Divide: Self-Affirmation Reduces Ideological Closed-Mindedness and Inflexibility in Negotiation', *Journal of Personality and Social Psychology*, vol. 93, 2007, pp. 415–30; D. K. Sherman and G. L. Cohen, 'Accepting Threatening Information: Self-Affirmation and the Reduction of Defensive Biases', *Current Directions in Psychological Science*, vol. 11, 2002, pp. 119–23.

34 Ziva Kunda, 'The Case for Motivated Reasoning'.

35 R. E. Petty and J. T. Cacioppo, *Communication and Persuasion*, Springer, 1986, pp. 1–24.

36 Kevin Munger, 'Tweetment Effects on the Tweeted: Experimentally Reducing Racist Harassment', *Political Behavior*, vol. 39, no. 3, 2016. The only treatment that

significantly decreased the rate of racist language use was the in-group/high follower treatment.

37 E. L. Paluck, H. Shepherd and P. M. Aronow, 'Changing Climates of Conflict: A Social Network Experiment in 56 schools', *PNAS*, vol. 113, no. 3, 2016, pp. 566–71.

38 I. P. Levin and G. J. Gaeth, 'How Consumers Are Affected by the Framing of Attribute Information Before and After Consuming the Product', *Journal of Consumer Research*, vol. 15, no. 3, 1988, pp. 374–78.

39 T. M. Marteau, 'Framing of Information: Its Influence Upon Decisions of Doctors and Patients', *British Journal of Social Psychology*, vol. 28, 1989, pp. 89–94; B. J. McNeil, S. G. Pauker, H. C. Sox et al., 'On the Elicitation of Preferences for Alternative Therapies', *The New England Journal of Medicine*, vol. 306, no. 21, 1982, pp. 1259–62; D. K. Wilson, R. M. Kaplan and L. J. Schneiderman, 'Framing of Decisions and Selections of Alternatives in Health Care', *Social Behaviour*, vol. 2, 1987, pp. 51–9.

40 D. J. Hardisty, E. J. Johnson and E. U. Weber, 'A Dirty Word or a Dirty World?: Attribute Framing, Political Affiliation, and Query Theory', *Psychological Science*, 2010, vol. 21, pp. 86–92.

41 A. Lerman, M. Sadin and S. Trachtman, 'Policy Uptake as Political Behavior: Evidence from the Affordable Care Act'.

42 Katie Patrick, 'Vegans, You're Doing it Wrong: How to Get People to Eat Less Meat, with Gregg Sparkman', www.medium.com, 5 March 2018.

Chapter 9: Reshaping Ourselves

1 Alex Chesterfield, Ali Goldsworthy and Laura Osborne, 'Why Jo Swinson changed her mind about all women shortlists', *Changed My Mind*, www.opendemocracy. net, 19 January 2019.

2 T. A. Kreps, K. Laurin and A. C. Merritt, 'Hypocritical Flip-Flop, or Courageous Evolution? When Leaders Change Their Moral Minds', *Journal of Personality and Social Psychology*, vol. 113, no. 5, 2017, pp.730–52, www.doi.org.

3 Kerwin Swint, *Mudslingers: The Twenty-five Dirtiest Political Campaigns of All Time*, Sterling, 2006, pp. 3–4.

4 Richard Hanania, 'Does Apologizing Work? An Empirical Test of the Conventional Wisdom', *Behavioural Public Policy*, 1 September 2015, www.doi.org.

5 U. Waldenström and E. Schytt, 'A Longitudinal Study of Women's Memory of Labour Pain From 2 Months to 5 Years After the Birth', *BJOG*, vol. 116, no. 4, 2009, pp. 577–83, www.doi.org.

6 Michael B. Wolfe and Todd J. Williams, 'Poor Metacognitive Awareness of Belief Change', *Quarterly Journal of Experimental Psychology*, vol. 71, no. 9, 2018, www.doi.org.

7 'People Rationalize Policies as Soon as They Take Effect', www.psychologicalscience.org, 26 February 2018; K. Laurin, 'Inaugurating Rationalization: Three Field Studies Find Increased Rationalization When Anticipated Realities Become Current', *Psychological Science*, vol. 29, no. 4, 2018, pp. 483–95, www.doi.org.

8 'People Rationalize Policies as Soon as They Take Effect', www.psychologicalscience.org.

9 Alex Chesterfield, Ali Goldsworthy and Laura Osborne, 'Why Jo Swinson changed her mind about all women shortlists'.

10 Tom Gilovich, Dacher Keltner, Serena Chen et al., *Social Psychology*, p. 313.

11 Known as the Zaller model: people rarely have fixed attitudes on specific issues and instead construct preferences as they go along.

12 'Societies change their minds faster than people do', www.economist.com, 2 November 2019.

13 John Zaller, *The Nature and Origins of Mass Opinion*, Cambridge University Press, 1992.

14 Even so, Zaller argues individual political predispositions matter a lot; they are 'the critical intervening variable between the communications people encounter in the mass media, on one side, and their statements of political preferences, on the other.' Political predispositions are rooted in life experiences, childhood socialisation, direct involvement in the raw ingredients of policy issues, social and economic status, inherited personality factors, and tastes.

15 Ziva Kunda, 'The Case for Motivated Reasoning'.

16 D. J. Flynn, B. Nyhan and J. Reifler, 'The Nature and Origins of Misperceptions: Understanding False and Supported Beliefs about Politics'.

17 Some studies find effects (e.g. Martin Gilens, 'Political Ignorance and Collective Policy Preferences', *The American Political Science Review*, vol. 95, no. 2, 2001; John Sides, Michael Tesler and Lynn Vavreck, 'The Electoral Landscape of 2016', *AAPSS*, vol. 667, 2016; Alexis Grigorieff, Christopher Roth and Diego Ubfal, 'Does Information Change Attitudes Towards Immigrants?', www.ssrn.com, 25 April 2016) and some don't (e.g. J. Kuklinski, P. Quirk, J. Jerit et al., 'Misinformation and the Currency of Democratic Citizenship', *The Journal of Politics*, vol. 62, no. 3, 2000; Adam J. Berinsky, 'Assuming the Costs of War: Events, Elites, and the American Public Support for Military Conflict', *The Journal of Politics*, vol. 69, no. 4, 2007; D. J. Flynn, B. Nyhan and J. Reifler, 'The Nature and Origins of

Misperceptions: Understanding False and Supported Beliefs about Politics'). See also William G. Howell, Martin R. West and Paul E. Peterson, 'The Persuadable Public', www.educationnext.org, 30 September 2009.

18 Alex Chesterfield, Ali Goldsworthy and Laura Osborne, 'Steve Martin: Changing your ways is easier than changing your mind', *Changed My Mind*, www.opendemocracy.net, 14 February 2019.

19 Alex Chesterfield, Ali Goldsworthy and Laura Osborne interview Deborah Mattinson, 'Over 80% of the UK and US think their country's divided: our new podcast considers why', *Changed My Mind,* www.opendemocracy.net, 14 November 2018.

20 Daniel J. Hopkins, John Sides and Jack Citrin, 'The Muted Consequences of Correct Information about Immigration', *The Journal of Politics*, vol. 81, 2019, pp. 315–20.

21 Brendan Nyhan and Jason Reifler, 'When Corrections Fail: The Persistence of Political Misperceptions', *Political Behaviour*, vol. 32, 2010, pp. 303–33, www.doi. org; Brendan Nyhan and Jason Reifler, 'The Roles of Information Deficits and Identity Threat in the Prevalence of Misperceptions', *Journal of Elections, Public Opinion and Parties*, vol. 29, no. 2, 2018, pp. 222–44, www.tandfonline.com.

22 Brendan Nyhan, 'New Surveys Show the Persistence of Misperceptions', www. huffpost.com, 30 July 2012.

23 D. J. Flynn, B. Nyhan and J. Reifler, 'The Nature and Origins of Misperceptions: Understanding False and Supported Beliefs about Politics'; Brendan Nyhan and Jason Reifler, 'When Corrections Fail: The Persistence of Political Misperceptions'.

24 Brendan Nyhan and Jason Reifler, 'Misinformation and Fact-Checking: Research Findings from Social Science', *New American Foundation*, 2012.

25 Ibid.

26 Bertram Gawronski, Roland Deutsch, Sawsan Mbirkou et al., 'When "Just Say No" is Not Enough: Affirmation Versus Negation Training and the Reduction of Automatic Stereotype Activation', *Journal of Experimental Social Psychology*, vol. 44, 2008, pp. 370–7.

27 Leonid Rozenblit and Frank Keil, 'The Misunderstood Limits of Folk Science: An Illusion of Explanatory Depth', *Cognitive Science*, vol. 26, no. 5, 2002, pp. 521–62.

28 Philip M. Fernbach, Todd Rogers, Craig R. Fox et al., 'Political Extremism Is Supported by an Illusion of Understanding', *Psychological Science*, vol. 24, no. 6, 2013.

29 Keith E. Stanovich, 'The Bias that Divides Us', www.quillette.com, 26 September 2020.

30 J. Kaplan, S. Gimbel and S. Harris, 'Neural Correlates of Maintaining One's Political Beliefs in the Face of Counterevidence', *Scientific Reports*, vol. 6, 2016, www.doi.org.

31 D. R. Johnson, M. P. Murphy and R. M. Messer, 'Reflecting on Explanatory Ability: A Mechanism for Detecting Gaps in Causal Knowledge', *Journal of Experimental Psychology: General*, vol. 145, no. 5, pp. 573–88, www.doi.org.

32 Alex Chesterfield and Kate Coombs, 'To Fight Polarization, Ask, "How Does That Policy Work?"', www.behavioralscientist.org, 25 November 2019.

33 Keith Stanovich and Richard West first used these terms to describe dual-process models of thinking. Kahneman then popularised them in his book *Thinking Fast and Slow*; K. E. Stanovich and R. F. West, 'Individual Difference in Reasoning: Implications for the Rationality Debate?'; Daniel Kahneman, *Thinking Fast and Slow*, Penguin Books, 2011.

34 Gordon Pennycook and David G. Rand, 'Lazy, Not Biased: Susceptibility to Partisan Fake News is Better Explained by Lack of Reasoning Than by Motivated Reasoning', *Cognition*, vol. 188, 2019, pp. 39–50, www.doi.org.

35 Joseph Seering, Tianmi Fang, Luca Damasco et al., 'Designing User Interface Elements to Improve the Quality and Civility of Discourse in Online Commenting Behaviors', in *Proceedings of the 2019 CHI Conference on Human Factors in Computing Systems*, 2019, pp. 1–14, www.doi.org.

36 Louise Perry, 'It's good to talk', www.thecritic.co.uk, May 2020.

37 Eric Barker, 'This Is How To Change Someone's Mind: 6 Secrets From Research', www.bakadesuyo.com, 16 December 2019.

38 Famke Louise, 'About', www.famkelouise.nl.

39 Daniel Boffey, 'Dutch celebrities backtrack after Covid restraints rebellion', www.theguardian.com, 24 September 2020.

40 Ibid.

41 'Pop stars, actors say they "will no longer be part of" efforts to combat coronavirus', www.dutchnews.nl, 23 September 2020.

42 'The odd couple: Singer and intensive care doctor launch Covid campaign', www.dutchnews.nl, 5 October 2020.

43 Niels Klaassen, 'Famke Louise now works with ICU doctor Gommers: face masks campaign begins today', www.ad.nl, 5 October 2020.

44 Alex Chesterfield, Ali Goldsworthy and Laura Osborne interview Jordan Blashek and Chris Haugh, 'Changed my Mind: A Republican's journey to backing criminal justice reform', *Changed My Mind*, www.opendemocracy.net, 20 August 2020.

45 K. G. Kugler and P. T. Coleman, 'Get Complicated: The Effects of Complexity on Conversations Over Potentially Intractable Moral Conflicts', *Negotiation and Conflict Management Research*, vol. 13, no. 3, 2020, pp. 211–30, www.doi.org.

46 Alex Chesterfield, Ali Goldsworthy and Laura Osborne, 'Negotiations expert Margaret Neale on changing her mind about conflict'.

47 Alex Chesterfield, Ali Goldsworthy and Laura Osborne, 'Daniel Finkelstein on changing political allies', *Changed My Mind*, www.opendemocracy.net, 6 August 2020.

Chapter 10: Changed My Mind

1 Pamela Toler, 'The Emperor Changes His Mind', www.wondersandmarvels.com, 18 July 2013.

2 Thatcher's famous moniker was in fact first used in an irony-laden Russian newspaper article in the 1970s. She was able to twist it to her advantage.

3 Sir Geoffrey Howe, 'Sir Geoffrey Howe Resignation Speech 1990', www.britpolitics.co.uk.

4 Martin Sixsmith, *Russia: A 1,000-Year Chronicle of the Wild East*, BBC Books, 2021, p. 444.

5 Alex Chesterfield, Ali Goldsworthy and Laura Osborne interview Leah Garcés, 'When an animal rights activist met a factor farmer', *Changed My Mind*, www.opendemocracy.net, 4 June 2020; see also Elizabeth Dohms-Harter, 'Animal Rights Activist's New Purpose Is Helping Factory Farmers', www.wpr.org, 14 February 2020.

6 Alison is now Derek's partner. Alex Chesterfield, Ali Goldsworthy and Laura Osborne, 'Derek Black on why he left the White Nationalist movement'.

7 Ibid. For more on Derek's story, see Eli Saslow, *Rising Out of Hatred*, Anchor, 2019.

Afterword

1 R. S. Foa, A. Klassen, D. Wenger, A. Rand, and M. Slade, 'Youth and Satisfaction with Democracy: Reversing the Democratic Disconnect?' Cambridge, United Kingdom: Centre for the Future of Democracy, 2020.

2 M. Krupenkin, 'Does Partisanship Affect Compliance with Government Recommendations?', *Political Behavior*, vol. 43, pp. 451–472, 2021. https://doi.org/10.1007/s11109-020-09613-6.

3 Allyson Chiu, *Washington Post*, 'Goya's CEO said the US is 'truly blessed' with President Trump. Latinos are now boycotting', 1 July 2020.

4 '"Drug dealers, criminals, rapists": What Trump thinks of Mexicans', bbc.co.uk, 31 August 2016.

5 Raul A. Reyes, 'Goya was a staple in Latino households. It likely won't be anymore', cnn.com, 11 July 2020.

6 Jura Liaukonyte, Anna Tuchman and Xinrong Zhu, 'Spilling the Beans on Political Consumerism: Do Social Media Boycotts and Buycotts Translate to Real Sales Impact?', 11 January 2022. http://dx.doi.org/10.2139/ssrn.4006546.

7 Jacqueline Alemany and Marianna Sotomayor, 'The "GOP Impeachment 10" try to navigate Cheney's demise and their own futures', *Washington Post*, 10 May 2021.

8 Lucien Bruggeman, 'Republican Liz Cheney calls Trump "clearly unfit for future office"', *ABC News*, 2 January 2022.

9 Meredith McGraw, 'Trump moves to close off Liz Cheney's political escape hatch', *Politico*, 17 February 2022.

10 Paul LeBlanc, 'Liz Cheney says she "was wrong" to oppose same-sex marriage in wide-ranging interview', CNN, 27 September 2021.

11 C. Puryear, E. Kubin, C. Schein, Y. Bigman, and K. Gray, 'Bridging Political Divides by Correcting the Basic Morality Bias', 11 January 2022. https://doi.org/10.31234/osf.io/fk8g6.

12 Magdalena Wojcieszak, and Benjamin R. Warner, 'Can Interparty Contact Reduce Affective Polarization? A Systematic Test of Different Forms of Intergroup Contact', *Political Communication*, 37:6, pp. 789-811, 2020. https://doi.org/10.1080/10584609.2020.1760406.

13 O. Simonsson, J. Narayanan and J. Marks,' Love thy (partisan) neighbor: Brief befriending meditation reduces affective polarization', *Group Processes & Intergroup Relations*, July 2021. https://doi.org/10.1177/13684302211020108.

INDEX